AF788779

C++ Programming:

From Problem Analysis to Program Design, Fifth Edition

Lab Manual

C++ Programming:
From Problem Analysis to Program Design, Fifth Edition
Lab Manual

by Judy Scholl and Gerard Nugent

COURSE TECHNOLOGY
CENGAGE Learning™

Australia • Brazil • Japan • Korea • Mexico • Singapore • Spain • United Kingdom • United States

COURSE TECHNOLOGY
CENGAGE Learning™

C++ Programming: From Problem Analysis to Program Design, Fifth Edition Lab Manual

Judy Scholl and Gerard Nugent

Executive Editor: Marie Lee

Acquisitions Editor: Amy Jollymore

Senior Product Manager: Alyssa Pratt

Editorial Assistant: Zina Kresin

Content Project Manager: Matthew Hutchinson

Art Director: Faith Brosnan

Print Buyer: Julio Esperas

Copyeditor: Camille Kiolbasa

Proofreader: Green Pen Quality Assurance

Cover Designer: Roycroft Design/
www.roycroftdesign.com

Cover Photo: © Guntmar Fritz/Masterfile

Compositor: Integra

© 2011 Course Technology, Cengage Learning

ALL RIGHTS RESERVED. No part of this work covered by the copyright herein may be reproduced, transmitted, stored or used in any form or by any means graphic, electronic, or mechanical, including but not limited to photocopying, recording, scanning, digitizing, taping, Web distribution, information networks, or information storage and retrieval systems, except as permitted under Section 107 or 108 of the 1976 United States Copyright Act, without the prior written permission of the publisher.

For product information and technology assistance, contact us at
Cengage Learning Customer & Sales Support, 1-800-354-9706
For permission to use material from this text or product, submit all requests online at **cengage.com/permissions**
Further permissions questions can be emailed to
permissionrequest@cengage.com

Library of Congress Control Number: 2010922619

ISBN-13: 978-0-538-79810-5

ISBN-10: 0-538-79810-6

Course Technology
20 Channel Center Street
Boston, MA 02210
USA

Cengage Learning is a leading provider of customized learning solutions with office locations around the globe, including Singapore, the United Kingdom, Australia, Mexico, Brazil, and Japan. Locate your local office at:
international.cengage.com/region

Cengage Learning products are represented in Canada by Nelson Education, Ltd.

To learn more about Course Technology, visit **www.cengage.com/coursetechnology**

Purchase any of our products at your local college store or at our preferred online store **www.CengageBrain.com**

Some of the product names and company names used in this book have been used for identification purposes only and may be trademarks or registered trademarks of their respective manufacturers and sellers.

Any fictional data related to persons or companies or URLs used throughout this book is intended for instructional purposes only. At the time this book was printed, any such data was fictional and not belonging to any real persons or companies.

Course Technology, a part of Cengage Learning, reserves the right to revise this publication and make changes from time to time in its content without notice.

The programs in this book are for instructional purposes only.

They have been tested with care, but are not guaranteed for any particular intent beyond educational purposes. The author and the publisher do not offer any warranties or representations, nor do they accept any liabilities with respect to the programs.

Printed in the United States of America
1 2 3 4 5 6 16 15 14 13 12 11

TABLE OF CONTENTS

CHAPTER ONE
AN OVERVIEW OF COMPUTERS AND PROGRAMMING LANGUAGES 1

Chapter 1: Assignment Cover Sheet 2
Lab 1.1 Learning about Different Types of Computers 3
Lab 1.2 Exploring the Hardware and Software Components of a Computer System 4
Lab 1.3 Storing Information Electronically 6
Lab 1.4 Processing a C++ Language Program 8
Lab 1.5 Programming with the Problem Analysis-Coding-Execution Cycle 11

CHAPTER TWO
BASIC ELEMENTS OF C++ 15

Chapter 2: Assignment Cover Sheet 16
Lab 2.1 Identifying Basic Elements of a C++ Program 17
Lab 2.2 Identifying Data Types 20
Lab 2.3 Using Arithmetic Operators, Operator Precedence, and the `string` Data Type 23
Lab 2.4 Using `cin`, Allocating Memory, and Writing Assignment Statements 26
Lab 2.5 Using `cout`, the `endl` Manipulator, and Common Escape Sequences 30
Lab 2.6 Using Preprocessor Directives, the `string` Data Type, and Writing a C++ Program Using Good Programming Style and Form 34

CHAPTER THREE
INPUT/OUTPUT 51

Chapter 3: Assignment Cover Sheet 52
Lab 3.1 Examining Predefined Input Functions 53
Lab 3.2 Examining and Formatting Output 67
Lab 3.3 Understanding Input Failure 73
Lab 3.4 Using Files for Input and Output 77

CHAPTER FOUR
CONTROL STRUCTURES I (*SELECTION*) 83

Chapter 4: Assignment Cover Sheet 84
Lab 4.1 Using Relational and Logical Operators to Evaluate Logical (Boolean) Expressions 85
Lab 4.2 Using the Selection Control Structures `if` and `if...else` 88
Lab 4.3 Using Nested `if` and `if...else` Statements 93
Lab 4.4 Using the `if` Statement with Input Failure 98
Lab 4.5 Confusing the Assignment Operator (=) with the Equality Operator (==) 109
Lab 4.6 Using the Conditional Operator (?:) 111
Lab 4.7 Using the `switch` Selection Control Structure 113
Lab 4.8 Using the `assert` Function to Terminate a Program 122

CHAPTER FIVE
CONTROL STRUCTURES II (*REPETITION*) 127
Chapter 5: Assignment Cover Sheet 128
Lab 5.1 Using the `while` Looping (Repetition) Structure 129
Lab 5.2 Using the `for` Looping (Repetition) Structure 142
Lab 5.3 Using the `do...while` Looping (Repetition) Structure 151
Lab 5.4 Using `break` and `continue` Statements 158
Lab 5.5 Using Nested Control Structures 165
Lab 5.6 Converting between `while`, `do...while`, and `for` Loops 172

CHAPTER SIX
USER-DEFINED FUNCTIONS I 181
Chapter 6: Assignment Cover Sheet 182
Lab 6.1 Exploring Other Standard (Predefined) Functions 183
Lab 6.2 Adding User-Defined, Value-Returning Functions 189
Lab 6.3 Using User-Defined, Value-Returning Functions 194
Lab 6.4 Testing and Debugging a Program with User-Defined, Value-Returning Functions 198

CHAPTER SEVEN
USER-DEFINED FUNCTIONS II....205
Chapter 7: Assignment Cover Sheet 206
Lab 7.1 Calling Void Functions without Parameters 207
Lab 7.2 Calling Void Functions with Value Parameters 212
Lab 7.3 Calling Void Functions with Value and Reference Parameters 220
Lab 7.4 Accessing an Identifier by Its Scope 227
Lab 7.5 Using Static and Automatic Variables 234
Lab 7.6 Using Function Overloading 239
Lab 7.7 Using Default Parameters 244

CHAPTER EIGHT
USER-DEFINED SIMPLE DATA TYPES, NAMESPACES, AND THE `string` TYPE 249
Chapter 8: Assignment Cover Sheet 250
Lab 8.1 Creating and Manipulating Enumerated Data Types 251
Lab 8.2 Using the `typedef` Statement 254
Lab 8.3 Using the `namespace` Mechanism 257
Lab 8.4 Using the `string` data type and `string` functions 259
Lab 8.5 Challenge Programming Using `string` Manipulations 264

CHAPTER NINE
ARRAYS AND STRINGS 265

Chapter 9: Assignment Cover Sheet 266
Lab 9.1 Declaring and Manipulating Data into Arrays 267
Lab 9.2 Checking Index Bounds and Initializing Arrays 272
Lab 9.3 Passing Arrays as Parameters to Functions 280
Lab 9.4 Coding with C-strings 285
Lab 9.5 Inputting and Outputting Data Using C-strings 288
Lab 9.6 Coding with Parallel Arrays 292
Lab 9.7 Manipulating Data in a Two-Dimensional Array 299
Lab 9.8 Using a Multidimensional Array 304

CHAPTER TEN
APPLICATIONS OF ARRAYS (SEARCHING AND SORTING) AND THE `vector` TYPE 309

Chapter 10: Assignment Cover Sheet 310
Lab 10.1 Implementing the Sequential Search Algorithm 311
Lab 10.2 Sorting an Array Using Selection Sort 316
Lab 10.3 Implementing the Binary Search Algorithm 322
Lab 10.4 Implementing the Insertion Sort 326
Lab 10.5 Using the **`vector`** Data Type 329

CHAPTER ELEVEN
RECORDS (`structs`) 335

Chapter 11: Assignment Cover Sheet 336
Lab 11.1 Defining **`structs`** and Declaring **`struct`** Variables 337
Lab 11.2 Manipulating Data Using a **`struct`** 341
Lab 11.3 Using Arrays in **`structs`** 346
Lab 11.4 Using **`structs`** in **`vectors`** 351

CHAPTER TWELVE
CLASSES AND DATA ABSTRACTION 357

Chapter 12: Assignment Cover Sheet 358
Lab 12.1 Describing Classes Using the Unified Modeling Language (UML) Notation and Declaring Objects 359
Lab 12.2 Manipulating and Accessing Data within the Class 363
Lab 12.3 Designing Driver Programs 368
Lab 12.4 Invoking Default Constructors, Constructors with Parameters, and Constructors with Default Parameters 372
Lab 12.5 Invoking Destructors 377
Lab 12.6 Using the Abstract Data Type (ADT) and Information Hiding 378
Lab 12.7 Using Static Members of a Class 380

CHAPTER THIRTEEN
INHERITANCE AND COMPOSITION 385
Chapter 13: Assignment Cover Sheet 386
Lab 13.1 Overriding Member Functions of the Base Class 387
Lab 13.2 Using Constructors of Derived and Base Classes 393
Lab 13.3 Creating Header Files for the Base Class and the Derived Classes 395
Lab 13.4 Using Protected Members of a Class in Inheritance 400
Lab 13.5 Relating Classes through Composition 404
Lab 13.6 Defining Object-Oriented Design (OOD) and Object-Oriented Programming (OOP) 406

CHAPTER FOURTEEN
POINTERS, CLASSES, AND VIRTUAL FUNCTIONS 409
Chapter 14: Assignment Cover Sheet 410
Lab 14.1 Declaring Pointer Variables, the Address Of Operator (&), and the Dereferencing Operator (*) 411
Lab 14.2 Accessing Pointers to Classes and Structs 413
Lab 14.3 Using Dynamic Variables and Dynamic Arrays 416
Lab 14.4 Understanding Shallow versus Deep Copy and Pointers 420
Lab 14.5 Understanding Peculiarities of Classes with Pointer Data Members 421
Lab 14.6 Using Inheritance, Pointers, and Virtual Functions 422

CHAPTER FIFTEEN
OVERLOADING AND TEMPLATES 427
Chapter 15: Assignment Cover Sheet 428
Lab 15.1 Using Operator Overloading 429
Lab 15.2 Overloading Binary Operators 432
Lab 15.3 Overloading Unary Operators 435
Lab 15.4 Understanding Templates 438

CHAPTER SIXTEEN
EXCEPTION HANDLING 443
Chapter 16: Assignment Cover Sheet 444
Lab 16.1 Catching Exceptions and Processing Exceptions During Program Execution Using `try` and `catch` Blocks 445
Lab 16.2 Using C++ Exception Classes 449
Lab 16.3 More About Exception Handling 453
Lab 16.4 Creating Your Own Exception Classes 458

CHAPTER SEVENTEEN
RECURSION 463
Chapter 17: Assignment Cover Sheet 464
Lab 17.1 Using a Recursive Algorithm 465
Lab 17.2 Designing a Recursive Algorithm for a Power Function 470
Lab 17.3 Recursion and Iteration 473

INTRODUCTION

The objective of this lab manual is to give students step-by-step examples to become familiar with programming concepts, design, and coding. This text is designed to be used with *C++ Programming: From Problem Analysis to Program Design, Fifth Edition*, but it also can be used to supplement any CS1 C++ textbook. This manual is written to be used in a classroom lab environment.

FEATURES

To ensure a successful experience for instructors and students alike, this book includes the following features:

- **Lab Objectives** — Every lab has a brief description and list of learning objectives.
- **Materials Required** — Every lab includes information on hardware, software, and other materials you will need to complete the lab.
- **Completion Times** — Every lab has an estimated completion time, so that you can plan your activities more accurately.
- **Activity Sections** — Labs are presented in manageable sections. Where appropriate, additional Activity Background information is provided to illustrate the importance of a particular project.
- **Step-by-Step Instructions** provide steps to enhance technical proficiency.
- **Review Questions** help reinforce concepts presented in the lab.

SOFTWARE REQUIREMENTS

- Computer running Windows 2000, Windows XP, Vista, or Windows 7.
- Microsoft Visual C++ .NET or Bloodshed Dev-C++. Dev-C++ is another IDE that can be freely downloaded.

Completing the Lab Assignments

Some lab assignments require written answers to complete an exercise, while others are programming assignments that require you to work with a C++ compiler.

- To complete the written assignments, remove the pages that your instructor assigns, and then write your answers directly on the pages of the Lab Manual.
- To complete the programming assignments, use the compiler that your instructor recommends or requires. Print all the documentation assigned, including program code, program prompts, input and output displayed on the screen, input files, and output files. You can submit your written answers and the printed documentation with a lab cover sheet for grading.

  If your instructor requires an electronic copy of your work, e-mail the completed assignment to your instructor or include a CD or flash drive with your work. Your instructor will tell you what is needed, but be sure to submit the .cpp, .exe, and any .h files that you create, as well as any input and output files. Also include your name or ID in the titles of all your files.
- To provide program documentation, compile and run your program, copy the prompts, input, and output (if appropriate), and paste them as a block comment at the end of your program.

  In Windows 2000, click the Mark button on the toolbar of the output window. (The toolbar appears by default; if the output window does not have a toolbar, follow the instructions for Windows XP.) Drag to select the text you want to copy, and then click the Copy button. Open your program in a text editor, such as the program editor in your SDK, click at the end of the program, and type /* to begin a block comment. Press Ctrl+V to paste the text in the program file, and then type */ to end the block comment.

  In Windows XP or Vista, right-click the title bar of the output window, point to Edit, and then click Mark. Drag to select the text you want to copy, and then press Enter. Open your program in a text editor, such as the program editor in your SDK, click at the end of the program, and type /* to begin a block comment. Press Ctrl+V to paste the text in the program file, and then type */ to end the block comment.

  After you paste the comment in the program, either print the program file from your text editor or submit the program file to your instructor electronically.

About the Author

Judy Scholl has been a Professor of Computer Science at Austin Community College in Austin, Texas since 1988. She currently teaches programming languages and Web authoring courses. She received her Ph.D. from the University of Texas at Austin.

Gerard Nugent is a Lecturer in the CIS Department of the McCoy School of Business at Texas State University–San Marcos where he teaches Microcomputer Applications. He is also an Adjunct Professor at Austin Community College, Austin, Texas where he teaches programming languages. He received his Masters of Science in Computer Science from Texas State University–San Marcos and holds a J.D. from the University of Texas at Austin.

C++ Programming:
From Problem Analysis to Program Design, Fifth Edition
Lab Manual

1 An Overview of Computers and Programming Languages

In this chapter, you will:

- Learn about different types of computers
- Explore the hardware and software components of a computer system
- Learn about the language of a computer
- Learn about the evolution of programming languages
- Examine high-level programming languages
- Discover what a compiler is and what it does
- Examine a C++ program
- Examine how a C++ program is processed
- Learn what an algorithm is and explore problem-solving techniques
- Become aware of structured design and object-oriented design programming methodologies
- Become aware of Standard C++ and ANSI/ISO Standard C++

Chapter 1: Assignment Cover Sheet

Name ______________________ Date ______________________

Section ______________________

Lab Assignments	Assigned	Grade
Lab 1.1 Learning about Different Types of Computers		
Lab 1.2 Exploring the Hardware and Software Components of a Computer System		
Lab 1.3 Storing Information Electronically		
Lab 1.4 Processing a C++ Language Program		
Lab 1.5 Programming with the Problem Analysis-Coding-Execution Cycle		
Total Grade		

See your instructor or the introduction to this book for instructions on submitting your assignments.

Lab 1.1 Learning about Different Types of Computers

Computers and software can help you perform many tasks, such as maintaining a bank account and writing assignments or reports. Software is developed using programming languages. This book uses the C++ programming language to develop software that can accomplish specific tasks.

Computers have evolved from their introduction in the 1950s, when there were very few computers, through the 1960s, when manufacturers produced very large, expensive computers, to the 1970s, when people began to use cheaper, smaller computers. Today, computers are even more affordable and faster. Regardless of the type, mainframe, midsize, and micro (personal) computers share some basic elements, including input, output, storage, and performance of arithmetic and logical operations.

A mainframe computer was once one of the largest, fastest, and most powerful computers available. However, to put this in perspective, a mainframe in 1960 was less powerful than today's personal computer. During the next decade, the midsize computer was introduced as a less expensive, less powerful, smaller, and more affordable alternative to mainframes. The introduction of micro computers, or personal computers (PCs), brought all of these efficiencies to a level that made computers a household commodity. PCs are usually sold with descriptions of their features to help consumers (who are often not computer experts) match the computer's features with their needs.

Objectives

In this lab, you become acquainted with the different types of computers that have evolved and identify how each is used.

After completing this lab, you will be able to:

- Identify and define the different types of computers.
- Identify the capabilities of the different types of computers.

Estimated completion time: **5 minutes**

Learn about Different Types of Computers

Match the following terms with the appropriate definitions.

1. 1950s	a) Personal computer
2. 1960s	b) When computers became affordable for non-specialists
3. 1990s	c) A less expensive and smaller computer than a mainframe that allowed more companies to afford computers
4. Mainframe	d) When accessibility to computers was limited to very few people
5. Midsize computer	e) When large companies began to use computers
6. Microcomputer	f) Until recently, one of the largest, fastest, and most powerful computers

Lab 1.2 Exploring the Hardware and Software Components of a Computer System

A computer is an electronic device made up of physical components (hardware) and programs (software). Major hardware components include the following:

- central processing unit (CPU), which contains the control unit (CU), arithmetic logic unit (ALU), and various registers for special purposes such as the instruction register (IR) and program counter (PC);
- main memory (MM), also called random access memory (RAM); and
- input/output devices and secondary storage.

The CPU is the brain of the computer and determines the computer's speed. The ALU, an important component of the CPU, carries out all arithmetic and logical operations. The accumulator (ACC) holds the results of the operations performed by the ALU. Main memory is directly connected to the CPU. Main memory is an ordered sequence of cells, called memory cells. Each cell has a unique location in main memory, called the address of the cell. Both data and instructions (programs) are stored in main memory. All instructions (programs) and data must be loaded into main memory before they can be executed, or performed. Programs and data are transferred to secondary storage when they are not being executed.

Programs are commands that perform input (get data), produce output (display results), provide storage, and calculate arithmetic and logical operations. There are two types of programs, system programs and application programs. System programs control the computer and monitor activities of the computer. Application programs perform a specific task. Examples of application programs include word processing, spreadsheets, and games.

Objectives

In this lab, you become acquainted with common computer terminology regarding hardware and software components.

After completing this lab, you will be able to:

- Identify and define hardware components.
- Distinguish between types of programs.
- Recognize addressing, storage, input, and output.

Estimated completion time: **15–20 minutes**

Explore the Hardware Components of a Computer System

Match the following terms with the appropriate definitions.

1. Accumulator	a) An electronic device that can perform commands to input, output, or store data and can calculate arithmetic and logical expressions
2. Address	b) Computer components including the central processing unit (CPU), main memory (MM), input/output devices, and secondary storage
3. Arithmetic logic unit	c) The brain of the computer, containing several components such as the control unit (CU), program counter (PC), instruction register (IR), arithmetic logic unit (ALU), and accumulator (ACC)

4. Computer	d) Controls a program's overall execution
5. CPU	e) Points to the next instruction to be executed
6. CU	f) Holds the instruction that is currently being executed
7. Hardware	g) Holds the results of the operations performed by the arithmetic logic unit
8. Input devices	h) The component of the CPU that performs arithmetic and logical operations
9. Instruction register	i) A unique location in main memory
10. Output devices	j) Stores information permanently
11. Program counter	k) Devices including the keyboard, mouse, and secondary storage
12. Secondary storage	l) Devices including monitor, printer, and secondary storage

Explore the Software Components of a Computer System

1. Application program	a) Computer instructions used to solve a problem
2. Program	b) Programs run by the computer
3. Software	c) Used to monitor the overall activity of the computer and provide services
4. System program	d) Used to perform a specific task; examples include word processing, spreadsheets, and games

Answer the following questions about the computer in your computer lab:

1. What is the computer's operating system?

2. How much memory does the computer have?

3. What type of CPU does the computer have?

4. How much secondary storage does the computer have?

Lab 1.3 Storing Information Electronically

A computer is an electronic device that processes digital signals, which represent information with a sequence of 0s and 1s—binary code. These digital signals are called the language of a computer, or machine language. The digit 0 or 1 is called a binary digit, or bit. A sequence of eight bits is called a byte.

All data is stored and manipulated as binary codes. Inside the computer, every character is represented as a sequence of bits, each having a unique representation. Encoding schemes need either one or two bytes to store characters, depending on the scheme. Although most computers perform the same kinds of operations, the machine language of one computer is not necessarily the same as the machine language of another computer.

Machine language code, or programs written in binary code, are very difficult to write and are error-prone. Assembly languages, instructions written in an easy-to-remember form called a mnemonic, were developed to make programming easier. However, assembly language instructions must be translated into machine language before being executed. A program called an assembler translates the assembly language instructions into machine language.

The next step toward making programming easier was the creation of high-level languages that were closer to natural languages. To run a program written in a high-level language, the instructions must first be translated into machine language using a program called a compiler.

Objectives

In this lab, you become acquainted with electronic signals and the representative code used to interpret these signals.

After completing this lab, you will be able to:

- Identify machine representation of computer code.

Estimated completion time: **15–20 minutes**

Storing Information Electronically

Fill in the blank with the appropriate term.

1. The two types of electrical signals are ______________ and ______________.
2. ______________ signals represent information with a sequence of 0s and 1s.
3. The digits 0 and 1 are used to represent ______________.
4. The digits 0 and 1 are called ______________ or the shortened term ______________.
5. The sequence of 0s and 1s is referred to as ______________.
6. A sequence of eight bits is called a(n) ______________.
7. The most common encoding scheme on personal computers is ______________ and is abbreviated as ______________.
8. Refer to the appendices in your text: The character represented by the decimal number 97 is ______________.
9. Refer to the appendices in your text: The character represented by the decimal number 65 is ______________.
10. C++ differentiates between uppercase and lowercase characters. True or False?

11. Machine language that used binary code made programming prone to errors. True or False?
12. Assembly language is used to make instructions easy to remember. True or False?
13. A program that translates assembly language instructions into machine language is called a(n) ________________.
14. A program that translates instructions written in a high-level language into machine code is called a(n) ________________.

Give the ASCII code for the following integers and characters.

1. 'A'
2. 4
3. '4'
4. 'a'
5. '\n'
6. '\0'
7. 0
8. '0'

LAB 1.4 PROCESSING A C++ LANGUAGE PROGRAM

The following is an example of a C++ program:

```
1 #include <iostream>
2 using namespace std;
3
4 int main()
5 {
6        cout << "Welcome to the C++ Programming" << endl << endl;
7        cout << "Anything in double quotes is a string." << endl;
8        cout << "Numbers in quotes are a string like 8 + 7" << endl;
9        cout << "Numbers not in quotes like " << 8 << " or "
              << 7 << "have their values printed." << endl;
10       cout << "Numbers not in quotes with arithmetic operators are "
              << "evaluated " << 8 + 7 << endl;
11       return 0;
12 }
```

When compiled, linked, and executed, this program will display:

```
Welcome to C++ Programming
Anything in double quotes is a string.
Numbers in quotes are a string like 8 + 7
Numbers not in quotes like 8 or 7 have their values printed.
Numbers not in quotes with arithmetic operators are evaluated 15
```

The line numbers along the left margin of the code are not part of the program but are used to identify the line; each numbered line refers to a statement in the code, as explained in the following.

Line 1 is a statement that begins with a `#`. This is a preprocessor directive. There can be multiple preprocessor directives, each of which represents prewritten code in a C++ library. The iostream library contains code needed for program input and output operations.

Line 2, `using namespace std;`, is required in order to use **`cout`** (the predefined object) and **`endl`** (the m1nipulator); **`cout`** is used for output, and **`endl`** is used for moving the insertion point to the next line.

Line 3 is an empty line, often called "whitespace."

Line 4 identifies the beginning of the main function, **`int main ()`**. All programs are functions in C++.

Line 5, the opening brace ({), is the beginning of the body of the main function. All functions begin with an opening brace and end with a closing brace (}).

Lines 6, 7, & 8. The **`cout`** object and the **`insertion`** operator (<<) cause the values between double quotes, referred to as a string, to be displayed exactly as written. Each string, expression, or manipulator is preceded by the insertion operator (<<) within the cout statement.

Line 9 is an output statement that contains both a string and literal numbers (numbers not in quotes) as separate data items (called expressions). Numbers are displayed as their literal values.

Line 10 is another output statement that contains a string and an arithmetic operation (expression). The arithmetic operation is evaluated and displayed as evaluated. Lines 9 and 10 are continued on the next line but remain part of the same statement.

Line 11 contains the reserved word **`return`**. When the program finishes, a return value of 0 tells the operating system that the program has completed.

Line 12 contains the closing brace (}) that indicates the end of the body of the main function.

C++ is up one language level from assembly language. It is one of many high-level programming languages that use parts of a natural language to make it easier to understand. Six steps are necessary to process a program written in a high-level language:

1. Use a text editor to create source code in the high-level language. The text editor is contained in the SDK. The source code must follow the rules (syntax) of the language. Save the source code of the program in a file that has a .cpp file extension. The text editor is contained in the SDK.
2. Begin with the preprocessor directives needed for the program. This statement is processed by a program called the preprocessor.
3. The compiler is a program that verifies that the source code obeys the rules of the programming language (the syntax). When the program is syntactically correct, the compiler translates the program into a machine language program called an object program. The compiler is part of a software development kit (SDK).
4. Another program in the SDK is called a linker, which combines the object program with prewritten code from libraries, such as iostream, creating an executable program. This is usually performed with the "Build" or "Make" command in the SDK.
5. An additional program in the SDK is called the loader, which loads the executable program into main memory.
6. Finally, execute or run the program.

Objectives

To become familiar with the different programs in the SDK by creating a program written in a high-level language program.

After completing this lab, you will be able to:

- Identify the process needed to convert a high level language program, in this case C++, to an executable program.

Estimated completion time: **15–20 minutes**

Process a C++ Language Program

Answer the following questions by circling the correct answer:

1. An SDK is primarily used to create an assembly program. True or False
2. Every C++ program will contain a function. True or False
3. A high-level source code file can be loaded into main memory and executed. True or False
4. The numbers contained in a string can be mathematically evaluated in a program output statement. True or False
5. A compiler directive is executed by the preprocessor program. True or False
6. High-level language source code is more easily read than machine code. True or False

Select the correct answer to the following questions:

7. A program that combines the source code with prewritten code is
   a) the preprocessor.
   b) the loader.
   c) the linker.
   d) the compiler.

8. A file that contains the program after it has been translated into machine code is
   a) the editor file.
   b) the source code file.
   c) the object file.
   d) the .cpp file.

9. An assembler is
   a) a high-level language that uses a natural language.
   b) a program in the SDK that links source code with prewritten code.
   c) a program that translates assembly code into machine code.
   d) a program that places a source code file into main memory.

10. The rules for correctly writing a C++ source code program are known as
   a) the grammar.
   b) the syntax.
   c) the preprocessing.
   d) the SDK.

11. The program that places the executable program into main memory is
   a) the compiler.
   b) the editor.
   c) the preprocessor.
   d) the loader.

Lab 1.5 Programming with the Problem Analysis-Coding-Execution Cycle

To become a good programmer, you must learn good problem-solving techniques. To develop a program, you start by analyzing a problem, outlining the problem requirements, and designing steps, called an algorithm, to solve the problem. Secondly, you implement the algorithm in a programming language. You follow the six steps listed in Lab 1.4 to run the program and verify that the algorithm works. Thirdly, you maintain the program by using and modifying it if the problem domain changes.

Running a program successfully does not necessarily mean that the program processes the data correctly. You need to test your program with sample data or perform some mathematical analysis to test whether it runs correctly. If it does not, then you must examine the code, the algorithm, or the initial problem analysis.

Dividing a problem into smaller subproblems is called structured design. In structured design, you analyze a subproblem and then produce a solution for the subproblem. The process of implementing a structured design is called structured programming, top-down design, stepwise refinement, or modular programming. To develop a program to solve a problem, you start by analyzing the problem. Next, you code the program and then execute it. Structured programming breaks a problem into smaller problems and applies the problem analysis-coding-execution cycle to each small problem.

Objectives

In this lab, you learn problem-solving and design steps to solve problems.

After completing this lab, you will be able to:

- Analyze problems and produce the steps necessary to solve the problem.

Estimated completion time: **45 minutes**

Program with the Problem Analysis-Coding-Execution Cycle

Answer the following questions or complete the steps for problem solving.

1. What are the three steps required in problem solving in the programming environment?

2. Draw a diagram showing the problem analysis-coding-execution cycle steps. Include arrows that indicate the flow when an error occurs and when there is no error.

3. What is the most important step in program development? Why?

4. What are three other names used to represent structured design? What is the basis for structured design?

5. Once a problem has been divided into subproblems, what step must occur next?

6. Converting your design into a high-level language only occurs after your design has been checked to be logically sound. What steps do you take once you have created your source code from your design?

7. Even if a program executes successfully, how do you know that it is correct?

8. Consider the problem of converting miles to kilometers. To find the equivalent kilometers, the number of miles is divided by 0.62. Write the steps involved in calculating the mileage conversion when the number of miles is 12.

9. Consider the problem of calculating a paycheck. The pay is calculated by multiplying the number of hours worked by the rate of pay. All hours greater than 40 are calculated at time and a half. Correct any steps below that are in error.

   a. Get the number of hours worked.

   b. Get the rate of pay.

   c. Get the amount of pay.

   d. Find the amount of pay at the base salary.

   e. Find the number of overtime hours.

   f. Find the number of hours at regular pay.

   g. Find the amount of pay at overtime rate.

   h. Calculate the paycheck using the following equation:

      pay = hoursWorked * rateOfPay + overtimeHours * pay * 1.5

2 Basic Elements of C++

In this chapter, you will:

- Become familiar with the basic components of a C++ program, including functions, special symbols, word symbols, and identifiers
- Explore simple data types and examine the string data type
- Discover how to use arithmetic operators
- Examine how a program evaluates arithmetic expressions
- Learn what an assignment statement is and what it does
- Discover how to input data into memory using input statements
- Become familiar with the use of increment and decrement operators
- Examine ways to output results using output statements
- Learn how to use preprocessor directives and learn why they are necessary
- Explore how to structure a program properly, including using comments to document a program
- Learn how to write a C++ program

Chapter 2: Assignment Cover Sheet

Name ______________________________ Date ______________________________

Section ______________________________

Lab Assignments	Assigned	Grade
Lab 2.1 Identifying Basic Elements of a C++ Program		
Lab 2.2 Identifying Data Types		
Lab 2.3 Using Arithmetic Operators,Operator Precedence, and the `string` Data Type		
Lab 2.4 Using `cin`, Allocating Memory, and Writing Assignment Statements		
Lab 2.5 Using `cout`, the `endl` Manipulator, and Common Escape Sequences		
Lab 2.6 Using Preprocessor Directives, the `string` Data Type, and Writing a C++ Program Using Good Programming Style and Form (Critical Thinking Exercises)		
Total Grade		

See your instructor or the introduction to this book for instructions on submitting your assignments.

LAB 2.1 IDENTIFYING BASIC ELEMENTS OF A C++ PROGRAM

A computer program is a sequence of statements whose objective is to accomplish a task that requires planning and creating a program. These statements in C++ are grouped into functions. Some functions, called predefined or standard functions, are provided as part of the system. Other functions are written by programmers. Each C++ program must have one and only one function named main and may have other functions. The following is a sample C++ program that displays "Welcome to C++ Programming" on the screen:

```
#include <iostream>
using namespace std;

int main()
{
cout <<"Welcome to C++ Programming" << endl;
return 0;
}
```

To write meaningful programs, you must learn the special symbols, words, and syntax rules of any programming language. You must also learn semantic rules, which determine the meaning of the instructions. Additionally, you should learn the tokens, which are the smallest units of a program written in any programming language. C++ tokens are divided into special symbols, word symbols, and identifiers.

Some special symbols in C++ are:

+	-	*	/
.	;	?	,
<=	!=	==	>=

(the blank is also a special symbol)

Some word symbols (reserved words or keywords) in C++ are:

`int, float, double, char, const, void, public, return`

Keywords and reserved words are names of the data types, which cannot be used for any other purpose in the C++ programming language.

The third category of C++ tokens, identifiers, are used to name things. A C++ identifier can only consist of letters, digits, and the underscore character (_). Identifiers cannot start with a digit and are case sensitive. Identifiers can be of any length; however, each computer system has a maximum significant number of characters, which restricts the length of an identifier. Additionally, some software development kits (SDKs) may conflict with identifiers that start with an underscore; therefore, avoid using identifiers beginning with an underscore.

Two predefined identifiers are `cout`, which is used when generating output, and `cin`, which is used to input data. Predefined identifiers can be redefined, but it would not be wise to do so.

Objectives

In this lab, you become acquainted with tokens used in C++ statements, which are the special symbols, word symbols, and identifiers used in C++ statements.

After completing this lab, you will be able to:

- Recognize special symbols.
- Recognize word symbols.
- Recognize identifiers.
- Recognize invalid symbol representations.
- Write a simple C++ program that displays a message to the screen.

Estimated completion time: **10–20 minutes**

Identifying Basic Elements of a C++ Program

Indicate whether each of the following representations is a special symbol, word symbol, or identifier or is invalid.

Token	Special symbol	Word symbol	Identifier	Invalid
1. ABC				
2. xy!				
3. double				
4. $2ft				
5. &&ab				
6. ab*				
7. return				
8. c3po				
9. void				
10. 123z				
11. FLOAT				
12. date				
13. qr&				
14. first name				
15. *				
16. R2D2				
17. 5day				
18. !=				
19. +xy				
20. hello				

Question	Answer (Circle the correct answer.)	
21. Given: `int number;` `int` is a keyword.	True	False
22. Given: `date today;` `date` is a keyword.	True	False
23. Given: `int date;` `int` is a keyword.	True	False
24. The syntax to declare a named constant is: `const dataType identifier = value;`	True	False
25. The order-of-precedence rules for arithmetic operators are semantic-based rules.	True	False
26. The semantics of the following statements are the same: `2 + 3 * 5` and `(2 + 3) * 5`	True	False

27. Write the statements needed for a C++ program that will display "Hello World" on the screen.

LAB 2.2 IDENTIFYING DATA TYPES

The purpose of computer programs is to manipulate data. Data is entered and becomes the input. The program then manipulates the data in some way, and the result is the output. The data entered is composed of symbols, such as alphabetic letters, characters, digits, words, images, etc., each of which represents certain values. Programming languages categorize data into specific data types, according to the type of values the symbols represent. All data used in a programming language will be organized as belonging to a specific data type. Additionally, each data type has a certain set of operations that can be used with it. A data type, therefore, consists of a set of values together with a set of operations.

In C++, there are three groups of data types: simple, structured, and pointers. This exercise deals only with simple data types. Simple data types are further classified into integral, floating-point, and enumerated data types. The integral data type has integers or whole numbers (no decimals). The floating-point data type consists of real (decimal) numbers. Enumerated is a user-defined data type covered later in the text and this lab manual. The names of the data types are keywords or reserved words, which cannot be used for any other purpose in the C++ programming language.

Integral Data Types

There are nine categories of integral data types, each of which has a specified amount of memory allocated and range of values. This exercise deals with only the **char**, **int**, **short**, and **bool** types. Different compilers may designate a different memory allocation and have a different range of values other that those shown below.

Integer Data Types		
name	memory (storage in bytes)	range of values
int	4	-2147483648 to 2147483647
short	2	-32768 to 32767
bool	1	true or false
char	1	-128 to 127

The **int** data type can be positive or negative numbers. Positive numbers can have, but do not need, a + in front of them. Negative numbers must be preceded by a minus (–) sign. No commas are used to separate thousands, millions, etc. Examples are 15070, 0, -567, and +755.

The **bool** data type is often referred to as a logical or Boolean type that can have only a true or false value. True and false are reserved words or keywords.

The **char** data type consists of characters (letters, digits, or special symbols). Most, but not all, of these can be found as keys on the keyboard. All char values consist of only one character and are enclosed in single quote marks, e.g., 'A', 'a', '4' (note, in this case, 4 is not an integer but the character 4), '&', ' ' (a character space is represented as a space between two single quote marks).

char values come from character data sets, the most common of which is the American Standard Code for Information Interchange (ASCII, pronounced "askey") containing 128 ordered values. Each character has a position on the ASCII chart, which is used to compare characters. 'A' has an ASCII value 65, and 'a" has an ASCII value 97. Some nonprintable character representations on the ASCII chart require the use of a backslash character with another character, such as the new line character '\n'.

Floating-Point Data Types

Floating-point data types are decimals that can be represented in both scientific and fixed notations. The fixed notation real number 668.492 is represented as 6.684920E2 in scientific notation. Another example is the fixed notation real number 0.0055, which is represented as 0.550000E-2 in scientific notation. Fixed notation real number -5.25 would become -5.250000E0 in scientific notation.

Two of the floating-point data types are **float** and **double**. The **float** is sometimes called single precision, and **double** is called double precision. The term precision refers to the number of significant digits to the right of the decimal point. The **float** type is thus accurate up to six or seven decimal places, whereas the **double** type is accurate up to fifteen decimal places. In C++, floating-point numbers are considered **double** by default. Use of the **float** data type may generate compiler warnings such as "truncation from double to float." This can be avoided by simply using the **double** data type.

The following chart shows the memory allocation and value ranges for the **float** and **double** data types.

Float Data Types		
name	memory (in storage bytes)	range of values
float	4	-3.4E+38 to 3.4E+38
double	8	-1.7E+308 to 1.7E+308

Objectives

In this lab, you become acquainted with simple data types–**int**, **char**, **bool**, **float**, and **double**–and keywords.

After completing this lab, you will be able to:

- Identify integral, character, Boolean, floating-point data types, and keywords.

Estimated completion time: **10 minutes**

Identify the data type of the following examples:

1. '\n' ____________________
2. 24 ____________________
3. 5 ____________________
4. '9' ____________________
5. true ____________________
6. 0.00532 ____________________
7. -5.496720E3 ____________________
8. 66.0 ____________________
9. -7 ____________________
10. 'L' ____________________
11. '?' ____________________
12. 1.343000+E6 ____________________

Give an example of a value for the following data types:

13. char ____________________
14. fixed notation float ____________________
15. int ____________________
16. negative double number in scientific notation ____________________
17. bool ____________________
18. short ____________________

LAB 2.3 USING ARITHMETIC OPERATORS, OPERATOR PRECEDENCE, AND THE `string` DATA TYPE

In computer programming, there are five arithmetic operators: + addition, – subtraction, * multiplication, / division, and % modulus operator (remainder). Arithmetic expressions and precedence are evaluated as they are in mathematics with multiplication, division, and modulus having the same precedence and a higher precedence than addition and subtraction, which have the same precedence. However, the symbols—the operators—used in evaluation have minor differences. For instance, in mathematics, "a times b" can be written as a × b, ab, a(b) (a)b, or (a)(b). In C++, "a times b" can only be written using the * operator. Parentheses can be used in computer programming, such as a*b, (a*b), or (a)*(b), but they do not indicate multiplication.

The numbers or variables in the expression are called operands. Operators that have two operands are called binary operators. Operators that have only one operand are called unary operators. When evaluated, mixed expressions with mixed operands change integers to floating-point numbers.

Integer division truncates the result. For example, in integer division, the expression 5/2 results in 2 (with no decimal). In floating-point division, the expression 5.0/2.0 results in 2.5. In a mixed expression of either 5/2.0 or 5.0/2, the result is 2.5. The result of 3⁄4 is 0, not 0.75. The result of 3.0⁄4.0 is 0.75.

The modulus operator works with integers to find the whole number remainder. Using the same example 5%2, the remainder is 1, not 0.5. The remainder of 3/4 (written 3%4) is 3, not 0.75. The expression 3.0%4.0 is invalid.

The operators *, /, and % have the same level of precedence, meaning that the operation occurs as it is encountered, left to right (unless overridden by parentheses), when evaluating the expression. The operators + and – have the same level of precedence, and that level is below the level of the operators *, /, and %.

Since the `char` data type is also an integral data type, C++ allows you to perform arithmetic operations on `char` data. The character '8' differs in representation from the integer 8. The integer value of 8 is 8, whereas the integer value of the character '8' is 56. Be careful when using the `char` data type for arithmetic operations.

If all operands (that is, numbers) in an expression are integers, the expression is called an integral expression. If all operands in an expression are floating-point numbers, the expression is called a floating-point or decimal expression. An expression that has operands of different data types is called a mixed expression. When evaluating an operator in a mixed expression, keep the following guidelines in mind:

- If the operator has the same types of operands, the operator is evaluated according to the type of operands.
- If the operator has both types of operands, then during calculation, the integer is changed to a floating-point number with the decimal part of zero, and the operator is evaluated. The result is a floating-point number.

Operators having the same level of precedence are evaluated from left to right.

A value of one data type can be automatically changed to another data type, as in a mixed expression. This process is called implicit type coercion. To avoid implicit type coercion, C++ provides for explicit type conversion through the use of the cast operator, also called type conversion or type casting. Type casting does not change the actual value of a variable; type casting changes the value of an expression. The cast operator takes the following forms, with the first example being more stable:

- `static_cast<dataTypeName>(expression)`
- `dataType(expression)`

The data type `string` is a programmer-defined data type. To use this data type, you need to access program components from the library. A string is a sequence of zero or more characters enclosed in double quotation marks. Every character has a relative position in the string. The length of a string is the number of characters in it. The data type `string` may not be available in Standard C++. To process strings effectively, C++ provides the library `string`, which contains various operations to manipulate a string.

Every character in a string has a relative position in the string. The position of the first character is 0, the position of the second character is 1, and so on. The length of a string is the number of characters in it. Remember that a space is a character.

Objectives

In this lab, you learn the mathematical representation in C++ of arithmetic expressions, precedence, and the `string` data type. Additionally, you learn to evaluate expressions using type conversion (casting).

After completing this lab, you will be able to:

- Evaluate arithmetic expressions using addition, subtraction, multiplication, division, and remainder.
- Use type conversion (casting) in arithmetic evaluations.
- Evaluate arithmetic expressions by precedence.
- Evaluate mixed arithmetic expressions.
- Identify the `string` data type.

Estimated completion time: **20–30 minutes**

Using Arithmetic Operators, Operator Precedence, and the `string` Data Type

Evaluate the following expressions or indicate that they are invalid if an illegal operator is used with the incorrect operand:

Expression	Result
1. 20 % (4 – 2)	
2. 20 / 4.0 * 6.4 / 2	
3. 4 % 5	
4. 3.0 * (6 / 24)	
5. 3 – (3 + 3.0) * 10 / 3	
6. 12.0 % 4	
7. 7 * 6 / 21 / 3.0	
8. 11 % 4 * 3.0	
9. 17 % 4 / 3	
10. 5 % 6 / 4	

Expression	Result
11. 5 / 4.0 * 5	
12. 6 + 2 / 4	
13. (2 – 3 + (2 * (3 / 3) % 1))	
14. 5 % 4	
15. 5 – (2.0 + 5) * 10 / 2	
16. static_cast<float>(4)/3	
17. static_cast<int>(3.7)+5.3	
18. static_cast<int>(3.7+5.3)	
19. static_cast<double>(5/2)	
20. static_cast<char>(65)	

Question	Answer (Circle the correct answer.)
21. The explicit conversion of one data value to another data value is called type ______________.	a. casting b. coercion
22. The implicit conversion of one data value to another data value is called type ______________.	a. casting b. coercion
23. The following is an example of type casting: `static_cast<double>5`	True False
24. The following is an example of type coercion: `static_coercion<double>5`	True False

25. Given the following code, type casting occurs:
`int number;`
`double value = 8.6;`
`number = value;`
	True False

26. Given the following code, type coercion occurs:
`int number;`
`double value = 8.6;`
`number = value;`
	True False

27. The following is an example of the `string` data type: `"6"`	True False
28. The following is an example of the `string` data type: `false`	True False
29. The following is an example of the `string` data type: `"Hello World"`	True False
30. The following is an example of the `string` data type: `" "`	True False

LAB 2.4 USING `cin`, ALLOCATING MEMORY, AND WRITING ASSIGNMENT STATEMENTS

Data must be loaded into main memory before it can be manipulated. Storing data into the computer's memory is a two-step process:

1. Instruct the computer to allocate memory.
2. Include statements in the program to put data into the allocated memory.

When you allocate memory, you use a unique name to identify each memory location that is being allocated. Additionally, you indicate the type of data that is to be stored in those memory locations. A memory location whose value cannot be changed is called a named constant. It is customary to use all uppercase characters for memory location identifiers (names) that are named constants. This is not required but sets them apart from memory locations whose values can be changed. Named constants do not change their values and must be initialized at declaration. You declare a memory location as a named constant with the following syntax:

```
const dataType identifier = value;
```

In C++, const is a reserved word that specifies that the value stored in the memory location is fixed and cannot be changed.

In C++, memory locations that can be changed are called variable memory locations or variables. Variables can be initialized at declaration and can be given different values through execution. You declare a variable with the following syntax:

```
dataType identifier1, identifier2, …, identifierN;
```

A simple data type is a variable or named constant that can store only one value at a time. When another value is assigned to the same variable (you cannot assign another value to a named constant), that is called destructive replacement.

Data is stored in variables either through an assignment statement or through an input statement. Assignment statements use the = assignment operator. C++ evaluates the expression to the right of the assignment operator and then stores the result in the memory address identified by the variable to the left of the operator. The expression on the right must evaluate to a value compatible with the data type of the variable on the left. Initialization occurs the first time a value is placed in the variable. Tracing values through a sequence of statements, called a walk-through or desk checking, is a valuable tool to learn and practice.

Memory that has been reserved and not assigned a value contains the sequence of bits that remain from system functions or prior use. You must, therefore, either assign a value or read a value into a variable after you declare it; otherwise, the program uses the leftover bits as the value of the variable.

When the computer receives data from the keyboard, the user is said to be acting interactively. Putting data into variables from the standard input device is done by using `cin` and the stream extraction operator (>>). By using more than one variable with `cin`, more than one value can be read at a time. When reading multiple values, these values must be separated by at least one blank or tab or must be entered one per line.

Variables can obtain values either through input or through assignment. Inputting data offers the program more flexibility and requires a prompt to the user to enter the data. Assignments are used in calculations.

The increment operator (++) and decrement operator (--) are used in assignment statements or used alone with the variable name to increase or decrease a variable by one. Increment and decrement operators each have two forms, pre and post. The syntax of the increment operator is:

Pre-increment: `++variable`

Post-increment: `variable++`

If ++x is used in an expression, first the value of x is incremented by 1, and then the new value of x is used to evaluate the expression. On the other hand, if x++ is used in an expression, first the current value of x is used in the expression, and then the value of x is incremented by 1. When the increment and decrement operators with a variable are used in a stand-alone statement, it does not matter if you use the pre-increment or post-increment format.

Objectives

In this lab, you learn that allocating memory with both variables and named constants results in the program assigning a name and type to the memory location. You must initialize named constants when you declare them; initialization is optional for variables. Additionally, you learn that the value of variables can be changed through assignment or through the process of inputting data. When changing a variable by the value 1, you can use increment and decrement operators.

After completing this lab, you will be able to:

- Allocate memory with both variables and named constants.
- Assign values to variables when expressions are evaluated.
- Assign values to variables through input.
- Use the decrement and increment operators.

Estimated completion time: **20 minutes**

Using `cin`, Allocating Memory, and Writing Assignment Statements

Describe the following declarations, assignments, and input statements. Indicate the value in memory after each statement is executed. Write "invalid" if the statement is not executable.

`cin`, Memory Allocation, and Assignment Statements	Show the Variable Name and Value of Each Statement
1. `int a, b = 9;` `a = b;`	
2. `int d = 2, x = 3, y = 1;` `y + 4 = d - x;`	
3. `short number = 10;` `number = 0;`	

4. `short number = 0;`
`number = 10;`
`number = number + 5;`	

`cin`, Memory Allocation, and Assignment Statements	Show the Variable Name and Value of Each Statement

5. `double value = 12.0;`
`value = 10.0;`
`value = value + 0.5;`	

6. `const int b = 9;`	

7. `double x = -14.5, y = 22.5;`
`int d = 3;`
`y = d - x + y;`	

8. `double ans = 4;`	

9. `int n;`
`cin >> n;`
//Assume the user enters 3.24	

10. `char a;` `cin >> a;` Assume the user enters 'b'	

11. `double x;`
`cin >> x;`
//Assume the user enters 3.24	

12. `double a, b, c = 0.0;`	
13. `int d = 2, x = 3, y = 4;` `4 = d – x + y;`	
14. `double def = 123.5; int y;` `y = def;`	
15. `int b = 9.0;`	

16. `int num1= 8, num2 = 3, temp = 0;`
`temp = num1;`
`num1 = num2;`
`num2 = temp;`	

cin, Memory Allocation, and Assignment Statements	Show the Variable Name and Value of Each Statement

17. `int num;`
`cin >> num;`
`//Assume the user enters 8`
`num++;`	

18. `int c = 8;`
`++c;`
`c--;`	

19. `double x = 5.0;`
`int y = 4;`
`x = x + y / 4;`	

20. `double x = 5.0;`
`int y = 4;`
`y = x + y/4;`	

21. `int count = 0;`
`cout << ++count << endl;`
`cout << count++ << endl;`
`cout << count << endl;`	

Question	Answer (Circle the correct answer.)

22. There is no difference between the following two statements:
`count++;`
`++count++;`
	True False

23. Given:
`int num1 = 2;`
the following statements are equivalent statements:
`num1 = num - 1;`
`num1--;`
	True False

24. The statement num- subtracts 1 from, num and the statement num-- subtracts 2 from num.	True False

25. Given:
`int count = 5;`
`--count++;`
`cout << count << endl;`
the number 5 will be displayed.
	True False

LAB 2.5 USING cout, THE endl MANIPULATOR, AND COMMON ESCAPE SEQUENCES

In C++, to output on the standard output device (usually the screen), you use `cout` and the stream insertion operator (<<). C++ evaluates the expression used with the stream insertion operator and prints its value at the current cursor position on the output device. You use a manipulator to format the output. The `endl` (the lowercase letter l (el), not the number 1) manipulator moves the cursor to the beginning of the next line and is called a newline character. You can accomplish the same action using the newline escape sequence \n as a character by itself or within a string. You can use multiple stream insertion operators in a single `cout` statement. Do not use a line wrap if an output string is too long. Close the string, go to the next line, use another insertion operator, and start a new string. If you break a string this way, remember to include blanks if appropriate.

There are many escape sequences in C++ that allow you to control the output. The following are some of the commonly used escape sequences:

\n	Newline	Cursor moves to the beginning of the next line.
\t	Tab	Cursor moves to the next tab stop.
\b	Backspace	Cursor moves one space to the left.
\r	Return	Cursor moves to the beginning of the current line (not the next line).
\\	Backslash	Backslash is printed.
\'	Single quotation	Single quotation mark is printed.
\"	Double quotation	Double quotation mark is printed.

Comments appear in a program as explanations to the programmer and are ignored by the compiler. A single-line comment begins with // anywhere in the line. Everything encountered on that line after // is ignored by the compiler. Multiple-line comments are enclosed between /* and */.

Objectives

In this lab, you learn to use `cout` and the insertion stream operator to display expressions or manipulators on the screen.

After completing this lab, you will be able to:

- Display expressions on the screen.
- Use the `endl` manipulator.
- Use common escape sequences.

Estimated completion time: **30–40 minutes**

Using cout, the endl Manipulator, and Common Escape Sequences

Describe the following declaration, assignment, input, and output statements, or write C++ code to implement the comment statements. Describe what is contained in memory, and show what is displayed on the screen after each `cout` statement is executed.

1.
```
const double PI = 3.1416;

double radius = 2.5;

cout << "The area of the circle is " << PI * radius * radius << endl;
```

2. Write the appropriate C++ statement to match the description in each of the following comments:

   // declare an integer variable for the width of a rectangle

   // declare an integer variable for the length of a rectangle

   // prompt the user for the width and length

   // input the width and length values

   // output the area of the rectangle found by multiplying length times width

3. Indicate the purpose of the declaration statements and each pair of input and output statements by writing a comment above each statement.

```
double balance;

double deposit;

double checks;

cout << "Enter your beginning checkbook balance: ";

cin >> balance;                //assume 536.25 is entered

cout << "Enter your deposits for the month: ";

cin >> deposit;                //assume 64.75 is entered

cout << "Enter your checks for the month: ";

cin >> checks;                 //assume 425.50 is entered

cout << "Your ending check balance is: " << balance + deposit - checks
<< endl;
```

4. Write the appropriate C++ statement to match the description in each of the following comments:

   // declare three double variables called num1, num2, num3

   // declare a variable called average

   // ask the user to input values separated by a space for 3 values

   // input the values into num1, num2, num3

   // assign average the sum value of num1, num2, and num3 divided by 3

   // output a statement with a message describing the values input and the average

5. When a value is assigned in memory, whatever value was previously in memory is replaced by the new assigned value. This is called destructive replacement. If you want two memory locations to exchange values, you need to save a value in a third location to prevent losing the original value. The following code shows how to swap two values in memory. Explain the purpose of each of the following lines:

```
int num1 = 10, num2 = 5, temp;

cout << "num1 is " << num1 <<", num2 is "<< num2 << endl;

temp = num1;

num1 = num2;

num2 = temp;

cout << "Now the numbers swap and num1 is " << num1 <<", num2 is "
     << num2 << endl;
```

6. Write the appropriate C++ statements to match the descriptions in the following comments:

   // declare two integer variables in feet and inches

   // ask the user how many feet and inches tall he or she is (no fraction)

   // input the feet and inches

   // assign inches the value of inches plus feet times 12

   // output with an appropriate message the number of inches the person is tall

7. Write the output of the following code:

```
int x = 2, y = 3, z = 5;

cout << "This is my report in columns\n"

     << '\t' << x << '\t' << x * x << endl

     << '\t' << y << '\t' << y * y << endl

     << '\t' << z << '\t' << z * z << endl;
```

8. Write a C++ statement to match the descriptions in the following comments:

   // output a heading that has your name used as a possessive noun (use a single quote)

   // followed by the words, favorite movie

   // output a newline that shows your favorite movie title in double quotes

LAB 2.6 USING PREPROCESSOR DIRECTIVES, THE `string` DATA TYPE, AND WRITING A C++ PROGRAM USING GOOD PROGRAMMING STYLE AND FORM

C++ provides a collection of libraries, called header files, with functions and symbols needed to run programs. To indicate which header file to use, you insert the pound symbol (#), the preprocessor directive *include*, and the name of the header file between left and right angle brackets <>. There is no ending semicolon with preprocessor directives. Preprocessor directives are placed as the first lines of a program.

Standard C++ and ANSI/ISO Standard C++ differ in the declaration of header files. This book follows the rules for ANSI/ISO Standard C++. In ANSI/ISO Standard C++, header files do not have file extensions. Additionally, the cin and cout identifiers are declared within a namespace. One way to use the identifiers `cin` and `cout` declared in the namespace `std` is to refer to them as `std::cin and std::cout` throughout the program. Another option is to include the statement `using namespace std;` after the preprocessor directive.

Programs that have structure are easier to understand and modify. C++ programs consist of preprocessor directives and program statements creating the C++ source code. Source code must be saved in a file with the extension .cpp. When compiled successfully, the compiler generates the object code saved in a file with the extension .obj. When the object code is linked with system resources, executable code is produced and saved in a file with the extension .exe. (Note: Extensions are system dependent. The SDK that you use might use different naming conventions.)

C++ programs must contain the function `main` and follow syntax, or grammar, rules. All function statements consist of a heading and a body. The statements are in the body and are enclosed in curly braces. The heading indicates if the function returns a value and, if it does, what data type the value is. Additionally, the function contains declaration statements and executable statements. Declaration statements are used to declare elements, such as variables. Executable statements perform calculations, manipulate data, create output, accept input, and so on. C++ programs follow not only C++ syntax, but also semantics, which is the set of rules that apply to the statements and operations. For ease of use, programs should be well documented both with comments and meaningful identifier names and have an easy-to-read format. Use comments to document a program and explain its purpose, identify who wrote the program, and explain the purpose of particular statements. A single-line comment begins with // anywhere in the line. Everything encountered on that line after // is ignored by the compiler. Multiple line comments are enclosed between /* and */.

In skeleton form, a C++ program looks like:

```
preprocessor directives to include header files

using statement

declare named constants

int main()

{

      statement1

         .

         .

         .

      statementn

      return 0;

}
```

Some characters have defined uses in a C++ program. Spaces are used as separators. Spaces must never appear within a reserved word or identifier. The semicolon is a statement terminator. Brackets are delimiters and have other uses in addition to enclosing the body of a function, which will be discussed as necessary. Commas are used to separate items in a list.

Using meaningful identifier names is another way to document the program. Although not required for a program to run, you should use lowercase letters for variable names, use uppercase letters for constant names, begin a class name with an uppercase letter, and join multiple words for a name using the underscore character (_). For example, a typical variable name is hat_size or hatSize, whereas a typical constant name is CIRCLE_RADIUS. The examples in this book follow these standards.

Good documentation uses clearly written prompts that are executable statements and tell users what to do when they interact with a program. A prompt should not only tell the user what to enter, but also state the limits of the input. Another helpful documentation practice is the use of comments.

The computer does not require comments or an easy-to-read style. However, good form and style should be used to make the program easier to understand and modify.

In addition to simple assignment statements, you can use a compound assignment statement for more concise notation. The compound operators are +=, -=, *=, /=, and %=.

Objectives

In this lab, you learn to write complete programs with ANSI/ISO Standard C++ header files.

After completing this lab, you will be able to:

- Read a complete program and determine the output.
- Write a complete program including preprocessor directives for `iostream` and `string` header files.
- Use a readable format in a C++ program.
- Use meaningful identifiers.
- Use comments for documentation.

Estimated completion time: **60–80 minutes**

Using Preprocessor Directives, the `string` Data Type, and Writing a C++ Program Using Good Programming Style and Form

1a. Read the following C++ program. The line numbers are for descriptive purposes only and are not part of the actual program. Write the appropriate comments for lines 1, 3, 5, 6, 7, 20, 23, 26, 29, 32, 34, 37, 39, and 42. Next to each `cout` statement, show what is to be displayed on the screen. In the memory chart, show what value is contained in memory as the variable values change.

```
1. // Enter your name as a comment for program identification
```

```
// Enter program assignment StuInfo1.cpp
// Enter your class section and time

// Describe the purpose of this program

// Describe what input is expected

// Describe what output is expected

// header files
#include <iostream>
#include <string>
using namespace std;

int main()
{
// Declare variables:
string firstName, lastName, classification, major;
double gpa;

// Describe the use of the prompt line

cout << “Please enter your first name and last name separated by a space.\n”
     << “Limit your input to 2 names. ”;
```

```
//Describe the use of the input statement



cin >> firstName >> lastName;

// Describe the use of the prompt line



cout << "Please enter your classification:\n"
        << "freshman, sophomore, junior, senior, special, or graduate: ";
//Describe the use of the input statement



cin >> classification;

// Describe the use of the prompt line



cout << "Please enter your major (one word only): ";
//Describe the use of the input line



cin >> major;

// Describe the use of the prompt line



cout << "Please enter your grade point average: ";
```

```
//Describe the use of the input statement

cin >> gpa;

// Describe the use of the output line

cout << “\nYou have entered the following information:\n”
     << “\nClassification:\t” << classification
     << “\nMajor:\t\t” << major
     << “\ngpa:\t\t” << gpa << endl;

return 0;
}
```

1b. Step through the code by hand. Then use the following memory table to show what occurs in memory when the C++ code is executed.

To fill out the memory table, use two lines for each variable. On one line, enter declaration information. Write the name of the declared variable, its data type, and the line number at declaration. On the next line in the memory table, enter test data for that variable. The variable firstName is entered as an example.

Variable Name	Data Type	Value in Memory	Line Number at Declaration	Line Number When Initialized
sandwich	string	?	17	
		Ham		24

In the following space, show what is displayed on the screen after executing the output message.

1c. Use your SDK to enter the program with your comment changes. For readability, preserve the blank lines that separate parts of the program. Do not enter the line numbers; they are for description purposes only. Save the program as **StuInfo1.cpp** in the Chap02 folder on your Student Disk. Compile, link, and execute the program.

To compile your program, check with your instructor regarding the specific instructions for the SDK that you are using. Correct any errors until your program successfully compiles.

To link your program, check with your instructor regarding the specific instructions for the SDK that you are using. Correct any errors, re-compile, and re-link until your program successfully links.

To execute your program, check with your instructor regarding the specific instructions for the SDK that you are using. Check your output for accuracy. If necessary, correct any errors, re-compile, re-link, and re-execute until your output is accurate.

Make necessary changes until your program is successful. Select and copy everything that appears on your screen. Paste the copied text into a comment block at the end of your program. Then compare the output of the actual program to the output you predicted.

2a. Using Exercise 1 as an example, create a design for a program that prompts the user to select a lunch from several sandwich choices.

The user should be prompted with the following information:

- Identification of the program and an explanation of how to use it
- Sandwich choices: Ham, Beef, Reuben, PBJ, Cheese, or Vegetarian
- Bread choices: Rye, Wheat, White, Sourdough, or Pumpernickel
- Condiment choices: Mayo, Mustard, Ketchup, or none
- Drink choices: Coke, Diet Coke, Tea, Coffee, or Water
- The price of a half sandwich or a whole sandwich: 3.99 or 5.99

Then the user enters his or her choice.

After all data has been entered, output the complete selection. Include comments to identify the program author, describe the program, and describe program statements. Additionally, remember to include all preprocessor directives that you need.

Write your design in the following space. Your design should be a list of C++ comments without any code.

2b. Write a C++ program based on the design you created in Exercise 2a, and name it **Deli.cpp**. Step through the code by hand.

Use the following memory table to show what occurs in the computer's memory when the C++ code is executed. (Include line numbers in your documentation only. Do not use line numbers when entering your final program.) To fill out the memory table, use one or two lines for each variable as needed. On one line, enter declaration information. Write the name of the declared variable, its data type, and the line number at declaration. On the next line in the memory table, enter test data for that variable. The variable sandwich is entered as an example; your design might use different line numbers.

Variable Name	Data Type	Value in Memory	Line Number at Declaration	Line Number When Initialized
sandwich	string	?	17	
		Ham		24

In the following space, show what is displayed on the screen after executing the output message.

2c. Enter, compile, link, and execute **Deli.cpp**. Then copy the output and save it in a block comment at the end of your program. Save **Deli.cpp** in the Chap02 folder on your Student Disk.

The following is a copy of the screen results that might appear after running your program, depending on the data entered. The input entered by the user is in bold.

```
Welcome to the Sandwich Corral
You will be given choices for building your sandwich.
Please enter your selection after each prompt and then press
the Enter key.
Please enter your sandwich choice:
Ham, Beef, Reuben, PBJ, Cheese, or Vegetarian: Ham
Please enter your bread choice:
Rye, Wheat, White, Sourdough, or Pumpernickel: Rye
Please enter your choice of condiment (one only):
Mayo, Mustard, Ketchup, or none: Mustard
Please enter your drink choice:
Coke, Diet, Tea, Coffee, or Water: Water
Please enter 3.99 for a half sandwich or 5.99 for a whole
sandwich: 3.99

You have entered the following information:
Sandwich:       Ham
Bread:          Rye
Condiment:      Mustard
Drink:          Water

Tab:            3.99
```

3a. *Critical Thinking Exercise*: Using Exercise 1 as an example, create the design for a program that prompts the user to enter two names. Display the two names the user enters—this is called echo printing. Then swap the values of the names. For example, the value of name1 will become the value of name2, and the value of name2 will become the value of name1. (Consider the value of each memory location and how many memory locations are needed to accomplish this task.) Display the two names after they have been swapped.

Include comments to identify the program author, to describe the program, and to describe program statements. Additionally, remember to include all preprocessor directives that you need.

Write your design in the following space. Your design should be a list of C++ comments without any code.

3b. Write a C++ program based on the design you created in Exercise 3a, and name it **Swap.cpp**. Step through the code by hand.

Use the following memory table to show what occurs in the computer's memory when the C++ code is executed. (Include line numbers as documentation only. Do not use line numbers when entering your final program.) To fill out the memory table, use two or three lines for each variable. On one line, enter declaration information. Write the name of the declared variable, its data type, and the line number at declaration. On the next line in the memory table, enter test data for that variable. On the third line for each variable, show where the value has changed if it changes. The variable name1 is entered as an example; your design might use different line numbers.

Variable Name	Data Type	Value in Memory	Line Number at Declaration	Line Number when Initialized or Changed
name1	string	?	17	
		Boubacar		21
		Celine		30

In the following space, show what is displayed on the screen after executing the output message.

3c. Enter, compile, link, and execute **Swap.cpp**. Then copy the output and save it in a block comment at the end of your program. Save **Swap.cpp** in the Chap02 folder on your Student Disk.

The following is a copy of the screen results that might appear after running your program, depending on the data entered. The input entered by the user is in bold.

```
Enter two names separated by a space: Boubacar Celine

The first name is: Boubacar
The second name is: Celine

The first name is: Celine
The second name is: Boubacar
```

Critical Thinking

4a. *Critical Thinking Exercise*: Imagine that you are a real estate agent and make your living from sales commissions. House commissions paid to sell a house through multiple listings are 6%. The listing agency receives 3%, and the selling agency receives 3%. Of that 3%, each agency receives 1.5%, and the selling agent or listing agent receives 1.5%. As a real estate agent, you want to know how much you will receive for a house that you either list or sell. For your records, identify the house by the owner's last name.

Design a program that asks the user for the name and selling price of the home. Calculate the amount paid by the home owner to sell the home and the amount of the commission you will receive. Use constants for the entire cost to sell the home and for the listing agent's commission rate.

Write your design in the following space. Your design should be a list of C++ comments without any code.

4b. Write a C++ program based on the design you created in Exercise 4a, and name it **Realtor.cpp**. Step through the code by hand.

Use the following memory table to show what occurs in memory when the C++ code is executed. (Include line numbers as documentation only. Do not use line numbers when entering your final program.) To fill out the memory table, use two lines for each variable. On one line, enter declaration inforsmation. Write the name of the declared variable, its data type, and the line number at declaration. On the next line in the memory table, enter test data for that variable. The variable name is entered as an example, but you may use different line numbers in your design.

Variable Name	Data Type	Value in Memory	Line Number at Declaration	Line Number when Initialized or Changed
name	string	?	24	
				31

In the following space, show what is displayed on the screen after executing the output message.

4c. Enter, compile, link, and execute **Realtor.cpp**. Then copy the output and save it in a block comment at the end of your program. Save **Realtor.cpp** in the Chap02 folder of your Student Disk.

The following is a copy of the screen results that might appear after running your program, depending on the data entered. The input entered by the user is in bold.

```
Please enter the owner's last name: Garcia
Please enter the sales price of the home: 100000

The Garcia's home sold for $100000
The cost to sell the home is $6000
The selling or listing agent commission is $1500
```

3 Input/Output

In this chapter, you will:

- Learn what a stream is and examine input and output streams
- Explore how to read data from the standard input device
- Learn how to use predefined functions in a program
- Explore how to use the input stream functions `get`, `ignore`, `putback`, and `peek`
- Become familiar with input failure
- Learn how to write data to the standard output device
- Discover how to use manipulators in a program to format output
- Learn how to perform input and output operations with the string data type
- Become familiar with file input and output

Chapter 3: Assignment Cover Sheet

Name ______________________________ Date ______________________________

Section ______________________________

Lab Assignments	Assigned	Grade
Lab 3.1 Examining Predefined Input Functions		
Lab 3.2 Examining and Formatting Output (Critical Thinking Exercise)		
Lab 3.3 Understanding Input Failure (Critical Thinking Exercise)		
Lab 3.4 Using Files for Input and Output (Critical Thinking Exercise)		
Total Grade		

See your instructor or the introduction to this book for instructions on submitting your assignments.

Lab 3.1 Examining Predefined Input Functions

In C++, I/O is accomplished through a stream, which is a sequence of bytes (characters) from the source to the destination. The exception occurs when using images and sound. To receive data from the keyboard and send output to the screen, every C++ program must use the header file `iostream`, which includes a set of functions to perform specific I/O tasks. To use the variables `cin` and `cout`, use the preprocessor directive `#include <iostream>` with the statement `using namespace std;`.

You use the variable `cin` with the extraction operator >> to input data from the keyboard. Additionally, C++ allows the `cin` statement to read more than one data item by using the extraction operator several times. The extraction operator >> is binary and thus takes two operands. The left operand must be an input stream variable such as `cin`. The right operand is a variable. The extraction operator >> skips all whitespace characters. When reading a `char` variable, after the program ignores whitespace, it reads only the next character. When reading an `int` or a `float`, a program reads digits (including possible leading + or - signs) until it finds whitespace or a character. The `int` type also stops at a decimal point. If no decimal is entered for a `float` type, the value is converted to a `float` type when the receiving variable is of the `float` type.

The main function executes automatically when you run a program. Other functions execute only when they are activated or called. C++ comes with predefined functions and variables that are already included in header files. The `iostream` header file contains a variable declaration for `cin`. A useful predefined function found in the `cmath` header file is the `pow` function, which is used to calculate a base number raised to an exponent. To use a predefined function in a program, you need to know the name of the header file containing the specifications of the function and include that header file in the program. In addition, you need to know the name of the function, the number of parameters the function takes, and the type of each parameter. You must also be aware of what the function is going to do.

The variable `cin` has access to operators and functions that can extract data from the standard input device. You can use dot notation to associate the input stream variable name with the function name. The `get` function inputs the very next character, including whitespace characters, from the input stream and stores it in the memory location indicated by its argument. The `ignore` function allows the program to discard a portion of the input. The maximum number of characters to be ignored can be stipulated or input is ignored until a specified character is encountered, whichever comes first. Additionally, the `putback` function puts the last character extracted from the input stream by the `get` function back into the input stream. The `peek` function returns the next character from the input stream but does not remove the character from that stream.

The variables `cin` and `cout` are data types of the `istream` and `ostream` classes found in the `iostream` header file. These variables also have special names, called objects.

After the program terminates, any values left in the input stream are discarded. Other than a `float` type accepting integer input, no other mismatch of data is allowed. When a C++ program attempts to read invalid data, input failure occurs, causing the input stream to enter the fail state. Once an input stream enters a fail state, all further I/O statements using that stream are ignored. The stream function `clear` can restore the input stream to a working state.

Objectives

In this lab, you become acquainted with using I/O streams and the predefined functions `get`, `ignore`, `putback`, and `peek`.

After completing this lab, you will be able to:

- Use the I/O predefined functions `get`, `ignore`, `putback`, and `peek`.

Estimated completion time: **60–75 minutes**

Examining Predefined Input Functions

In the following exercises, you indicate whether statements are true or false. Then you design and write programs that use predefined input functions.

Question	Answer (Circle the correct answer)	
1. When using `cin` and the extraction operator for multiple input items, the items are separated by commas.	**True**	**False**
2. When using `cin` and the extraction operator to input numeric data, the + operator is optional.	**True**	**False**
3. The statements: `cin >> x;` `cin >> y;` require that items are input on different lines, whereas the statement: `cin >> x >> y` requires that items are input on the same line.	**True**	**False**
4. If the user is prompted to enter an integer value, press the Enter key and then enter another integer value; the `cin` statement to read those values is as follows: `cin >> x >> endl >> y;`	**True**	**False**
5. When using cin and the extraction operator, the newline character is treated the same as other whitespace characters.	**True**	**False**
6. When using the `get` function, whitespace characters are treated the same as other characters.	**True**	**False**
7. The `peek` function does not remove characters from the input stream.	**True**	**False**
8. To enter a newline character as part of a stream, you press the Enter key.	**True**	**False**
9. When input failure occurs, the program terminates.	**True**	**False**
10. The stream function `putback` lets you put the last character extracted from the input stream by the `get` function back into the input stream.	**True**	**False**

11a. Create the design for a program that prompts the user to enter a first name, middle name or initial, and last name, with each name separated by a space. Display only the user's initials on the screen. (Use a combination of the `get` and `ignore` functions.)

Write your design in the following space. Your design should be a list of C++ comments without any code.

11b. Write a C++ program based on the design you created in Lab 3.1, Exercise 11a, and name it **Initial1.cpp**. Step through the code by hand.

Use the following memory table to show what occurs in memory when the C++ code is executed. (Include line numbers as documentation only. Do not use line numbers when entering your final program.) To fill out the memory table, use one or two lines for each variable. On one line, enter declaration information. Write the name of the declared variable, its data type, and the line number at declaration.

Variable Name	Data Type	Value in Memory	Line Number at Declaration	Line Number when Initialized

In the following space, show what is displayed on the screen after executing the output message.

11c. Enter, compile, link, and execute **Initial1.cpp**. Then copy the output and save it in a block comment at the end of your program. Save **Initial1.cpp** in the Chap03 folder of your Student Disk.

The following is a copy of the screen results that might appear after running your program, depending on the data entered. The input entered by the user is shown in bold.

```
Enter your first name, middle name or initial, and last name separated
by spaces:
Jane Ann Doe
Your initials are: JAD
```

11d. What would occur if the user begins the input with one or more spaces?

11e. What would occur if the names were separated by more than one space?

12a. Create the design for a program that prompts the user to enter a first name, middle name or initial, and last name, with each name separated by a space. Display the user's first name, middle name or initial, and last name on the screen. On another line, display only the user's initials. (Use a combination of the `get` and `putback` functions.)

Write your design in the following space. Your design should be a list of C++ comments without any code.

12b. Write a C++ program based on the design you created in Exercise 12a and name it **Initial2.cpp**. Step through the code by hand.

Use the following memory table to show what occurs in memory when the C++ code is executed. (Include line numbers as documentation only. Do not use line numbers when entering your final program.) To fill out the memory table, use one or two lines for each variable. On one line, enter declaration information. Write the name of the declared variable, its data type, and the line number at declaration.

Variable Name	Data Type	Value in Memory	Line Number at Declaration	Line Number when Initialized

In the following space, show what is displayed on the screen after executing the output message.

12c. Enter, compile, link, and execute **Initial2.cpp**. Then copy the output and save it in a block comment at the end of your program. Save **Initial2.cpp** in the Chap03 folder of your Student Disk.

The following is a copy of the screen results that might appear after running your program, depending on the data entered. The input entered by the user is shown in bold.

```
Enter your first name, middle name or initial, and last name separated
by spaces:
Jane Ann Doe
Your initials are: JAD
Your name is: Jane Ann Doe
```

12d. What would occur if the user begins the input with one or more spaces?

12e. What would occur if the names were separated by more than one space?

13a. Create the design for a program that prompts the user to enter a first name, middle name or initial, and last name, with each name separated by a space. Display the user's first name, middle name or initial, and last name on the screen. On another line, display only the user's initials. (Use a combination of the `get` and `peek` functions.)

Write your design in the following space. Your design should be a list of C++ comments without any code.

13b. Write a C++ program based on the design you created in Exercise 13a and name it **Initial3.cpp**. Step through the code by hand.

Use the following memory table to show what occurs in memory when the C++ code is executed. (Include line numbers as documentation only. Do not use line numbers when entering your final program.) To fill out the memory table, use one or two lines for each variable. On one line, enter declaration information. Write the name of the declared variable, its data type, and the line number at declaration.

Variable Name	Data Type	Value in Memory	Line Number at Declaration	Line Number when Initialized

In the following space, show what is displayed on the screen after executing the output message.

13c. Enter, compile, link, and execute **Initial3.cpp**. Then copy the output and save it in a block comment at the end of your program. Save **Initial3.cpp** in the Chap03 folder of your Student Disk.

The following is a copy of the screen results that might appear after running your program, depending on the data entered. The input entered by the user is shown in bold.

```
Enter your first name, middle name or initial, and last name separated
by spaces:
Jane Ann Doe
Your initials are: JAD
Your name is: Jane Ann Doe
```

13d. What would occur if the user begins the input with one or more spaces?

13e. What would occur if the names were separated by more than one space?

LAB 3.2 EXAMINING AND FORMATTING OUTPUT

C++ has various output functions and manipulators you can use to format output. The floating-point number default output is in scientific notation, which is difficult to read. The manipulator `setprecision` formats the number of decimal places of floating-point numbers according to the number in the argument and requires the header file `iomanip`. The manipulator `fixed` formats floating-point to decimal output rather than scientific notation. Once set, the fixed-decimal format will apply throughout the program unless disabled. You can disable the manipulator `fixed` using the stream member function `unsetf`. The manipulator `showpoint` shows a decimal point and trailing zeros when the decimal amount is zero. The manipulator `setw` outputs the value of the next expression in an output statement in the number of columns specified by the argument and requires the `iomanip` header file. If the number of columns specified by the manipulator `setw` exceeds the number of columns required, the field width expands to accommodate the size. *Note*: The manipulator `setw` controls the output of only the next expression. The manipulator `flush` outputs all data in the buffer without including a newline character.

To get more formatting control, use the `fill` function or the manipulator `setfill` to fill the unused columns with the character used as the argument in the function call. The `setfill` manipulator works like the `fill` function except that it follows the stream manipulator in the `cout` statement and requires the `iomanip` header file. The manipulators `left` and `right` will left-justify or right-justify the output in the column specified by `setw`.

Objectives

In this lab, you become acquainted with the output formatting functions and manipulators and the `flush` function.

After completing this lab, you will be able to:

- Write programs using the functions and manipulators `setprecision`, `fixed`, `showpoint`, `setw`, `fill`, `setfill`, `left`, and `right` for formatting output.
- Use the `flush` function to clear the buffer.

Estimated completion time: **50–60 minutes**

Examining and Formatting Output

In the following exercises, you select the correct answer to a question. Then you design and write programs that produce formatted output.

Question	**Answer (Circle the correct answer.)**

1. Given the following statements:
`int number;`
`double value;`
`cout << "Enter two numeric values: ";`
`cin >> number >> value;`
`cout << number << ' ' << value << endl;`
if the user enters 8.5 6, which of the following is output?
	a. 8 .5
	b. 8.5 6
	c. there is no output; input failure occurs

2. Given the following statements:

```
int number = 6;
double value = 4.2
cout << setprecision(3) << number <<
     << ' ' << value << endl;
```

which of the following is output?

a. 6 4.200

b. 6.000 4.200

c. 6 4.2

3. Given the following statements:

```
int number = 6;
double value = 4.2
cout << showpoint << number <<
     << ' ' << value << endl;
```

which of the following is output?

a. 6 4.2

b. 6.0 4.2

c. 6 4.20

4. Given the following statements:

```
int number = 6;
double value = 4.2
cout << fixed << number <<
     << ' ' << value << endl;
```

which of the following is output?

a. 6 4.2

b. 6.00 4.20

c. 6 4.20

5. An `endl` may be placed after the << insertion operator anywhere in the `cout` statement. **True** **False**

6. Given the following statements:

```
string begin = "abc", end = "xyz";
cout << "1234567890\n"
     << setw(5) << begin << end << endl;
```

which of the following is output?

a. 1234567890
abc xyz

b. 1234567890
abc   xyz

c. 1234567890
abcxyz

d. 1234567890
  abc xyz

7. Given the following statements:

```
string begin = "abc", end = "xyz";
cout.fill('*');
cout << "1234567890\n"
     << setw(5) << begin << end << endl;
```

which of the following is output?

a. 1234567890
abc**xyz

b. 1234567890
abc****xyz

c. 1234567890
**abcxyz

d. 1234567890
abcxyz

8. The manipulator `setw` is used to output the value of an expression in specific columns. **True** **False**

9. Both the `flush` and `setw` manipulators position the cursor at the beginning of the next line on the output device. **True** **False**

10. Once the `setw` manipulator is used, the column width is set until `setw` is reset. **True** **False**

Critical Thinking

11a. *Critical Thinking Exercise*: (If you completed the program **Realtor.cpp**, which you stored in the Chap02 folder on your Student Disk, redesign that program in this exercise.) Create a new design for a program to produce a real estate report. As a real estate agent, you keep a record of homes you list, and you want to create a report that is easy to read. The report should also indicate the costs associated with selling the home, which include the total commission, the listing agency commission, the selling agency commission, and the selling agent's commission.

The information needed to sell the home includes the following:

- The last name of the owner of the home.
- The selling price of the home.

The costs are based on the following information:

- Home commissions paid to sell a home through multiple listings are 6%.
- The listing agency receives 3%, and the selling agency receives 3%.
- Of that 3%, each agency gets 1.5%, and the selling agent or listing agent gets 1.5%.

Your data is the sales amount entered as a double number with no fractional decimal value. Your calculations should consider the following:

- Calculate the amount paid by the homeowner to sell the home and the amount of the commission you will receive as the selling agent (not agency).
- Use a constant for the commission rate.

Display your output using the following guidelines:

- Display your output in columns using the `setw` function.
- Your first row of output should be headings. Use `setw(15)` for each item in the first row. When writing your string literals, be sure to include a blank at the end of the string to make sure that one string does not display directly next to another string.
- The second row should list your variables. For the second row, use a fixed format and two decimal places, and show the decimal point even when the fractional decimal value is 0.

Write your design in the following space. Your design should be a list of C++ comments without any code.

11b. Write a C++ program based on the design you created in Exercise 11a and name it **Realtor1.cpp**. Step through the code by hand.

Use the following memory table to show what occurs in memory when the C++ code is executed. (Include line numbers as documentation only. Do not use line numbers when entering your final program.) To fill out the memory table, use one or two lines for each variable. On one line, enter declaration information. Write the name of the declared variable, its data type, and the line number at declaration.

Variable Name	Data Type	Value in Memory	Line Number at Declaration	Line Number when Initialized

In the following space, show what is displayed on the screen after executing the output message.

11c. Enter, compile, link, and execute **Realtor1.cpp**. Then copy the output and save it in a block comment at the end of your program. Save **Realtor1.cpp** in the Chap03 folder of your Student Disk.

The following is a copy of the screen results that might appear after running your program, depending on the data entered. The input entered by the user is shown in bold.

```
Please enter owner's last name: Garcia
Please enter the sales price of the home: 100000
   Home Owner   Price of Home    Seller's Cost    Agent's Commission
       Garcia   100000.00              6000.00               1500.00
```

11d. The report output shows columns of values that could easily be altered. Change the **Realtor1.cpp** program to use the `fill` function or the manipulator `setfill` to put the '*' character in the blank spaces before all numbers so that the numbers cannot be altered. Save the program as **Realtor2.cpp** in the Chap03 folder of your Student Disk. Enter, compile, link, and execute **Realtor2.cpp**. Then copy the output and save it in a block comment at the end of your program.

The following is a copy of the screen results that might appear after running your program, depending on the data entered. The input entered by the user is shown in bold.

```
Please enter owner's last name: Garcia
Please enter the sales price of the home: 100000
   Home Owner   Price of Home            Seller's Cost  Agent's Commission
       Garcia*******100000.00****************6000.00************1500.00
```

11e. Although it is easier to read values when they are right-justified, it is difficult to read columns of strings that are right-justified. Rewrite **Realtor2.cpp** to left-justify the first field and right-justify all remaining fields using the `left` and `right` manipulators. Additionally, to test the `flush` function, remove one of your `endl` manipulators and call the flush function. Save the revised program as **Realtor3.cpp** in the Chap03 folder of your Student Disk. Enter, compile, link, and execute **Realtor3.cpp**. Then copy the output and save it in a block comment at the end of your program.

The following is a copy of the screen results that might appear after running your program, depending on the data entered. The input entered by the user is in bold.

```
Please enter owner's last name: Garcia
Please enter the sales price of the home: 100000
   Home Owner   Price of Home          Seller's Cost  Agent's Commission
   Garcia     *******100000.00***************6000.00***********1500.00
```

LAB 3.3 UNDERSTANDING INPUT FAILURE

Many things can go wrong during program execution. Even a program that is syntactically correct might produce incorrect results. For example, what would happen if you tried to input a letter into an `int` variable? If the input data did not match the corresponding variables, the program would run into problems. Attempting to read a letter into an `int` or `double` variable would result in an input failure. Consider the following statements:

```
int a, b, c;
double x;
```

If the input is:

```
W 54
```

then the statement:

```
cin >> a >> b;
```

would result in an input failure, because you are trying to input the character `'W'` into the `int` variable `a`. If the input were:

```
35 67.93 48
```

then the input statement:

```
cin >> a >> x > >b;
```

would result in storing `35` in `a`, `67.93` in `x`, and `48` in `b`.

Now consider the following read statement with the previous input (the input with three values):

```
cin >> a >> b >> c;
```

This statement stores `35` in `a` and `67` in `b`. The reading stops at . (the decimal point). Because the next variable `c` is of the data type `int`, the computer tries to read . into `c`, which is an error. The input stream then enters a state called the **fail state**.

What actually happens when the input stream enters the fail state? Once an input stream enters a fail state, all further I/O statements using that stream are ignored. Unfortunately, the program quietly continues to execute with whatever values are stored in variables and produces incorrect results.

When an input stream enters the fail state, the system ignores all further I/O using that stream. You can use the stream function `clear` to restore the input stream to a working state. The syntax to use the function `clear` is: `istreamVar.clear();`

Objectives

In this lab, you become familiar with input failure, the fail state, and how to detect and recover from that state.

After completing this lab, you will be able to:

- Determine whether an input string has entered the fail state.
- Recover from the fail state.

Estimated completion time: **15–20 minutes**

Understanding Input Failure

In the following exercises, you indicate whether statements are true or false. Then you design and write complete C++ programs that read user input, according to the instructions and output examples given.

Question	Answer (Circle the correct answer.)	
1. Entering a `char` value into an `int` variable causes C++ to automatically convert the data type.	True	False
2. A program that is syntactically correct will always produce correct results.	True	False
3. Trying to read a letter into a `double` variable would result in an input failure.	True	False
4. Once an input stream enters a fail state, all further I/O statements using that stream are silently ignored.	True	False
5. Once an input failure has occurred, you use the function `flush` to restore the input stream to a working state.	True	False

6a. *Critical Thinking Exercise:* The following program is a modified version of the program shown in Example 3-6. Enter the code in a file and name it **InputFailure.cpp**.

```
//Input Failure program
#include <iostream>
using namespace std;
int main()
{
    int a = 10; //Line 1
    int b = 20; //Line 2
    int c = 30; //Line 3
    int d = 40; //Line 4

    cout << "Line 5: cin = " << cin << endl; //Line 5

    cout << "Line 6: Enter four integers: "; //Line 6
    cin >> a >> b >> c >> d; //Line 7
    cout << endl; //Line 8
    cout << "Line 9: The numbers you entered are:"
        << endl; //Line 9
    cout << "Line 10: a = " << a << ", b = " << b
        << ", c = " << c << ", d = " << d << endl; //Line 10

    cout << "Line 11: cin = " << cin << endl; //Line 11
    cout << "Line 12: cin.fail() returns " << cin.fail() << endl; //Line 12

    cout << "Line 13: Now we will use cin.clear()." << endl; //Line 13
    cin.clear(); //Line 14
    cout << "Line 15: cin = " << cin << endl; //Line 15
    cout << "Line 16: cin.fail() returns " << cin.fail(); //Line 16

    return 0;
}
```

Compile, link, and execute **InputFailure.cpp**. Use `34 K 67 28` as the input values. Write the output that the program generates in the following space.

6b. What are the three values of the `cin` variable shown by your program?

6c. What are the two return values of the function `fail` shown by your program?

6d. Analyze the output of your program and your answers to questions 6b and 6c. Now answer the following questions using your own words: What happens to the stream variable `cin` after an input failure? What happens to the stream variable `cin` after using the function `clear`? How can you use the function `fail` to determine if an input failure has occurred?

Lab 3.4 Using Files for Input and Output

Data can be entered for processing by a computer program from the standard input device, the keyboard, and output to the standard output device, the screen or monitor. Using the keyboard for entering large amounts of data to be processed is not efficient. Instead, data can be read from files on storage media as program input. Likewise, outputting substantial amounts of information to the screen is not very practical. As an alternative, program output can be directed to files on secondary storage devices.

The C++ syntax for inputting and outputting data using files is similar to that for the input and output to the standard devices. File I/O requires five steps (1 through 5),

(1) Standard device I/O requires the preprocessor directive `#include <iostream>`. File I/O necessitates using the preprocessor directive `#include <fstream>`. (A program could get both standard and file input and output to both the screen and a file. If such is the case, both preprocessor directives, `iostream` and `fstream`, would be necessary.).

(2) Unlike standard I/O, stream variables must be declared for file I/O. The data type for file input variables is `ifstream`, and the data type for file output variables is `ofstream`.

(3) In addition, the stream variables must be associated with an input or output file. When an output file variable is associated with a physical file name, the file need not be in existence, and, if it is not, it will be created by default. Input file variables must be associated with a file name of a currently existing file. Both input and output files are set to a file mode, indicating how they are to be used in the program. The file mode can be included as a parameter in the `open` function. If no file mode is included as a parameter, the default is input when the input stream variable opens the input file and output when the output stream variable opens the ouput file. In the output mode, any data written to the output file will overwrite any data that is in the file. An append file mode parameter for an output file will allow data currently in the file to remain and will add or append new output to the end of the currently existing data.

(4) Like standard, the I/O file stream variables are used with the extraction operator >> and the insertion operator <<, as well as with other file functions such as `get`, `getline`, `ignore`, `putback`, and `peek`.

(5) The stream variables should be closed with the close function.

Objectives

After completing this lab you will be able to:

- Associate file stream variables with physical files.
- Open and close input and output files.
- Read data from input files.
- Write data to output files.

Estimated completion time: **50–60 minutes**

Using Files for Input and Output

In the following exercises, you are to design and write programs that will use files for input and/or output.

1a. *Critical Thinking Exercise*: You need to record the daily high and low temperatures (in Fahrenheit) for your city. Design a program that will that will accept the date and the high and low temperatures for that date. The program should average those temperatures for a daily average temperature and then output the date and the average temperature to a file. Use a string data type for the date and enter the date in the mm/dd/yy format. Use a double data type for the high, low, and average temperatures. The program should output the date and the average temperature to a file called temps.txt. Separate the date from the average with a space in the output. The output file should be in the same directory as the source code file. The output file will contain data only. Do not include column headings.

Write your design in the following space. For your design, write an algorithm (an English language description of the steps required to successfully write the program).

1b. Write the source code for the design you created in Exercise 1a and name it Fahrenheit.cpp. Use the following data sets to test your program.

Input			Output	
date	high	low	date	average
01/01/09	38	18	01/01/09	28
01/02/09	44	25	01/02/09	34.5

1c. Enter, compile, link, and run Fahrenheit.cpp. Save Fahrenheit.cpp and the output file temps.txt in the Chap03 folder of your Student Disk.

Print the output file and submit it with your work. You can open your files within your SDK. (*Hint:* In the Open dialog box, remember to change the "Look in" box to the proper drive and the "Files of type" box to All Files.)

2a. Create a design for a program that will get the input from the output file (temps.txt) that you created in Exercise 1. The program will read the date and average from the temps.txt file. Again, use a string data type for the date and a double for the average. The program should then convert the average (Fahrenheit) to Celsius. The conversion formula is subtract 32 from the average (Fahrenheit) and then multiply by five and divide by nine, e.g., (average – 32) * 5 / 9. Output the date and the Celsius temperature to a file (name the file Celsius.txt). Use the manipulators you have learned about in this chapter to format the output to one decimal space.

Write your design in the following space. For your design, write an algorithm (an English language description of the steps required to successfully write the program).

2b. Write a C++ program based on the design you created in Exercise 2a and name it Conversion.cpp.

2c. Enter, compile, link, and run Conversion.cpp. Print the output file (Celsius.txt) and submit it with your work.

4 Control Structures I (Selection)

In this chapter, you will:

- Learn about control structures
- Examine relational and logical operators
- Explore how to form and evaluate logical (Boolean) expressions
- Discover how to use the selection control structures `if`, `if...else`, and `switch` in a program
- Learn to use the `assert` function to terminate a program

Chapter 4: Assignment Cover Sheet

Name ______________________________ Date ______________________________

Section ______________________________

Lab Assignments	Assigned	Grade
Lab 4.1 Using Relational and Logical Operators to Evaluate Logical (Boolean) Expressions		
Lab 4.2 Using the Selection Control Structures `if` and `if else`		
Lab 4.3 Using Nested `if` and `if else` Statements		
Lab 4.4 Using the `if` Statement with Input Failure		
Lab 4.5 Confusing the Assignment Operator (=) with the Equality Operator (==)		
Lab 4.6 Using the Conditional Operator (?:)		
Lab 4.7 Using the `switch` Selection Control Structure (Critical Thinking Exercises)		
Lab 4.8 Using the `assert` Function to Terminate a Program		
Total Grade		

See your instructor or the introduction to this book for instructions on submitting your assignments.

Lab 4.1 Using Relational and Logical Operators to Evaluate Logical (Boolean) Expressions

A conditional statement is a control structure that allows a program to execute one of two alternative selections. A one-way alternative selection is executed depending on whether a condition is true. A two-way alternative selection is executed depending on whether the condition is true or false. The program evaluates a condition by comparing two operands. In C++, this condition is called a logical (Boolean) expression. Additionally, `true` and `false` are logical (Boolean) values. A conditional statement uses relational operators to perform the relational comparison, which applies to all three simple data types and to strings of the string class. It also uses the ASCII collating sequence. When C++ evaluates a logical expression, it returns a nonzero integer value if the logical expression evaluates to `true`; it returns an integer value of 0 otherwise. In C++, any nonzero value is treated as `true`. Table 4-1 describes each operator.

Table 4-1 C++ Relational Operators

Operators	Description
==	Equal to
!=	Not equal to
<	Less than
<=	Less than or equal to
>	Greater than
>=	Greater than or equal to

Comparison of real numbers for equality should be avoided because the results may not be accurate. When comparing strings, comparison is done character-by-character using the ASCII collating sequence, starting with the first character until a mismatch or the last characters have been compared. If all characters are the same until one string ends, the shorter string is evaluated as less than the larger string.

Logical (Boolean) operators enable you to combine logical expressions. The three logical operators are `and` (`&&`), `or` (||), and `not` (`!`). The binary logical operators (`&&`) and (||) combine logical expressions. The unary logical operator (`!`) reverses the value of the logical expression. The `&&` operator evaluates to `false` unless both Boolean expressions are true. The || operator evaluates to `true` unless both Boolean expressions are false.

Like mathematical expressions, relational expressions have an order of precedence for evaluation. The associativity of these operators is from left to right, but parentheses can override the precedence of these operators. After a program determines whether a compound expression is true or false, the rest of the expression is not evaluated. This is known as short-circuit evaluation. Table 4-2 lists the precedence of operators and the order of evaluation.

Table 4-2 Operator Precedence

Operators	Precedence
!, +, – (unary operators)	1
*, /, %	2
+, –	3
<, <=, >=, >	4
==, !=	5
&&	6
||	7
= (assignment operator)	Last

More recent versions of C++ contain a built-in data type, `bool`, that has the logical values `true` and `false`. The identifier `true` has the value 1, and the identifier `false` has the value 0.

Objectives

In this lab, you evaluate Boolean expressions using relational and Boolean operators. Additionally, you learn to evaluate these expressions by the order (or precedence) of operators.

After completing this lab, you will be able to:

- Evaluate logical expressions formed by the relationship of two operands.
- Use relational operators to evaluate all three simple data types and strings.
- Use logical (Boolean) operators to evaluate combined logical expressions.
- Evaluate logical expressions by the correct order of precedence.
- Recognize logical expressions that can be short-circuit evaluations.

Estimated completion time: **30–40 minutes**

Using Relational and Logical Operators to Evaluate Logical (Boolean) Expressions

Evaluate the logical (Boolean) expression in the Expression column, and circle all possible answers in the Result column. For `char` and `string` types, use the ASCII collating sequence.

Expression	Result (Circle all possible answers)
1. `int num1 = 3, num2 = 2;` `(num1 > num2)`	True False short-circuit
2. `double hours = 12.8;` `(hours > 40.2)`	True False short-circuit
3. `int funny = 7;` `(funny !=1)`	True False short-circuit
4. `char letter = 'A';` `('a' < letter)`	True False short-circuit
5. `short count = 1;` `count <=4;`	True False short-circuit
6. `double y = -2.3;` `y >=0.0;`	True False short-circuit

<table>
<tr><th>Expression</th><th>Result
(Circle all possible answers)</th></tr>
<tr><td>1. <code>! (false || false) || true</code></td><td>True False short-circuit</td></tr>
<tr><td>2. <code>false && true && false</code></td><td>True False short-circuit</td></tr>
<tr><td>3. <code>! false || (false || ! true)</code></td><td>True False short-circuit</td></tr>
<tr><td>4. <code>false || (true && (false || false))</code></td><td>True False short-circuit</td></tr>
<tr><td>5. <code>1 || ! true && false</code></td><td>True False short-circuit</td></tr>
<tr><td>6. <code>! (false || false) || false</code></td><td>True False short-circuit</td></tr>
<tr><td>7. <code>true && false && false</code></td><td>True False short-circuit</td></tr>
<tr><td>8. <code>! false || (false || ! true)</code></td><td>True False short-circuit</td></tr>
<tr><td>9. <code>false || (false && (false || true))</code></td><td>True False short-circuit</td></tr>
<tr><td>10. <code>0 || ! false && false</code></td><td>True False short-circuit</td></tr>
</table>

<table>
<tr><th>Expression
Use the values given:</th><th>Result
(Circle all possible answers)</th></tr>
<tr><td>1. <code>string name1 = Aaron ;</code>
<code>string name2 = aaron ;</code>
<code>(name1 == name2)</code></td><td>True False short-circuit</td></tr>
<tr><td>2. <code>string name1 = Aaron ;</code>
<code>string name2 = Aardvark ;</code>
<code>(name1 <= name2)</code></td><td>True False short-circuit</td></tr>
<tr><td>3. <code>bool flag = true;</code>
<code>int a = 2, b = 5, c = 10;</code>
<code>(a * b <= c && ! flag)</code></td><td>True False short-circuit</td></tr>
<tr><td>4. <code>char letter = 'A';</code>
<code>string word = A ;</code>
<code>(letter == word)</code></td><td>True False short-circuit</td></tr>
</table>

LAB 4.2 USING THE SELECTION CONTROL STRUCTURES `if` AND `if...else`

There are three selection control structures in C++: 1) the `if` structure provides one alternative branch or path; 2) the `if...else` structure has two alternative branches or paths; 3) the `switch` structure allows multiple branches or paths.

Which path or branch the program will take in an `if` or `if...else` structure is determined by evaluating a Boolean condition. The Boolean condition can be a simple Boolean expression or a compound condition, that is, two or more Boolean expressions joined by logical operators (the `and` or the `or` operators).

Objectives

In this lab, you will become acquainted with both the one way alternative `if` selection structure and the two way alternative `if...else` selection structure. You will create a program that uses the `if` and `if...else` structures.

After completing this lab you will be able to:

- Work with a one-way selection, which evaluates to either `true` or `false` and is followed by one or more statements.
- Work with a two-way selection, which evaluates to either `true` or `false` and is followed by one or more statements.
- Write a one-way selection structure followed by multiple statements.
- Write a two-way selection structure followed by one statement in each alternative.

Estimated completion time: **30–60 minutes**

Using the Selection Control Structure `if`

Write what the following statements display as output after the code executes. Use the following assignment statement for Exercises 1 through 8:

```
int x = 6;
```

1.
```
if (x > 10)
      cout << "x is greater than 10\n";
cout << "Selection allows decision making.\n";
```

2.
```
if (x == 6)
      cout << "A match is found.\n";
cout << "Sequence continues after selection is complete.\n";
```

3.
```
if (x < 8)
     {
        cout << "x is within the range.\n";
        cout << "This is a true statement.\n";
     }
cout << "And, after selection, the next statement is executed.\n";
```

4.
```
if (x > 0 && x < 10)
     cout << "x is in the range.\n";
cout << "the value of x is " <<  x;
```

Using the Selection Control Structure if...else

5.
```
if (x > 10)
     cout << "x is greater than 10.\n";
else
     cout << "x is less than or equal to 10.\n";
cout << "Selection allows decision making.\n";
```

6.
```
if (x < 8)
     {
        cout << "x is within the range.\n";
        cout << "This is a true statement.\n";
     }
else
     {
        cout << "x is out of range.\n";
        cout << "This is a false statement.\n";
     }
cout << "After selection, the next statement is executed.\n";
```

7.
```
if (x >= 5)
{
}
else
     cout << "Have a good day.\n";
```

8.
```
if (x > 0 && x < 10)
     cout << "x is in range.\n";
else
     cout << "x is not in range.\n";
```

Critical Thinking

9a. *Critical Thinking Exercise:* Design a program that will ask users to input their age and whether or not they have a discount coupon. If the age is greater than 17, set the ticket price to be eight dollars, and if the age is not greater than 17, set the ticket price to be six dollars. If the user has a discount coupon, reduce the ticket price by 25 percent. Output the ticket price. (*Hint*: use an `integer` variable for the price and a `char` variable for the discount, *i.e.,* ask the users to enter a y if they have a coupon and an n if they do not.)

Write your design in the following space. For your design, write an algorithm (an English language description of the steps required to successfully write the program).

9b. Write the source code for the design you created in Exercise 9a and name it Tickets.cpp.

9c. Enter, compile, link, and execute Tickets.cpp. Copy the output and save it in a block comment at the end of your program. Save Tickets.cpp in the Chap04 folder of your Student Disk.

The following is a copy of the screen results that might appear after running your program, depending on the data you entered.

Enter your age: 24
Do you have a discount coupon? (enter a y for yes and an n for no): y
Ticket Price: 6.00

Enter your age: 17
Do you have a discount coupon? (enter a y for yes and an n for no): n
Ticket Price: 6.00

LAB 4.3 USING NESTED `if` AND `if...else` STATEMENTS

The statement(s) executed in a selection can be any valid C++ statement(s). This includes an `if` statement located within another `if` or `if...else` statement. These statements are called nested statements. When the selection requires more than one alternative, use the nested `if` statement.

An `else` statement is not required; however, when used, all `else` statements must be paired with an `if`. In a nested `if` statement, C++ associates an `else` with the most recent incomplete `if structure`—that is, the most recent `if` that has not been paired with an `else`. The `if` and `if...else` structures control only one statement at a time. To permit more complex statements, C++ provides a structure called a compound statement or a block of statements. Some problems require the implementation of more than two alternatives. When one control statement is located within another, it is said to be nested.

A sequence of `if...else` statements can accomplish the same task as a series of `if` statements. However, a sequence of `if...else` statements is more efficient because once a match has been found, the remainder of the tests are skipped. In a series of `if` statements, all statements are evaluated. An alternative to writing nested `if...else` statements is to write compound Boolean expressions.

One method of program development is an informal mixture of C++ and ordinary language called pseudocode or pseudo. To find logical errors in your pseudo, you should always use a wide range of values in a walk-through to evaluate the code under as many different circumstances as possible. Once you have written your program, you should also test the program using data values that test all program paths.

Objectives

In this lab, you evaluate Boolean expressions in nested `if` statements.

After completing this lab, you will be able to:

- Match the `else` statement with the appropriate `if` statement.
- Know when to nest and when not to nest `if` statements.
- Write code using nested `if`s.
- Write compound Boolean expressions using `if...else` statements.
- Test all paths of your program.

Estimated completion time: **60–75 minutes**

Using Nested `if` and `if...else` Statements

Write what the following statements display as output after the program executes. Then design and write a program that uses nested `if` and `if...else` statements.

1a. Write what the following statements display as output after the program executes.

```
int temperature = 78;
int month = 6;
string name = "Pat Boone";
if (temperature >= 70 && month >=6)
    cout << "Wear white shoes.\n";
else if (name == "Pat Boone")
    cout << "Wear white shoes.\n";
else
    cout << "Wear black shoes.\n";
```

1b. What is the output of the program in Exercise 1a when temperature = 70, month = 5, and name = "Pat Boone"?

1c. What is the output of the program in Exercise 1a when temperature = 60, month = 5, and name = "Pat Boone"?

1d. What is the output of the program in Exercise 1a when temperature = 60, month = 5, and name = "Your name"?

2a. Design a program that prompts the user to enter three names separated by spaces. Using compound and nested `if` statements, display the names in alphabetical order.

Write your design in the following space. Your design should be a list of C++ comments without any code.

2b. Write a C++ program based on the design you created in Exercise 2a and name it **NameSort.cpp**. Step through the code by hand.

Use the following memory table to show what occurs in memory when the C++ code is executed. (Include line numbers as documentation only. Do not use line numbers when entering your final program.) To fill out the memory table, use two lines for each variable. On one line, enter declaration information. Write the name of the declared variable, its data type, and the line number at declaration.

Variable Name	Data Type	Value in Memory	Line Number at Declaration	Line Number when Initialized

In the following space, show what is displayed on the screen after executing the output message using the following data: **George Joe Adam**

2c. Enter, compile, link, and execute **NameSort.cpp**. Then copy the output and save it in a block comment at the end of your program. Save **NameSort.cpp** in the Chap04 folder of your Student Disk.

The following is a copy of the screen results that might display after running your program, depending on the data entered. The input entered by the user is shown in bold.

```
Please enter 3 names: George Joe Adam
The alphabetical order of the names is:
Adam
George
Joe
```

2d. Rerun **NameSort.cpp** with the names entered in this order: Joe Adam George

2e. Rerun **NameSort.cpp** with the names entered in this order: Adam Joe George

2f. Rerun **NameSort.cpp** with the names entered in this order: George Adam Joe

LAB 4.4 USING THE `if` STATEMENT WITH INPUT FAILURE

Attempting to read invalid data causes the input stream to enter a fail state. Once an input stream enters a fail state, all subsequent input statements associated with that input stream are ignored, and the computer continues to execute the program, which produces erroneous results. Other than reading invalid data, two common causes of input failure are:

- Attempting to open an input file that does not exist
- Attempting to read beyond the end of an input file

You can use the `if` statement to check the status of an input stream variable. If the input stream enters the fail state, you also can include instructions that stop program execution.

When you use the input stream variable as an expression in an `if` statement, it evaluates to `true` if the last input succeeded and to `false` if the last input failed. For example, `if (cin)` or `if (infile)` evaluates to `true` if the last input from the input device succeeded.

If an input fails, a message can be displayed, and a return statement is generated with the value of 1 included to terminate the program. A return value 0 indicates that the program ended correctly.

Objectives

In this lab, you evaluate the standard input device and an `ifstream` variable for input failure. If failure occurs, the programs terminate.

After completing this lab, you will be able to:

- Use the `if` statement to check for input failure.
- Evaluate the standard input variable for input failure.
- Evaluate the `ifstream` variable for input failure.
- Evaluate the `ofstream` variable for output failure.

Estimated completion time: **40–45 minutes**

Using the `if` Statement with Input Failure

Design and write a program that tests for input failure.

1a. Design a program that prompts the user to enter his or her age and first initial. Include code that checks for input failure in case the user enters character data for numeric data. If input failure occurs, display a message and return the value 1 from your main function. If no input failure occurs, display a message that echoes the data entered.

Write your design in the following space. Your design should be a list of C++ comments without any code.

1b. Write a C++ program based on the design you created in Exercise 1a and name it **Failure.cpp**. Step through the code by hand.

Use the following memory table to show what occurs in memory when the C++ code is executed. (Include line numbers as documentation only. Do not use line numbers when entering your final program.) To fill out the memory table, use two lines for each variable. On one line, enter declaration information. Write the name of the declared variable, its data type, and the line number at declaration.

Variable Name	Data Type	Value in Memory	Line Number at Declaration	Line Number when Initialized

In the following space, show what is displayed on the screen after executing the output message.

1c. Enter, compile, link, and execute **Failure.cpp**. Then copy the output and save it in a block comment at the end of your program. Save **Failure.cpp** in the Chap04 folder of your Student Disk.

The following is a copy of the screen results that might display after running your program, depending on the data entered. The input entered by the user is shown in bold.

```
Either
/*
Please enter your age and first initial: 19 J

Your age is 19 and your initial is J.
*/
or
/*
Please enter your age and first initial: J 19

You did not enter your age followed by your initial.
*/
```

2a. Create the design for a program that prompts the user to create a name and address file from a name, street address, city, state, and zip code entered. You should create the name and address file on a drive with a removable disk. Check for input failure in case the user does not have access to the drive (for example, if the disk is not inserted in the drive). If input failure occurs, display a message indicating the problem; otherwise, display a message indicating that the program ended successfully.

Write your design in the following space. Your design should be a list of C++ comments without any code.

2b. Write a C++ program based on the design you created in Exercise 2a and name it **NoDisk1.cpp**. Step through the code by hand. Specify that the output file is named **address.txt**.

Use the following memory table to show what occurs in memory when the C++ code is executed. (Include line numbers as documentation only. Do not use line numbers when entering your final program.) To fill out the memory table, use two lines for each variable. On one line, enter declaration information. Write the name of the declared variable, its data type, and the line number at declaration.

Variable Name	Data Type	Value in Memory	Line Number at Declaration	Line Number when Initialized

In the following space, show what is displayed on the screen after executing the output message.

2c. Enter, compile, link, and execute **NoDisk1.cpp**. Execute the program twice, once with no disk in the drive and once with a disk in the drive. After your program is executed, copy the output and save it in a block comment at the end of your program. Save **NoDisk1.cpp** in the Chap04 folder of your Student Disk.

The following is a copy of the screen results that might display after running your program, depending on the data entered. The input entered by the user is shown in bold.

```
/*
Cannot open output file. The program terminates.
*/

/*
Please enter a name: Judy Shaffer
Please enter a street address: 774 S. Main St.
Please enter a city, state, and zip code: Austin, Texas 78736

Your program ended successfully.
*/
```

3a. Create the design for a program that reads the **address.txt** file that you created in Exercise 2 from drive A (or another drive with a removable disk). Read in the name, street address, city, state, and zip code from **address.txt**, and display this information on the screen. Check for input failure in case the user does not have access to the drive (for example, if the disk is not inserted in the drive). If input failure occurs, display a message indicating the problem.

Write your design in the following space. Your design should be a list of C++ comments without any code.

3b. Write a C++ program based on the design you created in Exercise 3a and name it **NoDisk2.cpp**. Step through the code by hand.

Use the following memory table to show what occurs in memory when the C++ code is executed. (Include line numbers as documentation only. Do not use line numbers when entering your final program.) To fill out the memory table, use two lines for each variable. On one line, enter declaration information. Write the name of the declared variable, its data type, and the line number at declaration.

Variable Name	Data Type	Value in Memory	Line Number at Declaration	Line Number when Initialized

In the following space, show what is displayed on the screen after executing the output message.

3c. Enter, compile, link, and execute **NoDisk2.cpp**. Execute the program twice, once with no disk in the drive and once with a disk in the drive. After your program is executed, copy the output and save it in a block comment at the end of your program. Save **NoDisk2.cpp** in the Chap04 folder of your Student Disk.

The following is a copy of the screen results that might display after running your program, depending on the data entered. The input comes from **address.txt**.

```
Either
/*
Judy Shaffer
774 S. Main St.
Austin, Texas 78736
*/
or
/*
Cannot open input file. The program terminates.
*/
```

LAB 4.5 CONFUSING THE ASSIGNMENT OPERATOR (=) WITH THE EQUALITY OPERATOR (==)

Any Boolean expression evaluates to `true` or `false`. An assignment expression used in a Boolean expression is evaluated after the assignment occurs. Any nonzero value evaluates to `true`. An `if` statement erroneously consisting of an assignment statement evaluates to `true` any time the value is not zero; otherwise, it evaluates to `false`. C++ does not show this as a compile error. This error is a logical error.

Objectives

In this lab, you distinguish the assignment operator from an equality operator in a Boolean expression.

After completing this lab, you will be able to:

- Recognize the problems related to confusing the assignment operator with the equality operator.

Estimated completion time: **5–10 minutes**

Confusing the Assignment Operator (=) with the Equality Operator (==)

1. Write what the following statements display as output after the program executes:

```
int x = 8;
if (x == 10)
     cout << "x is equal to 10\n";
else
     cout << "x is not equal to 10\n";
```

2. The following code is the same as the code in Exercise 1 but uses the assignment operator rather than the equality operator. Write what the following statements display as output after the program executes:

```
int x = 8;
if (x = 10)
     cout << "x is equal to 10\n";
else
     cout << "x is not equal to 10\n";
```

LAB 4.6 USING THE CONDITIONAL OPERATOR (?:)

You can write certain `if...else` statements concisely by using the conditional operator in C++. The conditional operator, written as `?:`, is a ternary operator, which means that it takes three arguments. For example, examine the following code:

```
int x = 10, sum = 0;
if(x == 10)
   sum = x + 3;
else
   sum = x - 3;
Can be written as:
int x = 10, sum = 0;
(x==10) ? sum = x + 3 : sum = x - 3;
```

In the preceding examples, sum would be assigned 13 because x is equal to 10. Notice that this code does not use the reserved word `if` or a semicolon (;) after the true statement.

The conditional expression is evaluated as follows: If expression1 evaluates to `true`, the result of the conditional expression is expression2. Otherwise, the result of the conditional expression is expression3.

Objectives

In this lab, you rewrite `if...else` statements using the conditional operators (`?:`).

After completing this lab, you will be able to:

- Write `if...else` statements using the conditional operators (`?:`).

Estimated completion time: **10–15 minutes**

Using the Conditional Operator (?:)

Rewrite the following `if...else` statements using the conditional operator (`?:`). Assume these statements are part of a C++ program.

1.
```
if (x  > 10)
     cout << "x is greater than 10\n";
else
     cout << "x is less than or equal to 10\n";
```

2.
```
if (x==6)
    cout << "A match is found.\n";
else
    cout << "A match was not found.\n";
```

LAB 4.7 USING THE `switch` SELECTION CONTROL STRUCTURE

Another control structure, called the `switch` statement, gives the computer the power to choose from many alternatives.

A `switch` structure uses the reserved words `switch`, `case`, `break`, and `default`. First the expression is evaluated and then the value of the expression determines the actions performed as specified in the statements that follow the reserved word `case`. The value of the expression must be integral and is sometimes called the selector. An integral value is a value that evaluates to an integer value.

The syntax of the `switch` statement is as follows:

```
Switch (expression)
{
case value1: statements1
         break;
case value2: statements2
         break;
         ...
case valuen: statementsn
         break;
default: statements
}
```

The switch statement executes according to the following rules:

- When the value of the expression matches a case value, the statements execute until either a break statement is found or the end of the switch structure is reached.
- If the value of the expression does not match a case value, the statements following the default label execute. If there is no match and no default label, the entire switch statement is skipped.

The `switch` statement is an elegant way to implement multiple selections. If multiple selections involve a range of values, you should convert each range to a finite set of values. For instance, if the range of values includes 60–69, you could divide by 10 and then use the 6 as the finite value.

Objectives

In this lab, you write a `switch` statement using `break` statements and a `switch` statement using the fall-through capability.

After completing this lab, you will be able to:

- Write `switch` control statements using the `break` statement.
- Write `switch` control statements using the fall-through capability.

Estimated completion time: **30–40 minutes**

Using the `switch` Selection Control Structure

Write and test programs that use a `switch` statement, and then test them with different values.

1a. *Critical Thinking Exercise*: Design a program that prompts the user to select one of three television models and provides a description of the models. Using the `switch` statement's fall-through capability, display the model the user chooses, the description, and the price. The user should make a selection by model number.

The user should be prompted with the following information:

- Model 100: Remote control, timer, and stereo for $1000
- Model 200: The same as Model 100, plus picture-in-picture, for $1200
- Model 300: The same as Model 200, plus HDTV, flat screen, and a 16 x 9 aspect ratio, for $2400

Display all features of the model selected.

Write your design in the following space. Your design should be a list of C++ comments without any code.

1b. Write a C++ program based on the design you created in Exercise 1a and name it **TV.cpp**. Step through the code by hand.

Use the following memory table to show what occurs in memory when the C++ code is executed. (Include line numbers as documentation only. Do not use line numbers when entering your final program.) To fill out the memory table, use two lines for each variable. On one line, enter declaration information. Write the name of the declared variable, its data type, and the line number at declaration.

Variable Name	Data Type	Value in Memory	Line Number at Declaration	Line Number when Initialized

In the following space, show what is displayed on the screen after executing the output message.

1c. Enter, compile, link, and execute **TV.cpp**. Execute the program three times, selecting a different model with each execution. Then copy the output and save it in a block comment at the end of your program. Save **TV.cpp** in the Chap04 folder of your Student Disk.

The following is a copy of the screen results that might display after running your program, depending on the data entered. The input entered by the user is shown in bold.

```
Enter the model number of your choice:

Model 100: Remote control, timer, and stereo for $1000
Model 200: The same as Model 100, plus picture-in-picture, for $1200
Model 300: The same as Model 200, plus HDTV, flat screen,
           and a 16 x 9 aspect ratio, for $2400

100

You chose Model 100 TV with these features:
     remote control, timer, and stereo sound
```

```
Your price will be $1000.

Enter the model number of your choice:

Model 100: Remote control, timer, and stereo for $1000
Model 200: The same as Model 100, plus picture-in-picture, for
$1200
Model 300: The same as Model 200, plus HDTV, flat screen,
           and a 16 x 9 aspect ratio, for $2400

200

You chose Model 200 TV with these features:
     picture-in-picture
     remote control, timer, and stereo sound

Your price will be $1200.

Enter the model number of your choice:

Model 100: Remote control, timer, and stereo for $1000
Model 200: The same as Model 100, plus picture-in-picture, for
$1200
Model 300: The same as Model 200, plus HDTV, flat screen,
           and a 16 x 9 aspect ratio, for $2400

300

You chose Model 300 TV with these features:
     HDTV, flat screen, 16 x 9 aspect ratio
     picture-in-picture
     remote control, timer, and stereo sound

Your price will be $2400.

Enter the model number of your choice:

Model 100: Remote control, timer, and stereo for $1000
Model 200: The same as Model 100, plus picture-in-picture, for
$1200
Model 300: The same as Model 200, plus HDTV, flat screen,
           and a 16 x 9 aspect ratio, for $2400

400

Your choice is not available.
```

Critical Thinking

2a. *Critical Thinking Exercise*: Create a design for a program that prompts the user to select one of three flooring options for a home. The program also provides a description of the flooring options. Using the switch statement, display the option the user chooses, the description, and the price.

The user should be prompted with the following information:

- Option 1: Scored concrete for $3000
- Option 2: Carpeting for $5000
- Option 3: Wood floors in the living areas, carpeting in the bedrooms, and tile in the bath areas for $10,000

Write your design in the following space. Your design should be a list of C++ comments without any code.

2b. Write a C++ program based on the design you created in Exercise 2a and name it **Flooring.cpp**. Step through the code by hand.

Use the following memory table to show what occurs in memory when the C++ code is executed. (Include line numbers as documentation only. Do not use line numbers when entering your final program.) To fill out the memory table, use two lines for each variable. On one line, enter declaration information. Write the name of the declared variable, its data type, and the line number at declaration.

Variable Name	Data Type	Value in Memory	Line Number at Declaration	Line Number when Initialized

In the following space, show what is displayed on the screen after executing the output message.

2c. Enter, compile, link, and execute **Flooring.cpp**. Then copy the output and save it in a block comment at the end of your program. Save **Flooring.cpp** in the Chap04 folder of your Student Disk.

The following are copies of the screen results that might display after running your program, depending on the data entered. The input entered by the user is shown in bold.

```
Enter the number that matches your flooring choice:
Option 1: Scored concrete for $3000
Option 2: Carpeting for $5000
Option 3: Wood floors in the living areas, carpeting in the bedrooms,
          and tile in the bath areas for $10,000
1

You chose Option 1: Scored concrete for $3000.
```

The following shows another set of possible input and output:

```
Enter the number that matches your flooring choice:
Option 1: Scored concrete for $3000
Option 2: Carpeting for $5000
Option 3: Wood floors in the living areas, carpeting in the bedrooms,
          and tile in the bath areas for $10,000
2

You chose Option 2: Carpeting for $5000.
```

The following shows another set of possible input and output:

```
Enter the number that matches your flooring choice:
Option 1: Scored concrete for $3000
Option 2: Carpeting for $5000
Option 3: Wood floors in the living areas, carpeting in the bedrooms,
          and tile in the bath areas for $10,000
3

You chose Option 3: Wood floors in the living areas, carpeting in the
bedrooms, and tile in the bath areas for $10,000.
```

The following shows another set of possible input and output:

```
Enter the number that matches your flooring choice:
Option 1: Scored concrete for $3000
Option 2: Carpeting for $5000
Option 3: Wood floors in the living areas, carpeting in the bedrooms,
          and tile in the bath areas for $10,000
4

You chose Option 4:
Your selection is not available.
```

LAB 4.8 USING THE assert FUNCTION TO TERMINATE A PROGRAM

A predefined function, **assert**, stops program execution when certain elusive errors occur. Use the **assert** function to ensure that a program terminates with an appropriate error message indicating the type of error and the location in the program where the error occurred.

You can use the **assert** function with any logical expression. If the expression evaluates to **true**, the next statement executes. If the expression evaluates to **false**, the program terminates and indicates where the error occurred.

The **assert** function is included in the header file **cassert**. The **assert** function is useful during program development; however, a user would not understand what the error means. Therefore, you should remove **assert** statements when the program is ready for production. Rather than going through the code looking for the function, place the directive **#define NDEBUG** before the directive **#include <cassert>** to have the program ignore the **assert** function.

Objectives

In this lab, you use the **assert** function to test for division by 0. You then use the **#define NDEBUG** directive to ignore the **assert** function.

After completing this lab, you will be able to:

- User the **assert** function to ensure that a program terminates with an appropriate error message that indicates the type of error and the program location where the error occurred.
- Use the **#define NDEBUG** directive to ignore the **assert** function.

Estimated completion time: **50–60 minutes**

Using the assert Function to Terminate a Program

In the following exercises, design, write, and validate programs that use the **assert** function and the **#define NDEBUG** directive.

1a. Create a design for a program that evaluates a division problem and uses the **assert** function to determine whether an error occurs. Prompt the user for the numerator and denominator, but do not test to see whether the denominator is equal to 0. Display a message with the values entered and the decimal representation of the fraction.

Write your design in the following space. Your design should be a list of C++ comments without any code.

1b. Write a C++ program based on the design you created in Exercise 1a and name it **divZero1.cpp**. Step through the code by hand.

Use the following memory table to show what occurs in memory when the C++ code is executed. (Include line numbers as documentation only. Do not use line numbers when entering your final program.) To fill out the memory table, use two lines for each variable. On one line, enter declaration information. Write the name of the declared variable, its data type, and the line number at declaration.

Variable Name	Data Type	Value in Memory	Line Number at Declaration	Line Number when Initialized

In the following space, show what is displayed on the screen after executing the output message.

1c. Enter, compile, link, and execute **divZero1.cpp**. Then copy the output and save it in a block comment at the end of your program. Save **divZero1.cpp** in the Chap04 folder of your Student Disk.

The following is a copy of the screen results that might display after running your program, depending on the data entered. The input entered by the user is shown in bold.

```
Enter a numerator and a denominator: 2 0
Assertion failed: denominator, file C:\Chap04\divZero1.cpp, line 32

abnormal program termination
```

The following shows another set of possible input and output:

```
Enter a numerator and a denominator: 3 4

The decimal value of the numerator 3 divided by the denominator 4 is
0.75
```

1d. Revise **divZero1.cpp** using the #define NDEBUG directive and save as **divZero2.cpp**. Remember to place #define NDEBUG before #include <cassert>. Use the same data as you did in Step 1c to run your program. Depending on your compiler, your output will either be the same as for Lab 4.8, Exercise 1c or as follows:

```
Enter a numerator and a denominator: 2 0

The decimal value of the numerator 2 divided by the denominator 0 is
1.#INF
```

The following shows another set of possible input and output:

```
Enter a numerator and a denominator: 3 4

The decimal value of the numerator 3 divided by the denominator 4 is
0.75
```

5 Control Structures II *(Repetition)*

In this chapter, you will:

- Learn about repetition (looping) control structures
- Explore how to construct and use count-controlled, sentinel-controlled, flag-controlled, and EOF-controlled repetition structures
- Examine `break` and `continue` statements
- Discover how to form and use nested control structures
- Discover how to convert between different types of loops

Chapter 5: Assignment Cover Sheet

Name ______________________ Date ______________________

Section ______________________

Lab Assignments	Assigned	Grade
Lab 5.1 Using the `while` Looping (Repetition) Structure		
Lab 5.2 Using the `for` Looping (Repetition) Structure		
Lab 5.3 Using the `do...while` Looping (Repetition) Structure (Critical Thinking Exercise)		
Lab 5.4 Using `break` and `continue` Statements		
Lab 5.5 Using Nested Control Structures (Critical Thinking Exercises)		
Lab 5.6 Converting between `while`, `do...while`, and `for` loops (Critical Thinking Exercises)		
Total Grade		

See your instructor or the introduction to this book for instructions on submitting your assignments.

LAB 5.1 USING THE `while` LOOPING (REPETITION) STRUCTURE

The three looping (repetition) structures, **while**, **for**, and **do...while**, are reserved words in C++ and are used when you want a program to repeat a set of statements. The three different types of looping structures offer flexibility in coding. This lab focuses on the **while** loop.

The reserved word **while** acts on a Boolean expression and serves as a decision-maker. Generally, the work of the loop is accomplished within the body of the loop, which can include one or more statements, and is executed when the expression evaluates to **true**. The expression is reevaluated after each iteration of the statements until the expression evaluates to **false**. An exit condition must exist within a loop; otherwise, an infinite loop will occur.

A looping expression contains the loop control variable (LCV). The LCV must be initialized before it is evaluated and updated within the body of the loop to provide an exit condition. All loops with LCVs require the following:

1. An initialization of the loop control variable.
2. Evaluation of the loop condition. If the loop condition is **false**, the body of the loop never executes. If **true**, the body of the loop is executed.
3. An update of the loop control variable.
4. Repetition of Steps 2 and 3 until the loop condition evaluates to **false**.

There are four types of **while** loops: counter-controlled, sentinel-controlled, flag-controlled, and end of file (EOF)-controlled.

Objectives

In this lab, you become acquainted with all four types of **while** loops.

After completing this lab, you will be able to:

- Write a counter-controlled **while** loop when you know exactly how many pieces of data need to be read.
- Write a sentinel-controlled **while** loop that uses a special sentinel value to end the loop.
- Write an EOF-controlled **while** loop that continues until the program reaches the end of the file.

Estimated completion time: **60–75 minutes**

Using the `while` Looping (Repetition) Structure

Design and write code for the following program that uses **while** loops.

1a. Design a program that prompts the user to enter the number of students registered in a class. If the number is greater than 0, the program should use a counter-controlled **while** loop to prompt the user that same number of times for the students' names. Write the students' names to an output file named **students.txt**. Display a message to the user when the program is complete.

Write your design in the following space. Your design should be a list of C++ comments without any code.

1b. Write a C++ program based on the design you created in Exercise 1a and name it **Roster1.cpp**. Step through the code by hand.

Use the following memory table to show what occurs in memory when the C++ code is executed. (Include line numbers as documentation only. Do not use line numbers when entering your final program.) To fill out the memory table, use one or two lines for each variable. On one line, enter declaration information. Write the name of the declared variable, its data type, and the line number at declaration when initialized.

Variable Name	Data Type	Value in Memory	Line Number at Declaration	Line Number when Initialized

In the following space, show what is displayed on the screen after executing the output message.

1c. Enter, compile, link, and execute **Roster1.cpp**. Then copy the output and save it in a block comment at the end of your program. Save **Roster1.cpp** in the Chap05 folder of your Student Disk.

The following is a copy of the screen results that might display after running your program, depending on the data entered. The input entered by the user is shown in bold.

```
How many students may register for this class? 10
Enter the student's name: Yongrui Wuan
Enter the student's name: Marvella Garcia
Enter the student's name: Lola Zapata
Enter the student's name: Tony Pederzani
Enter the student's name: George Smith
Enter the student's name: John Patrick
Enter the student's name: Connor Bailey
Enter the student's name: Ryan Dennis
Enter the student's name: Susie Brown
Enter the student's name: Jack Cunningham

The program is complete.
```

2a. Design a program that simulates an order room of a factory. To fill an order, workers place items on a conveyer belt to be grouped, billed, and shipped. Each item has a UPC code that designates the name of the item and its price. When an order is complete, a worker places a bar on the conveyor belt to separate that order from the next order. The bar has a UPC code of 999. In programming, a specific value to designate the end of a loop is called a sentinel value. The UPC code of 999 is a sentinel value.

After the computer system scans the UPC code of each item, it records the name and price in a file named **invoice1.txt**. This output file contains the product name and price on one line, separated by a pound sign (#). For example, if a hammer is purchased for the price of 9.95, the program writes this line as `hammer#9.95`. The program does not write the sentinel value to the output file. In your program, use a `while` repetition construct.

Because this is a program simulation, prompt the user to enter the name and price of each item. On a real order-scanning machine, no prompt would be used. When the system reads the value 999, display a thank you message, the name of the output file, and each item and price added to the output file.

Write your design in the following space. Your design should be a list of C++ comments without any code.

2b. Write a C++ program based on the design you created in Exercise 2a and name it **Scan1.cpp**. Step through the code by hand.

Use the following memory table to show what occurs in memory when the C++ code is executed. (Include line numbers as documentation only. Do not use line numbers when entering your final program.) To fill out the memory table, use one or two lines for each variable. On one line, enter declaration information. Write the name of the declared variable, its data type, and the line number at declaration.

Variable Name	Data Type	Value in Memory	Line Number at Declaration	Line Number when Initialized

In the following space, show what is displayed on the screen after executing the output message.

2c. Enter, compile, link, and execute **Scan1.cpp**. Then copy the output and save it in a block comment at the end of your program. Save **Scan1.cpp** in the Chap05 folder of your Student Disk.

The following is a copy of the screen results that might display after running your program, depending on the data entered. The input entered by the user is shown in bold.

```
Please scan the name of the first item: hammer
Please scan the price of the hammer: 9.95


Please scan the name of the next item: saw
Please scan the price of the saw: 20.15


Please scan the name of the next item: shovel
Please scan the price of the shovel: 35.40


Please scan the name of the next item: 999


Thank you for your order.
invoice1.txt
hammer#9.95
saw#20.15
shovel#35.40
```

3a. Design a program that prompts the user to enter the name of an item, searches the file **invoice1.txt** that was created in Exercise 2 for the item, and then displays the name and the price associated with that item. When you get to the point that a search item is not in the list, you have reached the end of file. Use a compound flag-controlled `while` loop to search the list until either the item is found or the end of the file is reached. Display a message if the item is not found.

3b. Write a C++ program based on the design you created in Exercise 3a and name it **Scan2.cpp**. Step through the code by hand.

Use the following memory table to show what occurs in memory when the C++ code is executed. (Include line numbers as documentation only. Do not use line numbers when entering your final program.) To fill out the memory table, use one or two lines for each variable. On one line, enter declaration information. Write the name of the declared variable, its data type, and the line number at declaration.

Variable Name	Data Type	Value in Memory	Line Number at Declaration	Line Number where Value is Entered

In the following space, show what is displayed on the screen after executing the output message, depending on the data entered.

3c. Enter, compile, link, and execute **Scan2.cpp**. Then copy the output and save it in a block comment at the end of your program. Save **Scan2.cpp** in the Chap05 folder of your Student Disk.

The following is a copy of the screen results that might display after running your program, depending on the data entered. The input entered by the user is shown in bold.

```
Enter name of item for search: shovel


The item shovel costs 35.40
or
Enter name of item for search: hoe


The item hoe was not found
```

4a. Design a program that reads names and prices and then counts and accumulates all prices in the file **invoice1.txt**. Display each name and price, total count, and total of all prices in currency format.

Write your design in the following space. Your design should be a list of C++ comments without any code.

4b. Write a C++ program based on the design you created in Exercise 4a and name it **Scan3.cpp**. Step through the code by hand.

Use the following memory table to show what occurs in memory when the C++ code is executed. (Include line numbers as documentation only. Do not use line numbers when entering your final program.) To fill out the memory table, use one or two lines for each variable. On one line, enter declaration information. Write the name of the declared variable, its data type, and the line number at declaration.

Variable Name	Data Type	Value in Memory	Line Number at Declaration	Line Number where Value is Entered

In the following space, show what is displayed on the screen after executing the output message.

4c. Enter, compile, link, and execute **Scan3.cpp**. Then copy the output and save it in a block comment at the end of your program. Save **Scan3.cpp** in the Chap05 folder of your Student Disk.

The following is a copy of the screen results that might display after running your program, depending on the data entered.

```
Invoice


                 hammer    9.95
                    saw   20.15
                 shovel   35.40


Total    3 items      $   65.50
```

LAB 5.2 USING THE `for` LOOPING (REPETITION) STRUCTURE

The `for` looping structure, sometimes called a counted or indexed `for` loop, is a specialized form of the `while` loop that you use to simplify writing count-controlled loops.

To use the `for` looping structure, you write a `for` statement, in which `for` is followed by the initial statement, loop condition, and update statement enclosed within parentheses. The program executes a `for` loop in the following sequence:

1. The initial statement executes.
2. The loop condition is evaluated. If the loop condition is `false`, the body of the loop never executes. If the loop condition is `true`, the body of the loop is executed.
3. The update statement executes after the body of the loop ends.
4. Steps 2 and 3 are repeated until the loop condition evaluates to `false`.

Objectives

In this lab, you create programs that use the `for` loop.

After completing this lab, you will be able to:

- Write a `for` loop with an increment update condition.
- Write a `for` loop with a decrement update condition.

Estimated completion time: **40–50 minutes**

Using the `for` Looping (Repetition) Structure

In the following exercises, you design and write programs that use `for` loops.

1a. Design a program that prompts the user to enter a positive integer. Use a `for` loop to calculate and display the factorial value of that number. Increment the counter in your `for` loop. The factorial value of a number is a number multiplied by every factor between 1 and the number, inclusive. For instance, 3 factorial is 3 * 2 * 1. If the user enters a negative number, display a message indicating that the program calculates only positive numbers. Otherwise, display the result of the calculation.

Write your design in the following space. Your design should be a list of C++ comments without any code.

1b. Write a C++ program based on the design you created in Exercise 1a and name it **Factorial1.cpp**. Step through the code by hand.

Use the following memory table to show what occurs in memory when the C++ code is executed. (Include line numbers as documentation only. Do not use line numbers when entering your final program.) To fill out the memory table, use one or two lines for each variable. On one line, enter declaration information. Write the name of the declared variable, its data type, and the line number at declaration.

Variable Name	Data Type	Value in Memory	Line Number at Declaration	Line Number when Initialized

In the following space, show what is displayed on the screen after executing the output message.

1c. Enter, compile, link, and execute **Factorial1.cpp**. Then copy the output and save it in a block comment at the end of your program. Save **Factorial1.cpp** in the Chap05 folder of your Student Disk.

The following is a copy of the screen results that might display after running your program, depending on the data entered. The input entered by the user is shown in bold.

```
Enter a positive integer to find the factorial value: 5

The factorial of 5 is 120
```

2a. Redesign the program you wrote in Exercise 1 to use a decrement counter in your `for` loop. Write your design in the following space. Your design should be a list of C++ comments without any code.

2b. Write a C++ program based on the design you created in Exercise 2a and name it **Factorial2.cpp**. Step through the code by hand.

Use the following memory table to show what occurs in memory when the C++ code is executed. (Include line numbers as documentation only. Do not use line numbers when entering your final program.) To fill out the memory table, use one or two lines for each variable. On one line, enter declaration information. Write the name of the declared variable, its data type, and the line number at declaration.

Variable Name	Data Type	Value in Memory	Line Number at Declaration	Line Number when Initialized

In the following space, show what is displayed on the screen after executing the output message.

2c. Enter, compile, link, and execute **Factorial2.cpp**. Then copy the output and save it in a block comment at the end of your program. Save **Factorial2.cpp** in the Chap05 folder of your Student Disk.

The following is a copy of the screen results that might display after running your program, depending on the data entered. The input entered by the user is shown in bold.

```
Enter a positive integer to find the factorial value: 5

The factorial of 5 is 120
```

3a. Redesign the program you wrote in Lab 5.1, Exercise 1 to use a for loop. Write your design in the following space. Your design should be a list of C++ comments without any code.

3b. Write a C++ program based on the design you created in Exercise 3a and name it **Roster2.cpp**. Step through the code by hand.

3c. Enter, compile, link, and execute **Roster2.cpp**. Then copy the output and save it in a block comment at the end of your program. Save **Roster2.cpp** in the Chap05 folder of your Student Disk.

Your screen results should be the same for Roster1.cpp and Roster2.cpp when running the same data.

LAB 5.3 USING THE do...while LOOPING (REPETITION) STRUCTURE

The `while` and `for` loops are pretest loops. That is, the loop condition (Boolean test) occurs at the beginning or top of the loop structure. The condition is tested to determine whether it is `true` before the statements in the loop body are executed. If the condition tests `false`, the statements in the loop body are not executed and the program continues on to the statements that follow the loop structure. Consequently, if the condition tests `false` the first time it is tested, the statements in the body of the loop will never execute.

The `do...while` structure is a posttest loop. That is, the loop condition is located at the end or bottom of the loop structure. The loop condition is not tested until the statements in the body of the loop have been executed. Consequently, the statements in the body of the loop will always execute at least once.

The `do...while` loop structure will not generally be used unless the logic of the program requires the statements in the body of the loop to execute at least once. This structure is often used for data validation. A user is asked to input data in the body of the loop. If the data is invalid, it will cause the loop condition to be `true,` and the loop will be executed again, asking the user to input the data again. The loop will continue to execute until the user inputs valid data, which will cause the loop condition to be `false,` and the statements in the body of the loop will not be executed again.

Objectives

In this lab, you will create programs that use the `do...while` loop.

After completing this lab, you will be able to:

- Write a `do...while` sentinel-controlled loop that uses a special sentinel value or range of values to end the loop.
- Write a `do...while` counter-controlled loop when you know exactly how many pieces of data to read.
- Write a `do...while` loop that uses a compound Boolean loop condition that evaluates `false` if both of the following conditions evaluate to `false`:
  - a Boolean variable
  - a negated EOF (end of file) condition that evaluates to `false` when the program reaches the end of the file

Estimated completion time: **50–60 minutes**

Using the do...while Looping Repetition Structure

In the following exercises, you design and write programs that use `do...while` loops.

1a. Design a program that uses a `do...while` loop to validate that the input, a test score, has an integer value of at least zero but not greater than one hundred. The program will output that the test score is valid. (*Hint:* use a compound Boolean expression with the logical AND operator for the loop condition).

Write your design in the following space. For your design, write an algorithm (an English language description of the steps required to successfully write the program).

1b. Write the source code for the design you created in Exercise 1a and name it **ValidScore.cpp.**

1c. Enter, compile, link, and execute **ValidScore.cpp.** Copy the output and save it in a block comment at the end of your program. Save **ValidScore.cpp** in the Chap05 folder of your Student Disk. Enter at least one invalid test score and one valid test score.

The following is a copy of the screen results that might display after running your program, depending on the data you entered:

```
Enter a score: 105
Enter a score: 87
The score entered is 87.
```

2a. Design a program that uses a counter-controlled loop that asks the user to enter a student's last name and a test score. The program should ask for four names and four scores. Incorporate the design of the `do...while` loop you used in Exercise 1 to validate the test scores by nesting it inside of the counter-controlled `do...while` loop. Inside the counter-controlled `do...while` loop, write the student's last name and test score to an output file named Scores.txt. (*Hint:* output a space after writing a name to the output file and add an `endl` after writing a score to the output file.)

Write your design in the following space. For your design, write an algorithm (an English language description of the steps required to successfully write the program).

2b. Write the source code for the design you created in Exercise 2a and name it **TestScores.cpp.**

2c. Enter, compile, link, and execute TestScores.cpp. Print the Scores.txt file to check the output. Save TestScores.cpp in the Chap05 folder of your Student Disk.

The following is a copy of the output that might appear in the Scores.txt file after running your program, depending on the data you entered.

```
Smith 89
Jones 94
Craig 78
Tims 82
```

3a. Design a program that asks a user to enter a student's name using a `do...while` loop, which searches the Scores.txt output file that you wrote to in Exercise 2 to determine whether the student's name entered is in the Scores.txt file. To do this, the Scores.txt must now become an input file. Inside the loop, read a name and a score from the file. Use a selection structure to determine whether the name read from the input file matches the name input by the user. If it does, set a Boolean variable to `false` (*Hint:* the Boolean variable must be initialized to `true` when first declared). Then, output the student's name and test score to the screen. Use the Boolean variable and negate the eof function as a compound loop control condition. Use another if selection structure to determine whether the name was found in the file and if not, output a message to that effect.

Write your design in the following space. For your design, write an algorithm (an English language description of the steps required to successfully write the program).

3b. Write the source code for the design you created in Exercise 3a and name it **SearchScores.cpp.**

3c. Enter, compile, link, and execute **SearchScores.cpp.** Copy the output and save it in a block comment at the end of your program. Save **SearchScores.cpp** in the Chap05 folder of your Student Disk. Enter at least one name that is not in the file and one name that is in the file.

The following is a copy of the screen results that might display after running your program, depending on the data you entered:

```
Enter a name: Crosby
The name was not found in the file


Enter a name: Tims
Tims 82
```

Lab 5.4 Using `break` and `continue` Statements

The `break` and `continue` statements alter the flow of control in a program. When you use a break in a `switch` statement or in a repetition structure, you provide an immediate exit from the structure. The program continues to execute with the first statement after the structure.

Use a `continue` statement in a repetition structure to end the current iteration only and proceed with the next iteration of the loop. In a `for` loop, the next statement is the update statement. Use a `break` statement in a repetition structure to end the entire repetition. Use these constructs sparingly. They are introduced for informational purposes but are not suggested for general solutions.

Objectives

In this lab, you use `break` and `continue` statements to alter the control of a loop.

After completing this lab, you will be able to:

- Execute a loop until a `break` statement is encountered.
- Execute a loop, skip over the remaining loop statements when a `continue` statement is encountered, and proceed in the loop until the loop terminates.

Estimated completion time: **20–30 minutes**

Using `break` and `continue` Statements

In the following exercises, you evaluate the output in repetition control structures that use `continue` or `break` statements. You also write programs from designs that use `continue` or `break` statements.

1a. Design a program that prompts the user to enter 20 numbers. Add all positive numbers. Use a `for` loop with a `continue` statement to skip negative numbers. Output the total found.

Write your design in the following space. Your design should be a list of C++ comments without any code.

1b. Write a C++ program based on the design you created in Exercise 1a and name it **Continue.cpp**. Step through the code by hand.

Use the following memory table to show what occurs in memory when the C++ code is executed. (Include line numbers as documentation only. Do not use line numbers when entering your final program.) To fill out the memory table, use one or two lines for each variable. On one line, enter declaration information. Write the name of the declared variable, its data type, and the line number at declaration.

Variable Name	Data Type	Value in Memory	Line Number at Declaration	Line Number when Initialized

In the following space, show what is displayed on the screen after executing the output message.

1c. Enter, compile, link, and execute **Continue.cpp**. Then copy the output and save it in a block comment at the end of your program.

The following is a copy of the screen results that might display after running your program, depending on the data entered. The input entered by the user is shown in bold.

```
Enter a list of 20 numbers:
2 3 1 -6 10 2 6 5 9 -10 9 2 -4 3 1 2 -6 7 3 2

The sum of the positive numbers is: 67
```

2a. Modify the design and rewrite the **Continue.cpp** program you created in Exercise 1. The program should prompt the user to enter 20 numbers. Add all numbers until the user enters a negative number. Use a `for` loop with a `break` statement to end the loop when a negative number is entered. Output the total found.

Write your design in the following space. Your design should be a list of C++ comments without any code

2b. Write a C++ program based on the design you created in Exercise 2a and name it **Break.cpp**. Step through the code by hand.

Use the following memory table to show what occurs in memory when the C++ code is executed. (Include line numbers as documentation only. Do not use line numbers when entering your final program.) To fill out the memory table, use one or two lines for each variable. On one line, enter declaration information. Write the name of the declared variable, its data type, and the line number at declaration.

Variable Name	Data Type	Value in Memory	Line Number at Declaration	Line Number when Initialized

In the following space, show what is displayed on the screen after executing the output message.

2c. Enter, compile, link, and execute **Break.cpp**. Then copy the output and save it in a block comment at the end of your program. Save **Break.cpp** in the Chap05 folder of your Student Disk.

The following is a copy of the screen results that might display after running your program, depending on the data entered. The input entered by the user is shown in bold.

```
Enter a list of 20 numbers:
2 3 1 -6 10 2 6 5 9 -10 9 2 -4 3 1 2 -6 7 3 2

The sum of the positive numbers is: 6
```

Lab 5.5 Using Nested Control Structures

One control structure can be nested (contained) within another control structure, and, in turn, that structure can be nested within another control structure. The associated control structures do not have to be of the same type.

Inner control structures close before outer control structures.

Objectives

In this lab, you use a nested control structure within a control structure.

After completing this lab, you will be able to:

- Recognize the beginning and end of control structures.
- Recognize that when an inner control structure is a `for` loop, the loop is reinitialized with each iteration of an outer loop.

Estimated completion time: **60–75 minutes**

Using Nested Control Structures

In the following exercises, you design and write programs that use nested control structures.

1a. *Critical Thinking Exercise*: Design a program that prompts the user to enter a character and a sentence. Count the number of times the character you entered appears in the sentence. (Remember that an uppercase and a lowercase version of a letter are different letters.) Display a message that tells how often the specified character appears in the sentence. Your program should also allow the user to enter multiple sentences until the user chooses to quit the program.

Write your design in the following space. Your design should be a list of C++ comments without any code.

1b. Write a C++ program based on the design you created in Exercise 1a and name it **CountChar.cpp**. Step through the code by hand.

Use the following memory table to show what occurs in memory when the C++ code is executed. (Include line numbers as documentation only. Do not use line numbers when entering your final program.) To fill out the memory table, use one or two lines for each variable. On one line, enter declaration information. Write the name of the declared variable, its data type, and the line number at declaration.

Variable Name	Data Type	Value in Memory	Line Number at Declaration	Line Number when Initialized

In the following space, show what is displayed on the screen after executing the output message.

1c. Enter, compile, link, and execute **CountChar.cpp**. Then copy the output and save it in a block comment at the end of your program. Save **CountChar.cpp** in the Chap05 folder of your Student Disk.

The following is a copy of the screen results that might display after running your program, depending on the data entered. The input entered by the user is shown in bold.

```
Enter a character to count the number of times it is in a sentence: c

Enter a sentence to search for a specified character:
Learning to program in C++ is fun and challenging.

Your sentence had 1 c character(s)

Do you wish to enter another sentence (y/n)? y

Enter a sentence to search for a specified character:
Working with nested loops requires using braces.

Your sentence had 1 c character(s)

Do you wish to enter another sentence (y/n)? n
```

Critical Thinking

2a. *Critical Thinking Exercise*: Design a program that displays a table resembling a spreadsheet. The column headings should show the values A, B, C, D, and E, and the row headings should show 1, 2, 3, 4, and 5. The row values should be multiples of the value of the row number. Use a `for` loop to output the column headings. Use nested `for` loops to output the row number and the values within the rows and columns. The output should look like the following:

	A	B	C	D	E
1	1	2	3	4	5
2	2	4	6	8	10
3	3	6	9	12	15
4	4	8	12	16	20
5	5	10	15	20	25

Write your design in the following space. Your design should be a list of C++ comments without any code.

2b. Write a C++ program based on the design you created in Exercise 2a and name it **Table.cpp**. Step through the code by hand.

Use the following memory table to show what occurs in memory when the C++ code is executed. (Include line numbers as documentation only. Do not use line numbers when entering your final program.) To fill out the memory table, use one or two lines for each variable. On one line, enter declaration information. Write the name of the declared variable, its data type, and the line number at declaration.

Variable Name	Data Type	Value in Memory	Line Number at Declaration	Line Number when Initialized

In the following space, show what is displayed on the screen after executing the output message.

2c. Enter, compile, link, and execute **Table.cpp**. Then copy the output and save it in a block comment at the end of your program. Save **Table.cpp** in the Chap05 folder of your Student Disk.

The following is a copy of the screen results that might display after running your program.

```
         A      B      C      D      E
1        1      2      3      4      5
2        2      4      6      8      10
3        3      6      9      12     15
4        4      8      12     16     20
5        5      10     15     20     25
```

LAB 5.6 CONVERTING BETWEEN while, do...while, AND for LOOPS

In a while and for loop, the loop condition is evaluated before executing the body of the loop. Therefore, while and for loops are called pretest loops. On the other hand, the loop condition in a do...while loop is evaluated after executing the body of the loop. Therefore, do...while loops are called posttest loops.

Because the while and for loops both have entry conditions, these loops may never activate. The do...while loop, on the other hand, has an exit condition and therefore always executes the statement at least once.

All three loops have their place in C++. If you know, or the program can determine in advance, the number of repetitions needed, the for loop is the correct choice. If you do not know, and the program cannot determine in advance the number of repetitions needed, and it could be zero, the while loop is the right choice. If you do not know, and the program cannot determine in advance the number of repetitions needed, and it is at least one, the do...while loop is the right choice.

Note that although one of these three loops can often replace another in C++, the while and do...while structures differ from the for structure regarding the execution of a continue statement. When the continue statement is executed in a while or a do...while loop, the update statement may not execute. In a for structure, the update statement always executes.

Objectives

In this lab, you practice using and converting between the three looping structures available in C++.

After completing this lab, you will be able to:

- Change a type of loop to another type of loop and achieve the same results.
- Determine which loop is most effective for a particular problem.

Estimated completion time: **30–45 minutes**

Converting between while, do...while, and for Loops

The greatest common divisor (GCD) between two nonzero integers is the largest integer that divides both numbers (without a remainder). For example, the GCD between 18 and 48 is 6.

In the following exercises, you will write and test programs that calculate the GCD of two nonzero integers using Euclid's algorithm. The integers will be entered by the user at the command prompt.

Euclid's algorithm is based on the fact that the GCD of two numbers is also a divisor of their difference. For example:

48 / 18 = 2 (remainder is 12)

18 / 12 = 1 (remainder is 6)

Thus, the greatest common divisor between 48 and 18 is 6.

1a. The following program calculates the GCD of two integers input by the user using a while loop.

```
//Calculate the Greatest Common Divisor

#include <iostream>
using namespace std;

int main()
{
```

```
    int x; //first number
    int y; //second number
    int remainder = 0;

    cout << "Enter two integers greater than zero: ";
    cin >> x >> y;

    cout << "The Greatest Common Divisor of " << x << " and " << y <<
    " is: ";

    //Calculate the GCD using Euclid's algorithm
    while( y != 0 )
    {
      remainder = x % y;
      x = y;
      y = remainder;
    }

    //the GCD of the integers entered by the user is now in x
    cout << x << endl;

    return 0;
}
```

Compile, link, and execute **gcd.cpp**. What is the GCD calculated by the program if the user input is 18 48? Step through the code by hand.

Use the following memory table to show what occurs in memory when the C++ code is executed. (Include line numbers as documentation only. Do not use line numbers when entering your final program.) To fill out the memory table, use one or two lines for each variable. Enter declaration information on one line. Write the name of the declared variable, its data type, and the line number at declaration.

Variable Name	Data Type	Value in Memory	Line Number at Declaration	Line Number when Initialized

In the following space, show what is displayed on the screen after executing the program.

1b. Test the program with other values. Fill the following table with the results shown by your program:

Input Values	GCD
1 1	
1 2	
4 2	
13 3	
1984 17	
216 1024	

2a. *Critical Thinking Exercise*: Create a program named **gcd2.cpp** that uses a `for` loop instead of a `while` loop to calculate the GCD. Write your code below. Step through the code by hand.

Compile, link, and execute **gcd2.cpp**. What is the GCD calculated by the program if the user input is 18 48? Step through the code by hand.

Use the following memory table to show what occurs in memory when the C++ code is executed. (Include line numbers as documentation only. Do not use line numbers when entering your final program.) To fill out the memory table, use one or two lines for each variable. Enter declaration information on one line. Write the name of the declared variable, its data type, and the line number at declaration.

Variable Name	Data Type	Value in Memory	Line Number at Declaration	Line Number when Initialized

In the following space, show what is displayed on the screen after executing the program.

2b. Test the program with other values. Fill the following table with the results shown by your program:

Input Values	GCD
1 1	
1 2	
4 2	
13 3	
1984 17	
216 1024	

2c. Compare the loop used in **gcd.cpp** with the loop used in **gcd2.cpp**. Which loop (a `while` loop or a `for` loop) do you think is best for this problem and why?

3a. *Critical Thinking Exercise*: Create a program named **gcd3.cpp** that uses a `do...while` loop instead of a `while` loop to calculate the GCD. Write your code below. Step through the code by hand.

Compile, link, and execute **gcd3.cpp**. What is the GCD calculated by the program if the user input is 18 48? Step through the code by hand.

Use the following memory table to show what occurs in memory when the C++ code is executed. (Include line numbers as documentation only. Do not use line numbers when entering your final program.) To fill out the memory table, use one or two lines for each variable. Enter declaration information on one line. Write the name of the declared variable, its data type, and the line number at declaration.

Variable Name	Data Type	Value in Memory	Line Number at Declaration	Line Number when Initialized

In the following space, show what is displayed on the screen after executing the program.

3b. Test the program with other values. Fill the following table with the results shown by your program:

Input Values	GCD
`1 1`	
`1 2`	
`4 2`	
`13 3`	
`1984 17`	
`216 1024`	

3c. Compare the loop used in **gcd.cpp** with the loop used in **gcd3.cpp**. Which loop (a `while` loop or a `do...while` loop) do you think is best for this problem and why?

6 User-Defined Functions I

In this chapter, you will:

- Learn about standard (predefined) functions and discover how to use them in a program
- Learn about user-defined functions
- Examine value-returning functions, including actual and formal parameters
- Explore how to construct and use a value-returning, user-defined function in a program

Chapter 6: Assignment Cover Sheet

Name ______________________ Date ______________________

Section ______________________

Lab Assignments	Assigned	Grade
Lab 6.1 Exploring Other Standard (Predefined) Functions (Critical Thinking Exercise)		
Lab 6.2 Adding User-Defined, Value-Returning Functions (Critical Thinking Exercise)		
Lab 6.3 Using User-Defined, Value-Returning Functions (Critical Thinking Exercise)		
Lab 6.4 Testing and Debugging a Program with User-Defined, Value-Returning Functions		
Total Grade		

See your instructor or the introduction to this book for instructions on submitting your assignments.

Lab 6.1 Exploring Other Standard (Predefined) Functions

Functions are often called **modules**. They are like miniature programs; you can put them together to form a larger program.

The C++ standard library contains many predefined functions, named constants, and specialized data types. In C++, predefined functions are organized into separate libraries. For example, the header file `iostream` contains I/O functions, and the header file `cmath` contains math functions.

To use a predefined function in your programs, you need to know how to use the function and the name of the header file that contains the function's specification. You must include this header file in your program via the `include` statement. For example, to use the function `pow`, the program must include:

```
#include <cmath>
```

You can find a list of several useful predefined functions in Appendix F. For additional explanations and information on functions, named constants, and so on, you can check your system documentation or use online resources such as www.cplusplus.com/reference/clibrary/.

Objectives

In this lab, you practice using online resources to find information about predefined functions.

After completing this lab, you will be able to:

- Use online resources to find information about C++'s predefined functions.
- Use a predefined function with which you are unfamiliar.

Estimated completion time: **45–60 minutes**

Exploring Other Standard (Predefined) Functions

You can find a useful online reference of the C library (included in the C++ library) at www.cplusplus.com/reference/clibrary/. In this lab, you will learn how to use information available at this site to incorporate new predefined functions in your programs.

1a. Visit www.cplusplus.com/reference/clibrary/. Spend a few minutes browsing through the header files. In the following space, list three of these header files. Include a brief description of each of them.

1b. Click on the `ctime` header file. What are the time manipulation functions available in the C time library?

1c. Note that the `time` function can be used to get the current calendar (system) time. What is the signature of the `time` function?

1d. The `difftime` function returns the difference (in seconds) between two times. What is the signature of the `difftime` function?

2a. Recall that `pow` and `sqrt` are predefined mathematical functions available in C++. Given that $\sqrt{x} = x^{1/2}$, both of these functions can be used to calculate the square root of a number. The following program uses the `pow` and `sqrt` functions to calculate the square root of a number entered by the user. Save this program as **sqrt.cpp**.

```
//Calculate the square root of a number using sqrt and pow

#include <iostream>
#include <cmath>

using namespace std;

int main ()
{
    double x;
    double result;

    cout << "Enter a (double) value: ";
    cin >> x;

    result = pow(x, 0.5);
    cout << "pow(" << x << ", 0.5) = " << result << endl;

    result = sqrt(x);
    cout << "sqrt(" << x << ") = " << result << endl;

    return 0;
}
```

Compile, link, and execute **sqrt.cpp**. What is the square root calculated by the program if the user input is 81? Step through the code by hand.

Use the following memory table to show what occurs in memory when the C++ code is executed. (Include line numbers as documentation only. Do not use line numbers when entering your final program.) To fill out the memory table, use one or two lines for each variable. On one line, enter declaration information. Write the name of the declared variable, its data type, and the line number at declaration.

Variable Name	Data Type	Value in Memory	Line Number at Declaration	Line Number when Initialized

In the following space, enter what is displayed on the screen after executing the program.

2b. Test the program with other values. Fill the following table with the results from your program.

Input Values (x)	`pow(x, 0.5)`	`sqrt(x)`
1		
2		
4		
13		
121		
1029		

3a. You will now use the **time** and **difftime** functions to find out which function (pow or **sqrt**) is more efficient in calculating the square root of a number. Perform the indications in the following code to complete the program. Save it in a file named **sqrt2.cpp**.

```
//Calculate the square root of a number using sqrt and pow
#include <iostream>
#include <cmath>
#include <ctime>

using namespace std;

int main ()
{
    time_t before;
    time_t after;

    double x;
    double result;

    int i;

    //number of times pow and sqrt will be called:
    const int ITERATIONS = 1;

    cout << "Enter a (double) value: ";
    cin >> x;

    //your code goes here: record the time before using pow

    for (i = 0; i < ITERATIONS; i++)
        result = pow(x,0.5);
    //your code goes here: record the time after using pow

    cout << "pow(" << x << ", 0.5) = " << result << endl;
    //complete the following lines so that
    //the appropriate value is displayed
    cout << "Operation was calculated in ";
    cout << **your code goes here** << " seconds." << endl;

    //your code goes here: record the time before using sqrt

    for (i = 0; i < ITERATIONS; i++)
        result = sqrt(x);
    //your code goes here: record the time after using sqrt

    cout << "sqrt(" << x << ") = " << result << endl;
    //complete the following lines so that
    //the appropriate value is displayed
    cout << "Operation was calculated in ";
    cout << **your code goes here** << " seconds." << endl;

    return 0;
}
```

Compile and link **sqrt2.cpp**. Write your completed program in the following space.

3b. Test the program with several values. Fill the following table with the results from your program.

Input Values (x)	Time to Calculate `pow(x, 0.5)`	Time to Calculate `sqrt(x)`
1		
2		
4		
13		
121		
1029		

4a. *Critical Thinking Exercise*: In the previous exercise, it probably took your computer 0 seconds to use each of the functions for each of the input values. Both operations are so fast that we cannot determine which one is faster. In order to do so, you will modify the **sqrt2.cpp** program so that each function is called a significant number of times for the same input value. To do this, change the value of **`ITERATIONS`** to `100000000`. Save your program as **sqrt3.cpp**. Use the following space to enter the line(s) you modified in your program.

Compile, link, and execute the program. Fill the following table with the results from your program:

Input Values (x)	Time to Calculate `pow(x, 0.5)`, `100,000,000` Times	Time to Calculate `sqrt(x)`, `100,000,000` Times
1		
2		
4		
13		
121		
1029		

4b. Compare the results shown in the table above. Which function (`pow` or `sqrt`) is more efficient in calculating the square root of a number?

Lab 6.2 Adding User-Defined, Value-Returning Functions

Because C++ does not provide every function you might ever need, you can write your own functions, called user-defined functions. User-defined functions can be value-returning functions (those that have a data type) or void functions (those that do not have a data type).

You use, or call, a value-returning function in an expression. The expression can be part of an assignment statement or an output statement. A function call in a program causes the body of the called function to execute.

A value-returning function returns a value via the return statement. The data type of the value must match the function type.

Functions in a C++ program can appear in any order. When determining the best sequence for including user-defined functions in a program, remember the rule that you must declare an identifier before you can use it. The compiler compiles the program sequentially from beginning to end.

When using some functions, such as `main`, which you customarily place before other user-defined functions, you can place a function prototype before the function definition to work around the problem of undeclared identifiers. Because function prototypes appear before any function definition, the compiler translates the prototypes first so it can then correctly translate a function call.

```
functionType functionName(parameter list);
```

(Note that the function prototype ends with a semicolon.) You must have the data type of each parameter in the list. The name of the parameter is optional in the prototype.

The syntax of a value-returning function is:

```
functionType functionName(formal parameter list)
{
    statements
}
```

(Note that the function head does not end with a semicolon.) You must have both the data type and the name of each parameter in the list.

The statements enclosed between curly braces form the body of the function. The value-returning function must have a return statement and must return a value whose type matches the function type. That value may be a constant, variable, expression, or even a value returned from another function call.

The function call is part of an assignment statement, an expression, or a print statement. The function call has a parameter list, referred to as the actual parameter list. This actual parameter list matches the data type of each of the individual parameters, collectively called the formal parameter list, in the function head. The parameters must match in the exact order.

When a program executes, the first statement in the function `main` always executes first, regardless of where in the program the function `main` is placed. Other functions execute only when they are called.

A function call statement transfers control to the first statement in the body of the function. In general, after the last statement of the called function executes, control is passed back to the point immediately following the function call.

Objectives

In this lab, you include the prototype, call, and function header of user-defined void functions, implement the missing code, and then run and test the code.

After completing this lab, you will be able to:

- Use user-defined void functions with and without parameters.

Estimated completion time: **50–60 minutes**

Adding User-Defined, Value-Returning Functions

In the following exercise, you complete and test a C++ program that includes user-defined, value-returning functions.

1a. *Critical Thinking Exercise*: Examine the following C++ program that calls two user-defined value-returning functions. Provide the missing code by replacing the bold text with C++ statements, including the correct prototypes and calls to the functions. The program asks the user for today's year and month and his or her year and month of birth. The program calculates and displays the user's age.

```
// Enter your name as a comment for program identification
// Program assignment Age.cpp
// Enter your class section, and time

/* The program Age.cpp prompts the user to input today's
date and his/her birth date, then calculates and displays
the user's age. The program utilizes user-defined functions.*/
/* Dates are entered in integer format for month and year. */
/* An age, described in months and years, is displayed. */

//header files
/* use the correct preprocessor directives for input/output */
#include <iostream>
#include <string>

using namespace std;

// user-defined function prototypes
/* the function getValue returns an integer value
entered by the user in response to the prompt
in the string message */
 /* the function getLetter returns a character value
   entered by the user in response to the prompt
   in the string message */


int main()
{
// declare variables
/* declare integer variables thisYear, thisMonth,
year, month, and ageMonth and ageYear. declare a character
variable again to indicate if the process is
to continue. */
int thisYear, thisMonth, year, month, ageYear, ageMonth;
char again = 'y';

// display program instructions
cout << "This program asks you to enter today's year in 4 digits,\n"
<< "and today's month number in 2 digits.\n\n"
<< "Then it asks you to enter your birth year in 4 digits,\n"
<< "and your birth month in 2 digits.\n\n"
```

```
<< "The program will calculate and display your age in years and
months.\n";

// assign to thisYear the value returned from a call to getValue


// assign to thisMonth the value returned from a call to getValue



// loop until the user indicates to end
while (again == 'y')
{
// assign to year the value returned from a call to getValue

// assign to month the value returned from a call to getValue


// assign age the value of thisYear - year
ageYear = thisYear - year;
ageMonth = thisMonth - month;

/* test to see if thisMonth is less than month
if true
subtract 1 from age and add 12 to month
*/
if (thisMonth < month)
{
         ageYear–;
         ageMonth += 12;
}

// display the age in years and months
cout << "\nYou are " << ageYear << " years and " << ageMonth
        << "months old.\n";

// assign to again the value returned from getLetter

// convert the value of again to lowercase
again = tolower(again);

}

return 0;
}

/* the function getValue returns an integer value
   entered by the user in response to the prompt
   in the string message */
int getValue(string message)
{
// declare variables
// declare an integer value to enter a value
int value;

// prompt the user with the message passed to the function
cout << message;
// read in the value entered
cin >> value;
// return the value
```

```
return value;
}

/* the function getLetter returns a character value
   entered by the user in response to the prompt
   in the string message */
char getLetter(string message)
{
// declare variables
// declare a character value to enter a value
char letter;

// prompt the user with the message passed to the function
cout << message;
// read in the value entered
cin >> letter;
// return the value
return letter;
}
```

1b. Step through the code by hand. Then use the following memory tables (one for each function) to show what occurs in memory when the C++ code is executed. (Include line numbers as documentation only. Do not use line numbers when entering your final program.) To fill out the memory table, use one or two lines for each variable. On one line, enter declaration information. Write the name of the declared variable, its data type, and the line number at declaration.

main function

Variable Name	Data Type	Value in Memory	Line Number at Declaration	Line Number when Initialized

getValue function

Variable Name	Data Type	Value in Memory	Line Number at Declaration	Line Number when Initialized

getLetter function

Variable Name	Data Type	Value in Memory	Line Number at Declaration	Line Number when Initialized

In the following space, show what is displayed on the screen after executing the output message.

1c. Enter, compile, link, and execute **Age.cpp**. Then copy the output and save it in a block comment at the end of your program. Save **Age.cpp** in the Chap06 folder of your Student Disk.

The following is a copy of the screen results that might appear after running your program, depending on the data entered. The input entered by the user is shown in bold.

```
This program asks you to enter today's year in 4 digits,
and today's month number in 2 digits.

Then it asks you to enter your birth year in 4 digits,
and your birth month in 2 digits.

The program will calculate and display your age in years and months.

Enter today's 4-digit year: 2008
Enter today's month number: 07

Enter the 4-digit year of your birth: 1981
Enter the month number of your birth: 02

You are 27 years and 5 months old.

Do you want to enter more data? y/n y

Enter the 4-digit year of your birth: 1984
Enter the month number of your birth: 12

You are 23 years and 7 months old.

Do you want to enter more data? y/n y

Enter the 4-digit year of your birth: 1986
Enter the month number of your birth: 12

You are 21 years and 7 months old.

Do you want to enter more data? y/n n
```

Lab 6.3 Using User-Defined, Value-Returning Functions

All programs in C++ consist of at least one function, the main function. Simple tasks can be designed so that all of the steps needed to complete the tasks are contained within the main function. The more complex or lengthy a task, the more difficult and cumbersome it is to place all of the required steps into one main function. Programmers design and organize their programs by dividing the steps into separate subprograms or functions.

Larger programs are often written by more than one programmer. The use of separate functions can facilitate this division of labor. Different programmers or teams of programmers can be tasked with designing and developing separate functions that become components of a main program.

Objectives

In this lab, you will design and write a program using several functions.

After completing this lab, you will be able to:

- Design and write a program using predefined and user-defined, value-returning functions. Some of the user-defined, value-returning functions will have formal parameters, whereas others will not.

Estimated completion time: **40–50 minutes**

Using User-Defined, Value-Returning Functions

In the following exercise, you design and write a program that includes user-defined, value-returning functions to convert two units of measurement, weight and distance, from the U.S. Customary Units (American system) to the international standard metric system.

1a. *Critical Thinking Exercise:* Create the design for a program that prompts a user to enter a number representing a measurement and then identify whether it is pounds (enter a P) or yards (enter a Y). The program should convert that measurement into either kilograms or meters and output the result as a number with two decimal places.

Use four user-defined functions with the following names that accomplish the following:

- `getNumber` – obtains from the user a number representing a measurement. This function should use a loop to validate that the input is a number greater than zero.
- `identifyInput` – asks the user to identify the number input as pounds by entering a 'P' or yards by entering a 'Y'. This function should use a predefined function to convert the input to an uppercase letter and use a loop to validate that the input is a 'P' or a 'Y'.
- `getKilos` – converts pounds to kilograms by multiplying the pounds by 0.45359237 and returns the result.
- `getMeters` – converts yards to meters by multiplying the yards by 0.9144 and returns the result.

Write your design in the following space. For your design, write an algorithm (an English language description of the steps required to successfully solve the problem).

1b. Write a C++ program based on the design you created in Exercise 1a and name it UStoMetric.cpp.

1c. Enter, compile, link, and execute UstoMetric.cpp. Copy the output and save it in a block comment at the end of the source code. Save UStoMetric in the Chap06 folder of your Student Disk.

The following is a copy of the screen results that might display after running your program, depending on the data entered.

```
Enter a number greater than 0 that represents a
measurement in either pounds or yards: 15
Enter a P if the number you entered was pounds and a Y if the
number input was yards: P
15.00 pounds is equivalent to 6.80 kilograms

Enter a number greater than 0 that represents a
measurement in either pounds or yards: 23
Enter a P if the number you entered was pounds and a Y if the
number input was yards: Y
23.00 yards is equivalent to 21.03 meters
```

Lab 6.4 Testing and Debugging a Program with User-Defined, Value-Returning Functions

An advantage to modular programming is the capability to test functions and reuse them, confident that the coding is correct. By adding `cout` statements to display values before a function call, inside of a function, and after the return of a function, you can test the reliability of the function.

To debug a modular program, you should first correct any syntax errors found when compiling. One way to debug logic errors is to test the functions using `cout` statements before function calls, inside functions, and after function calls.

Objectives

In this lab, you test and debug a program with both syntax and logic errors.

After completing this lab, you will be able to:

- Write output statements to trace values in a logically incorrect program.

Estimated completion time: **40–50 minutes**

Testing and Debugging a Program with User-Defined, Value-Returning Functions

In the following exercises, you correct logic and syntax errors in a program.

1. Examine the following program, which contains logic and syntax errors.

   The purpose of the program is to calculate the cost to a company for a proposed raise. The program prompts for the number of employees and each employee's salary, and then calculates the individual raise and the total cost of raises. Employees earning $25,000 or less will receive a 5% raise. Employees earning between $25,001 and $35,000 will receive a 4% raise. Employees earning $35,001 or greater will receive a 3% raise. Display each employee's raise and the total raises.

   First, mark your changes in the following copy of **Buggy.cpp**.

```
// Enter your name as a comment for program identification
// Program assignment Buggy.cpp
// Enter your class section and time

/* The program Buggy.cpp calculates the cost to a
   company for a proposed raise. The program prompts
   for the number of employees and each employee's salary
   then calculates the individual raise and the total cost
   of raises. Employees earning $25,000 or less
   will receive a 5% raise. Employees earning
   between $25,001 and $35,000 will receive a 4%
   raise. Employees earning $35,001 or greater will receive
   a 3% raise. Display each employee's raise and
   the total raises. */
/* Input the number of employees and each employee's salary. */
/* Display each employee's raise and the total cost of raises. */

//header files
/* use the correct preprocessor directives for input/output */
#include <iostream>
#include <iomanip>
```

```
// user-defined function prototypes
/* the function getNumber returns an integer value
   entered by the user giving the number of employees */
int getNumber();
/* the function getSalary returns a float value
   entered by the user giving the employee's salary */
double getSalary(int empNumber);
/* the function calcRaise returns the raise
   calculated for the salary passed */
double calcRaise(double salary);
/* the function totalRaises returns the new
   total of raises using the current total and
   current raise being processed */
double totalRaises(double raise, double total);


int main()
{
         // declare variables
         /* declare an integer variable number to enter the
            number of employees, a float variable salary to
            enter the current employee's salary, a float variable
            raise to calculate raise amount, a float variable
            total to accumulate the total of employee raises */
         int number;
         double salary, raise, total;

         // set the formatting for output
         cout << fixed << showpoint << setprecision(2);

         // instruct the user regarding use of the program
         cout >> "This program asks the user to enter the number "
              >> "of employees and\nthe individual salary for each "
              >> "employee. \nThe individual employee's raise and "
              >> "the total raises are displayed.\n";

         // assign to number the value returned from getNumber
         number = getNumber();

         // loop until all employees are processed
         for (int count = 1; count < number; count++)
         {
             // assign to raise the value returned from getSalary
             salary = getSalary(count);
             // assign to raise the value returned from calcRaise
             raise = calcRaise(salary);
             // assign to total the accumulated raises
             total = totalRaises(total, raise);

             // display current employee raise
             cout << "Employee " << count << " receives a raise of $"
                << salary << endl;
         }

         // display total raises
         cout << "\n\nThe total cost of raises: $" << raise << endl;


return 0;
}
```

```
/* the function getNumber returns an integer value
   entered by the user giving the number of employees */
int getNumber()
{
         // declare variables
         /* declare an integer variable number to enter the
            number of employees */
         int number;
         // prompt the user for the number of employees
         cout << "\nEnter the number of employees: ";
         // read in the number of employees
         cin >> number;
         // return the number of employees
         return number;

}

/* the function getSalary returns a float value
   entered by the user giving the employee's salary */
double getSalary(int empNumber)
{
         // declare variables
         /* declare a double variable salary to enter the
            individual employee's raise */
         double salary;
         // prompt the user for the employee salary
         cout << "\nEnter the salary for an employee "
              << empNumber << ": ";
         // read in the employee salary
         cin >> salary;
         // return the employee salary
         return salary;

}

/* the function calcRaise returns the raise
   calculated for the salary passed */
int calcRaise(double salary)
{
         /* test salary value to calculate raise and
            return salary times percentage applicable */
         if (salary <= 25000)
             return salary * .05;
         else if (salary <= 35000)
             return salary * .04;
         else
             return salary * .03;

}

/* the function totalRaises returns the new
   total of raises using the current total and
   current raise being processed */
double totalRaises(double raise, double total);
{
         return total + raise;
}
```

After marking your changes, open the program named **Buggy.cpp** stored in the Chap06 folder of your Student Disk. Correct the syntax errors, and save your program as **TestRaises.cpp** in the Chap06 folder of your Student Disk. Compile, link, and execute **TestRaises.cpp**. Then copy the output and save it in a block comment at the end of your program.

2. As written, the output of **TestRaises.cpp** has no syntax errors but contains logic errors, as follows:

Output with logic errors, no syntax errors

```
This program asks the user to enter the number of employees and
the individual salary for each employee.
The individual employee's raise and the total raises are displayed.

Enter the number of employees: 2

Enter the salary for employee 1: 100000
Employee 1 receives a raise of $100000.00


The total cost of raises: $-
92559631349317831000000000000000000000000000000
0000000000.00
```

To help find logic errors, insert the following types of error-checking output statements in **TestRaises.cpp**:

- Output statements of arguments to functions
- Output statements of variables that are assigned values returning from functions

Save **TestRaises.cpp**, and then compile, link, and execute it. Copy the output and save it in a block comment at the end of your program.

The following is a copy of the screen results that might display after running your program, depending on the data entered. The input entered by the user is shown in bold.

```
/* output with test messages and no logic errors
This program asks the user to enter the number of employees and
the individual salary for each employee.
The individual employee's raise and the total raises are displayed.

Before getNumber, the number of employees entered is: -858993460
Enter the number of employees: 3
Inside getNumber, the number of employees entered is: 3
After getNumber, the number of employees entered is: 3

Before getSalary, the salary entered is: -
9255963134931783100000000000000000000
00000000000000000000000.00
Enter the salary for employee 1: 18600
Inside getSalary, salary is: 18600.00
After getSalary, the salary entered is: 18600.00

Before calcRaise, raise is: -
92559631349317831000000000000000000000000000000
00000000000.00
Inside calcRaise, raise is not defined.
After calcRaise, raise is: 930.00

Before totalRaises, total is: 0.00
```

```
Before totalRaises, raise is: 930.00
Inside totalRaises, total is: 930.00

Inside totalRaises, raise is: 0.00

After totalRaises, total is: 930.00

After totalRaises, raise is: 930.00
Employee 1 receives a raise of $930.00

Before getSalary, the salary entered is: 18600.00
Enter the salary for employee 2: 48000
Inside getSalary, salary is: 48000.00
After getSalary, the salary entered is: 48000.00

Before calcRaise, raise is: 930.00
Inside calcRaise, raise is not defined.
After calcRaise, raise is: 1440.00

Before totalRaises, total is: 930.00

Before totalRaises, raise is: 1440.00
Inside totalRaises, total is: 1440.00

Inside totalRaises, raise is: 930.00

After totalRaises, total is: 2370.00

After totalRaises, raise is: 1440.00
Employee 2 receives a raise of $1440.00

Before getSalary, the salary entered is: 48000.00
Enter the salary for employee 3: 31500
Inside getSalary, salary is: 31500.00
After getSalary, the salary entered is: 31500.00

Before calcRaise, raise is: 1440.00
Inside calcRaise, raise is not defined.
After calcRaise, raise is: 1260.00

Before totalRaises, total is: 2370.00

Before totalRaises, raise is: 1260.00
Inside totalRaises, total is: 1260.00

Inside totalRaises, raise is: 2370.00

After totalRaises, total is: 3630.00

After totalRaises, raise is: 1260.00
Employee 3 receives a raise of $1260.00


The total cost of raises: $3630.00
*/
```

3. Remove your error-checking output statements and save your program as **Raises.cpp** in the Chap06 folder of your Student Disk. Compile, link, and execute. **Raises.cpp**. Then copy the output and save it in a block comment at the end of your program.

The following is a copy of the screen results that might display after running your program, depending on the data entered. The input entered by the user is shown in bold.

```
This program asks the user to enter the number of employees and
the individual salary for each employee.
The individual employee's raise and the total raises are displayed.

Enter the number of employees: 7

Enter the salary for employee 1: 18600
Employee 1 receives a raise of $930.00

Enter the salary for employee 2: 24685
Employee 2 receives a raise of $1234.25

Enter the salary for employee 3: 32000
Employee 3 receives a raise of $1280.00

Enter the salary for employee 4: 48000
Employee 4 receives a raise of $1440.00

Enter the salary for employee 5: 21700
Employee 5 receives a raise of $1085.00

Enter the salary for employee 6: 19800
Employee 6 receives a raise of $990.00

Enter the salary for employee 7: 31500
Employee 7 receives a raise of $1260.00


The total cost of raises: $8219.25
```

7 User-Defined Functions II

In this chapter, you will:

- Learn how to construct and use void functions in a program
- Discover the difference between value and reference parameters
- Explore reference parameters and value-returning functions
- Learn about the scope of an identifier
- Examine the difference between local and global identifiers
- Discover static variables
- Learn function overloading
- Explore functions with default parameters

Chapter 7: Assignment Cover Sheet

Name ______________________________ Date ______________________________

Section ______________________________

Lab Assignments	Assigned	Grade
Lab 7.1 Calling Void Functions without Parameters		
Lab 7.2 Calling Void Functions with Value Parameters		
Lab 7.3 Calling Void Functions with Value and Reference Parameters		
Lab 7.4 Accessing an Identifier by Its Scope		
Lab 7.5 Using Static and Automatic Variables		
Lab 7.6 Using Function Overloading		
Lab 7.7 Using Default Parameters (Critical Thinking Exercise)		
Group Project: The payroll program written and refined in Labs 7.1, Ex. 8; 7.2, Ex. 7; 7.3, Ex. 6; and 7.5, Ex. 3 can be used for a Group Project. The group should work together to establish the use and purpose of each function, and then individual group members can be assigned different functions.		
Total Grade		

See your instructor or the introduction to this book for instructions on submitting your assignments.

LAB 7.1 CALLING VOID FUNCTIONS WITHOUT PARAMETERS

The order in which functions appear in a program does not matter if you use prototypes because the `main` function is always executed first. A void function does not have a data type and does not need a return statement. You can use the keyword `return` with no value to exit the program; otherwise, the program exits at the end of the function definition.

Void functions are not called as part of an expression; the call is a stand-alone statement. You can write a void function definition without parameters if you use the keyword `void` in place of the parameter list or if you leave the parameter list empty.

The general form (syntax) of the void function without parameters is as follows:

```
void functionName()
{
     statements
}
```

The function call has the following syntax:

```
functionName();
```

The function prototype has the following syntax:

```
void functionName();
```

Void functions are useful for displaying information about the program or printing statements.

Objectives

In this lab, you write two void functions with no parameters and include the function prototypes and the driver function (`main`) that calls the functions.

After completing this lab, you will be able to:

- Call a void function with no parameters from the `main` function.
- Write a prototype for a void function with no parameters
- Write a void function definition that has no parameters.

Estimated completion time: **20–30 minutes**

Calling Void Functions without Parameters

In the following exercises, you determine whether statements are true or false. You also begin to design and create a payroll program that you will refine throughout other labs in this chapter.

Question	Answer (Circle the correct answer)

1. Given the following prototype:
`void pageHeading ();`
The following statement is valid in the `main` function:
`pageHeading ();`
	True False

2. Using the same prototype given in Question 1, the following statement is valid in the `main` function: `cout << pageHeading() << endl;`	True False

3. Although void functions without parameters are legal in C++, they are not very useful because they do not communicate data between functions. **True** **False**

4. In C++, void is a reserved word. **True** **False**

5. Void functions with no parameters are very useful for writing reports. **True** **False**

6. Because void functions without parameters do not communicate data between functions, they are limited to containing only output statements. **True** **False**

7. Functions without parameters still require parentheses signifying a parameter list. **True** **False**

8a. When users run a program, they often need information concerning the purpose of the program and how they should use it. Additionally, after users run a program, they often want to view a report with the results. In this exercise, create the design for a program that has, in addition to the `main` function, two void functions with no parameters. Name one function `instruction`—it should provide information about the program to the user. Name the other function `reportTitle`—it should display the headings for a future report.

You will develop the program through several lab exercises so that it eventually processes a payroll by calculating paychecks for each employee. In this exercise, you work with a text file, **payroll.txt**, which is available in the Chap07 folder of your Student Disk. It contains the following information:

- Employee name
- Hourly rate of pay
- Number of hours worked
- Tax percentage to be deducted

The program will create a report in columnar format showing the following:

- Employee name
- Hourly rate of pay
- Number of hours worked
- Tax rate
- Gross pay
- Net pay

Manipulators are often included in the report title function because this function is used to set up a report. In this case, because it is a payroll program, use the manipulators `fixed`, `showpoint`, and `left`, and show values to two decimal points.

After all employees are processed, the program displays the total gross pay and the total net pay.

Write your design in the following space. Your design should be a list of C++ comments without any code. Use the report layout grid provided or graph paper to plan your report columns.

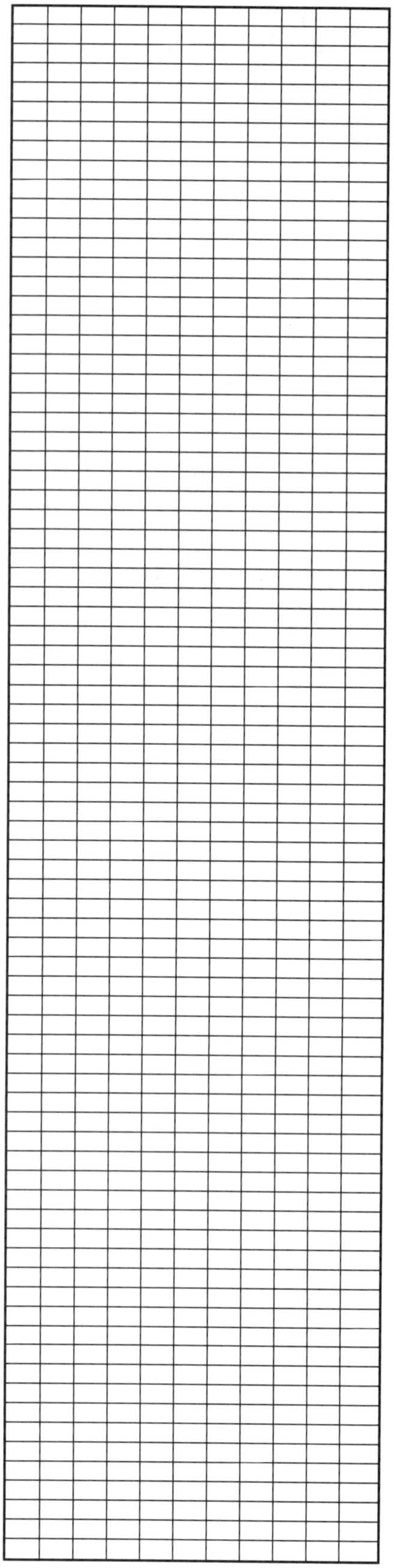

Report Layout Grid

8b. Write a C++ program based on the design you created in Exercise 8a and name it **Payroll1.cpp**. Step through the code by hand.

In the following space, show what is displayed on the screen after executing the output message.

8c. Enter, compile, link, and execute **Payroll1.cpp**. Then copy the output and save it in a block comment at the end of your program. Save **Payroll1.cpp** in the Chap07 folder of your Student Disk.

The following is a copy of the screen results that might display after running your program.

```
This payroll program calculates individual employee pay and
company totals using data from a data file payroll.txt.


A payroll report showing payroll information is displayed.

Employee            Hourly    Hours     Tax       Gross     Net
Name                Rate      Worked    Rate      Amount    Amount
```

LAB 7.2 CALLING VOID FUNCTIONS WITH VALUE PARAMETERS

Information is communicated between calling functions and called functions through a communication link called a parameter list. There are two types of parameters: value parameters and reference parameters. This lab focuses on functions with value parameters.

Parameters enable functions to manipulate different data each time they are called. A formal parameter that is a value parameter receives a copy of the content of the corresponding actual parameter. The formal parameter list found in the function definition lists the data type and the variable name. A void function definition with value parameters has the following syntax:

```
void functionName(formal parameter list)
```

The formal parameter list has the following syntax:

```
dataType variable, dataType variable, ...
```

A function call to a void function with value parameters has the following syntax:

```
functionName(actual parameter list)
```

The actual parameter list has the following syntax:

```
expression or variable, expression or variable, ...
```

The parameter lists must be in the same order to create a one-to-one correspondence.

If a formal parameter is a value parameter, after copying the value of the actual parameter, there is no connection between the formal parameter and actual parameter. Therefore, during program execution, the formal parameter manipulates the data stored in its own memory space.

Objectives

In this lab, you continue using stepwise refinement to build a program step by step. You build on the program you designed and wrote in the previous lab. You write a void function with value parameters, use the function prototype, and declare the variables needed to call a function with values.

After completing this lab, you will be able to:

- Use stepwise refinement as a program design technique.
- Call a void function with value parameters from the `main` function.
- Write a prototype for a void function with value parameters.
- Write a void function definition that has value parameters.
- Align a report in columnar format.

Estimated completion time: **30–45 minutes**

Calling Void Functions with Value Parameters

In the following exercises, you answer a series of multiple-choice questions. You also continue to design and create the payroll program that you began in Lab 7.1.

Question	Answer (Circle the correct answer)

1. Given the following function:

```
void increment (int x)
{
      x++;
}
```

and the following code in the main function:

```
int x = 5;
increment (x);
cout << x << endl;
```

The output is:

a. 5

b. 6

c. 7

d. a compiler error occurs

2. Using the increment function given in Question 1 and the following code in the `main` function:

```
const int x = 5;
increment(x);
cout << x << endl;
```

The output is:

a. 5

b. 6

c. 7

d. a compiler error occurs

3. Using the increment function given in Question 1 and the following code in the `main` function:

```
int x = 5;
increment(x + 1);
cout << x << endl;
```

The output is:

a. 5

b. 6

c. 7

d. a compiler error occurs

4. Given the following function:

```
void displayData (int x, char l)
{
      cout << "The number is " << x << endl
<< "The letter is " << l << endl;
}
```

and the following code in the main function:

```
int number = 80;
char letter = 'A';
displayData (letter, number);
```

The output is:

a. the number is 80, the letter is A

b. the number is 65, the letter is P

c. a compiler error occurs

5. Using the `displayData` function given in Question 4 and the following code in the `main` function:

```
int number = 80;
char letter = 'A';
displayData (static_cast<int>(letter),
static_cast<char>(number));
```

The output is:

a. the number is 80, the letter is A

b. the number is 65, the letter is P

c. a compiler error occurs

6. When a function parameter list contains value parameters, legal actual parameters are:

a. variables

b. expressions

c. constants

d. all of the above

7a. This lab exercise expands on the one you completed for Lab 7.1, Exercise 8 that gives instructions to use a payroll processing program and provides report titles for a report. Expand your design to read in data values from a data file for the following employee data:

- Employee name
- Hourly rate of pay
- Number of hours worked
- Tax percentage to be deducted

Using this data, calculate the gross pay and net pay for the employee, and call a function to display the information to a report. You can use the data in **payroll.txt** in the Chap07 folder of your Student Disk.

Write your design in the following space. Your design should be a list of C++ comments without any code. Use the report layout grid provided or graph paper to plan your report columns.

Report Layout Grid

7b. Write a C++ program based on the design you created in Exercise 7a and name it **Payroll2.cpp**. Step through the code by hand.

Use the following memory table to show what occurs in memory when the C++ code is executed. (Include line numbers as documentation only. Do not use line numbers when entering your final program.) To fill out the memory table, use one or two lines for each variable. On one line, enter declaration information. Write the name of the declared variable, its data type, and the line number at declaration.

main function

Variable Name	Data Type	Value in Memory	Line Number at Declaration	Line Number when Initialized

displayEmployeeInfo function

Variable Name	Data Type	Value in Memory	Line Number at Declaration	Line Number when Initialized

totalAmounts function

Variable Name	Data Type	Value in Memory	Line Number at Declaration	Line Number when Initialized

In the following space, show what is displayed on the screen after executing the output message.

7c. Enter, compile, link, and execute **Payroll2.cpp**. Then copy the output and save it in a block comment at the end of your program. Save **Payroll2.cpp** in the Chap07 folder of your Student Disk.

The following is a copy of the screen results that might display after running your program, depending on the data entered.

```
This payroll program calculates individual employee pay and
company totals using data from a data file payroll.txt.


A payroll report showing payroll information is displayed.

Employee                  Hourly    Hours      Tax      Gross       Net
Name                        Rate   Worked     Rate     Amount    Amount

John Smith                 10.45    40.00    15.00     418.00    355.30
Jane Doe                   12.50    45.00    15.00     843.75    717.19
Harry Morgan               20.00    40.00    20.00     800.00    640.00
Carmen Martinez            25.00    35.00    25.00     875.00    656.25
Jacintha Washington        50.85    60.00    35.00    4576.50   2974.72

Totals                                               7513.25   5343.46
```

Lab 7.3 Calling Void Functions with Value and Reference Parameters

Local variables are variables declared within a function. Variables in the formal parameter list are also considered to be local variables to the function. When using value parameters, new local variables are allocated in memory, and the value is copied into the new memory location. Reference parameters are parameters that are declared in the parameter list but do not use new memory locations. When using reference parameters, the address of the actual parameter passes to the called function, and the memory location from the calling function is used. When a function changes a reference parameter, the change is in the memory location passed through the parameter list.

You use the ampersand symbol (&) after the data type to designate a reference parameter; it stands for the address of operator. A formal value parameter receives a copy of the actual parameter. A reference parameter receives the location (memory address) of the corresponding actual parameter. You use reference parameters to share results with the calling function. Think of a reference parameter name as a synonym for the actual parameter name. The reference parameter name represents the same memory location. Stream variables must always be passed by reference.

It is not recommended that you use reference parameters in value-returning functions. If more than one value needs to be returned, use a void function with reference parameters. By combining all types of functions, you can create a modular program in which the work of the `main` function is done by calling multiple functions. You may have selection and repetition control structures in `main` that determine which functions are called, but little other work is done in `main`.

Objectives

In this lab, you continue to use all function types to modularize your program. You modify the program you designed and wrote in the previous labs. You add the use of a void function with reference parameters and the function prototype.

After completing this lab, you will be able to:

- Call a void function with reference parameters from the `main` function.
- Write a prototype for a void function with reference parameters.
- Write a void function definition with reference parameters.

Estimated completion time: **20–30 minutes**

Calling Void Functions with Value and Reference Parameters

In the following exercises, you answer a series of multiple-choice questions. You also continue to design and create the payroll program that you began in Lab 7.1.

Question	Answer (Circle the correct answer.)
1. Given the following function:	a. 5
`void increment (int &x) { x++; }`	b. 6
and the following code in the main function:	c. 7
`int x = 5; increment (x); cout << x << endl;`	d. a compiler error occurs
The output is:	

2. Using the increment function given in Question 1 and the following code in the `main` function:

```
const int x = 5;
increment(x);
cout << x << endl;
```

The output is:

a. 5
b. 6
c. 7
d. a compiler error occurs

3. Using the increment function given in Question 1 and the following code in the `main` function:

```
int x = 5;
increment(x + 1);
cout << x << endl;
```

The output is:

a. 5
b. 6
c. 7
d. a compiler error occurs

4. When a function parameter list contains reference parameters, legal actual parameters are:

a. variables
b. expressions
c. constants
d. all of the above

5. A function parameter list may contain either reference parameters or value parameters, but not both in the same parameter list. **True** **False**

6a. In **Payroll2.cpp** payroll, you wrote that input of data and payroll computations were carried out in your `main` function. Your `main` function should be a series of function calls with any control structures necessary to make those function calls. Using void functions with reference parameters, modify your program design to include a function to read in your data. Create another function with both value and reference parameters to perform your payroll calculations. Do not use reference parameters when value parameters will work.

Write your design in the following space. Your design should be a list of C++ comments without any code.

6b. Write a C++ program based on the design you created in Exercise 6a and name it **Payroll3.cpp**. Step through the code by hand.

Use the following memory table to show what occurs in memory when the C++ code is executed. (Include line numbers as documentation only. Do not use line numbers when entering your final program.) To fill out the memory table, use one or two lines for each variable. On one line, enter declaration information. Write the name of the declared variable, its data type, and the line number at declaration.

main function

Variable Name	Data Type	Value in Memory	Line Number at Declaration	Line Number when Initialized

main function (continued)

Variable Name	Data Type	Value in Memory	Line Number at Declaration	Line Number when Initialized

displayEmployeeInfo function

Variable Name	Data Type	Value in Memory	Line Number at Declaration	Line Number when Initialized

totalAmounts function

Variable Name	Data Type	Value in Memory	Line Number at Declaration	Line Number when Initialized

readData function

Variable Name	Data Type	Value in Memory	Line Number at Declaration	Line Number when Initialized

calculate function

Variable Name	Data Type	Value in Memory	Line Number at Declaration	Line Number when Initialized

In the following space, show what is displayed on the screen after executing the output message.

6c. Enter, compile, link, and execute **Payroll3.cpp**. Then copy the output and save it in a block comment at the end of your program. Save **Payroll3.cpp** in the Chap07 folder of your Student Disk. Compare the output from your Payroll3 to your output from your Payroll2 program. If the same data was entered into both programs, the output should be the same.

The following is a copy of the screen results that might display after running your program, depending on the data entered.

```
This payroll program calculates individual employee pay and
company totals using data from a data file payroll.txt.


A payroll report showing payroll information is displayed.

Employee                 Hourly     Hours       Tax      Gross        Net
Name                       Rate    Worked      Rate     Amount     Amount

John Smith                10.45     40.00     15.00     418.00     355.30
Jane Doe                  12.50     45.00     15.00     843.75     717.19
Harry Morgan              20.00     40.00     20.00     800.00     640.00
Carmen Martinez           25.00     35.00     25.00     875.00     656.25
Jacintha Washington       50.85     60.00     35.00    4576.50    2974.72

Totals                                                7513.25    5343.46
```

LAB 7.4 ACCESSING AN IDENTIFIER BY ITS SCOPE

The scope of an identifier refers to where an identifier is accessible in the program. Local identifiers are not accessible outside of the function (or block). An identifier declared within a block is accessible only within the block from the point at which it is declared until the end of the block. When a block is nested within another block, an identifier from the outer block is recognized in the inner block. The exception to this occurs if the inner block has an identifier of the same name.

The scope rules for variables declared in a `for` statement differ between standard C++ and ANSI C++. This book uses the ANSI C++ standard.

A global variable can be declared inside of a function if it is declared as an external variable and there is no other identifier with the same name.

If you use global variables, then the function is not independent and typically cannot be used in more than one program. It is recommended that you do not use global variables.

Objectives

The objectives of this lab are to demonstrate the differences between local and global variables and the scope of their identifiers.

After completing this lab, you will be able to:

- Differentiate between the scope of local and global variables.
- Use local and global variables in the same program.

Estimated completion time: **40–50 minutes**

Accessing an Identifier by Its Scope

In the following exercises, you answer a series of multiple-choice and true-or-false questions. You also continue to design and create the payroll program that you began in Lab 7.1.

Question	Answer (Circle the correct answer)
1. Given the following statements:	a. 2 3 4 b. 3 3 4 c. a compiler error occurs

```
{      // block 1
    int x = 2;
    int y = 3;
    int z = 4;
    .
    .
    {      // block 2
        int x = 3;
        cout << x << ' ' << y << ' '
             << z << endl;
    }
}
```

The output is:

2. Using the coding example in Question 1, which variables are global variables?	a. x b. y c. z d. none are global variables

3. To avoid the confusion that might occur between value and reference variables, you should code with global variables. **True** **False**
4. The terms global variable and reference variable mean the same thing. **True** **False**
5. Given the following function definition:

```
void swap (int &x, int &y)
{
   return;
}
```

and the following code in the main function:

```
int x = 5;
int y = 10;
swap (y, x)
cout << x << ' ' << y << endl;
```

The output is:

a. 5 10

b. 10 5

c. a compiler error occurs

6a. Create the design for a program that shows the scope of global and local variables. Your design should have three functions—`main`, parameters, and useGlobals. You should have two global integer variables named num1, initialized to 10, and num2, initialized to -5.

Your `main` function should have the following characteristics:

- Begin the program block
- Declare two local variables—num1, initialized to 20, and num2, initialized to 13
- Call the function parameters with the actual arguments num1 and num2
- Call the function parameters with the actual arguments num2 and num1
- Call the function useGlobals with no actual arguments
- Begin another program block
- Declare two local variables—num1, initialized to 94, and num2, initialized to 50
- Call the function parameters with the actual arguments num1 and num2
- Call the function parameters with the actual arguments num2 and num1
- Call the function useGlobals with no actual arguments
- End the second block
- Call the function parameters with the actual arguments num1 and num2
- Call the function parameters with the actual arguments num2 and num1
- Call the function useGlobals with no actual arguments
- Before each function call, display a message showing the value of num1 and num2
- After calling each function, display a message showing the value of num1 and num2

Your parameters function should have the following characteristics:

- Have the data type void
- Have two formal integer parameters num1 and num2
- Display a message showing the value of num1 and num2; in `main`, create two local integer variables named num1 and num2

Your useGlobals function should have the following characteristics:

- Have the data type void
- Have no formal parameters
- Display a message showing the value of num1 and num2; in `main`, create two local integer variables named num1 and num2

Write your design in the following space. Your design should be a list of C++ comments without any code.

6b. Write a C++ program based on the design you created in Exercise 6a and name it **Scope.cpp**. Step through the code by hand.

Use the following memory table to show what occurs in memory when the C++ code is executed. (Include line numbers as documentation only. Do not use line numbers when entering your final program.) To fill out the memory table, use one line for each variable. Write the name of the declared variable, its data type, the line number at declaration, and the line number at initialization.

global variables

Variable Name	Data Type	Value in Memory	Line Number at Declaration	Line Number when Initialized

main function

Variable Name	Data Type	Value in Memory	Line Number at Declaration	Line Number when Initialized

parameters function

Variable Name	Data Type	Value in Memory	Line Number at Declaration	Line Number when Initialized

useGlobals function

Variable Name	Data Type	Value in Memory	Line Number at Declaration	Line Number when Initialized

6c. Enter, compile, link, and execute **Scope.cpp**. Then copy the output and save it in a block comment at the end of your program. Save **Scope.cpp** in the Chap07 folder of your Student Disk.

The following is a copy of the screen results that might appear after running your program.

```
The following values refer to block 1 of main.


Calling parameters with num1 as the first argument
and num2 as the second argument block 1:
     Before calling function parameters block 1        num1: 20, num2: 13
     Inside function parameters                        num1: 20, num2: 13
     After calling function parameters block 1         num1: 20, num2: 13

Calling parameters with num2 as the first argument
and num1 as the second argument block 1:
     Before calling function parameters block 1        num1: 20, num2: 13
     Inside function parameters                        num1: 13, num2: 20
     After calling function parameters block 1         num1: 20, num2: 13

Calling useGlobals with no arguments block 1:
     Before calling function useGlobals block 1        num1: 20, num2: 13
     Inside function useGlobals                        num1: 10, num2: -5
     After calling function useGlobals block 1         num1: 20, num2: 13


The following values refer to block 2 of main.


Calling parameters with num1 as the first argument
and num2 as the second argument block 2:
     Before calling function parameters block 2        num1: 94, num2: 50
     Inside function parameters                        num1: 94, num2: 50
     After calling function parameters block 2         num1: 94, num2: 50
```

```
Calling parameters with num2 as the first argument
and num1 as the second argument block 2:
     Before calling function parameters block 2      num1: 94, num2: 50
     Inside function parameters                      num1: 50, num2: 94
     After calling function parameters block 2       num1: 94, num2: 50

Calling useGlobals with no arguments block 2:
     Before calling function useGlobals block 2      num1: 94, num2: 50
     Inside function useGlobals                      num1: 10, num2: -5
     After calling function useGlobals block 2       num1: 94, num2: 50
End of block 2

The following values refer to block 1 of main.


Calling parameters with num1 as the first argument
and num2 as the second argument block 1:
     Before calling function parameters block 1      num1: 20, num2: 13
     Inside function parameters                      num1: 20, num2: 13
     After calling function parameters block 1       num1: 20, num2: 13

Calling parameters with num2 as the first argument
and num1 as the second argument block 1:
     Before calling function parameters block 1      num1: 20, num2: 13
     Inside function parameters                      num1: 13, num2: 20
     After calling function parameters block 1       num1: 20, num2: 13

Calling useGlobals with no arguments block 1:
     Before calling function useGlobals block 1      num1: 20, num2: 13
     Inside function useGlobals                      num1: 10, num2: -5
     After calling function useGlobals block 1       num1: 20, num2: 13
```

Lab 7.5 Using Static and Automatic Variables

A variable for which memory is allocated at block entry and deallocated at block exit is called an automatic variable. A variable for which memory remains allocated as long as the program executes is called a static variable.

Static variables are declared within a block and are local to that block. Their scope is the same as that of any other local identifier of that block. However, because memory is allocated only once for static variables and not deallocated at the end of the function like automatic variables, the value of static variables remains with each function call, which prevents other functions from manipulating their values. Static variables are deallocated at the end of `main`.

Objectives

In this lab, you continue using stepwise refinement, and you recognize when to use static variables.

After completing this lab, you will be able to:

- Use static variables.

Estimated completion time: **15–25 minutes**

Using Static and Automatic Variables

In the following exercises, you answer a multiple-choice question and a true-or-false question. You also continue to design and create the payroll program that you began in Lab 7.1.

Question	Answer (Circle the correct answer)

1. Suppose function changeX has the statements
`static int x = 2;`
` x = x * 2;`
`cout << x << endl;`
If changeX is called three times from main, what is displayed?
	a. 4
	8
	16
	b. 4
	4
	4
	c. 16

2. Memory for static variables is allocated for all functions before execution of the `main` function.	**True** **False**

3a. In this lab, you continue to use stepwise refinement to revise your payroll program. You add a counter that is a static variable in your function and displays the employee information to count the number of employees receiving a paycheck. You add column headings to allow for an employee number, add the number of the employee being processed in each employee information data line, and adjust your total line to align correctly.

Write your design in the following space. Your design should be a list of C++ comments without any code.

3b. Write a C++ program based on the design you created in Exercise 3a and name it **Payroll4.cpp**. Step through the code by hand.

Use the following memory table to show the change to your displayEmployeeInfo function when the C++ code is executed. (Include line numbers as documentation only. Do not use line numbers when entering your final program.) To fill out the memory table, use one or two lines for each variable. On one line, enter declaration information. Write the name of the declared variable, its data type, and the line number at declaration. On the next line in the memory table, enter test data for that variable. The variable name is entered as an example but may use different line numbers in your design.

displayEmployeeInfo function

Variable Name	Data Type	Value in Memory	Line Number at Declaration	Line Number when Initialized

In the following space, show what is displayed on the screen after executing the output message.

3c. Enter, compile, link, and execute **Payroll4.cpp**. Then copy the output and save it in a block comment at the end of your program. Save **Payroll4.cpp** in the Chap07 folder of your Student Disk.

The following is a copy of the screen results that might display after running your program, depending on the data entered.

```
This payroll program calculates individual employee pay and
company totals using data from a data file payroll.txt.


A payroll report showing payroll information is displayed.

Emp.  Employee              Hourly    Hours     Tax      Gross      Net
No.   Name                    Rate   Worked    Rate     Amount   Amount

1     John Smith             10.45    40.00   15.00     418.00   355.30
2     Jane Doe               12.50    45.00   15.00     843.75   717.19
3     Harry Morgan           20.00    40.00   20.00     800.00   640.00
4     Carmen Martinez        25.00    35.00   25.00     875.00   656.25
5     Jacintha Washington    50.85    60.00   35.00    4576.50  2974.72

Totals                                                 7513.25  5343.46
```

LAB 7.6 USING FUNCTION OVERLOADING

In a C++ program, functions can have the same name, but they must have a different set of parameters. The types of parameters determine which function to execute. This is called function overloading. The return type or void is not considered a part of function overloading.

Objectives

In this lab, you use function overloading according to the type of data being processed.

After completing this lab, you will be able to:

- Use function overloading.

Estimated completion time: **15–20 minutes**

Using Function Overloading

In the following exercises, you determine whether statements are true or false. You also design and write a program that uses function overloading.

Question	Answer (Circle the correct answer)	
1. C++ function names, like other identifiers, must be unique.	**True**	**False**
2. In C++, if multiple functions have the same name, then the return type must be different.	**True**	**False**
3. Function overloading occurs when multiple functions have the same name but different parameter lists.	**True**	**False**

4a. Design a program that asks the user to enter a character, a string, an integer, and a float value. The user should be prompted for each data item in a separate function with the name getData and a reference parameter of the type of data item being read. Display the data entered twice, using a different function but each time named displayData, that have different parameter lists.

Write your design in the following space. Your design should be a list of C++ comments without any code.

4b. Write a C++ program based on the design you created in Exercise 4a and name it **Overload.cpp**. Step through the code by hand.

Use the following memory table to show what occurs in memory when the C++ code is executed. (Include line numbers as documentation only. Do not use line numbers when entering your final program.) To fill out the memory table, use one or two lines for each variable. On one line, enter declaration information. Write the name of the declared variable, its data type, and the line number at declaration. On the next line in the memory table, enter test data for that variable. The variable name is entered as an example but may use different line numbers in your design.

main function

Variable Name	Data Type	Value in Memory	Line Number at Declaration	Line Number when Initialized or Changed

getData function

Variable Name	Data Type	Value in Memory	Line Number at Declaration	Line Number when Initialized or Changed

getData function

Variable Name	Data Type	Value in Memory	Line Number at Declaration	Line Number when Initialized or Changed

getData function

Variable Name	Data Type	Value in Memory	Line Number at Declaration	Line Number when Initialized or Changed

getData function

Variable Name	Data Type	Value in Memory	Line Number at Declaration	Line Number when Initialized or Changed

displayData function

Variable Name	Data Type	Value in Memory	Line Number at Declaration	Line Number when Initialized or Changed

displayData function

Variable Name	Data Type	Value in Memory	Line Number at Declaration	Line Number when Initialized or Changed

In the following space, show what is displayed on the screen after executing the output message.

4c. Enter, compile, link, and execute **Overload.cpp**. Then copy the output and save it in a block comment at the end of your program. Save **Overload.cpp** in the Chap07 folder of your Student Disk.

The following is a copy of the screen results that might display after running your program, depending on the data entered. The input entered by the user is shown in bold.

```
Enter a character: x
Enter a word: hello
Enter a whole number: 5
Enter a number with a decimal point: 4.2

You entered the following data:
letter:  x
string:  hello
integer: 5
float:   4.2

Your data displayed again:
integer: 5
float:   4.2
letter:  x
string:  hello
```

LAB 7.7 USING DEFAULT PARAMETERS

Parameters may be passed to a function using default values. The default values are assigned to the parameter(s) the first time the function name appears in the program, and that usually occurs in the prototype. When default values have been assigned to parameters, the call to that function need not pass arguments for those default parameters if the logic of the program requires the function to use the default values. If, on the other hand, the logic requires values other than the default values then the call to the function must pass those values as parameters.

Several special rules apply to functions using default parameters. All parameters can be default parameters; however, if some of the parameters are not default parameters, the default parameters must be at the end (to the far right) of the parameter list. If there is more than one default parameter and a default parameter is not in the function call, then all default parameters to the right of that absent parameter must likewise be omitted. The default values assigned to parameters can be variables, constants, and other function calls; however, constants may not be assigned to a reference parameter.

Objectives

After completing this lab, you will be able to:

- Write a prototype for a function that has default parameters.
- Define a function that uses default and nondefault parameters.
- Design and write a program with calls to that function which will both include and omit the default parameters.

Estimated completion time: **50–60 minutes**

Using Default Parameters

Question

1. Given the following declarations and prototype choose the correct function call:

```
int x; sales;
void compute (string name, int& amount =
x, double rate = 0.5);
```

Answer

a. compute ("Joe", 15);

b. compute ("Joe," 15, 0.1);

c. compute ("Joe", 0.1);

d. compute ("Joe", sales);

2. Given the following prototype:

```
double calc (double bonus = 0.10, string
base = "xyz");
```

the output is:

a. result = calc ();

b. result = calc ("code", 2.0);

c. result = calc ("code");

d. result = calc (0.2, 15);

3. Write a prototype for a void function with one default parameter that outputs a line of characters. Assign the value '*' to the default parameter.

4. Write a call to the function you defined in 1a that outputs a line of dashes.

5a. *Critical Thinking.* Your school would like to develop a program that computes the maximum amount of financial aid a qualified student is entitled to receive in a semester if the student met certain income and grade point levels (on a 4.0 system). Specifically, if the student's GPA is at least a 2.0 but less than a 3.0, the student may receive half of the tuition cost in aid. If the student's GPA is at least 3.0, the student may receive aid up to all of the tuition cost.

Design a program that would get and validate in the `main` function the following input: 1) the tuition amount (not to exceed 2000) and 2) the GPA (which must be at least a 2.0). Use data validation loops. If the GPA is less than 2.0, output a message that the student doesn't qualify academically and end the program.

Use a value-returning function named computeAid that takes two parameters, tuition and GPA. Set the GPA parameter to a default value of 2.0. The function will calculate the amount of financial aid as follows: aid = tuition / 4 * GPA. If the GPA is less than 3.0, use a function call that passes only the tuition as an argument. If the GPA is 3.0 or greater, then pass two arguments, tuition and GPA.

Write your design in the following space. For your design, write an algorithm (an English language description of the steps required to successfully complete the task).

5b. Write a C++ program based upon the design you created in Exercise 5a and name it **FinancialAid.cpp.**

5c. Enter, compile, link, and execute **FinancilaAid.cpp**. Copy the output and save it in a block comment at the end of the source code. Save **FinancialAid.cpp** in the Chap07 folder of your Student Disk.

The following is a copy of the screen results that might display after running your program, depending on the data entered.

```
Enter the amount of your tuition costs, not to exceed $2,000.00: 500
Enter your GPA (a value between 0 and 4.0): 2.0
You are entitled to receive $500 in financial aid.

Enter the amount of your tuition costs, not to exceed $2,000.00: 1500
Enter your GPA (a value between 0 and 4.0): 4.0
You are entitled to receive $1,500 in financial aid.

Enter the amount of your tuition costs, not to exceed $2,000.00: 2000
Enter your GPA (a value between 0 and 4.0): 3.5
You are entitled to receive $1,750 in financial aid.

Enter the amount of your tuition costs, not to exceed $2,000.00: 1800
Enter your GPA (a value between 0 and 4.0): 1.9
Sorry, you do not qualify academically for financial aid.
```

8 User-Defined Simple Data Types, Namespaces, and the `string` Type

In this chapter, you will:

- Learn how to create and manipulate your own simple data type called the enumeration type
- Become familiar with the `typedef` statement
- Learn about the `namespace` mechanism
- Explore the `string` data type and learn how to use the various `string` functions to manipulate strings

Chapter 8: Assignment Cover Sheet

Name ______________________ Date ______________________

Section ______________________

Lab Assignments	Assigned	Grade
Lab 8.1 Creating and Manipulating Enumerated Data Types (Critical Thinking Exercise)		
Lab 8.2 Using the `typedef` Statement		
Lab 8.3 Using the `namespace` Mechanism		
Lab 8.4 Using the `string` Data Type and the `string` Functions		
Lab 8.5 Challenge Programming Using `string` Manipulations (Critical Thinking Exercise)		
Total Grade		

See your instructor or the introduction to this book for instructions on submitting your assignments.

LAB 8.1 CREATING AND MANIPULATING ENUMERATED DATA TYPES

The **enumeration data type** is an ordered set of distinct values defined by the user. Specifying your own data type allows you to determine what values of that type are allowed. In C++, the values specified must be identifiers, or enumerators, and are constants, not variables. The syntax for the enumeration type is:

```
enum typeName (value1, value2, ...);
```

Once a data type is defined, variables of that type can be declared. The syntax for declaring variables is the same as declaring any other variable:

```
dataType identifier, identifier, ...;
```

The default value of **enumerators** starts with the assigned value of the first identifier as 0 (zero) and the second value as 1, and so on. Within the same block, the same value (identifier) cannot be assigned to more than one enumerated type.

Although C++ does not allow arithmetic operations directly on the enumeration type, you can use type casting to perform arithmetic operations. Because enumerators are ordered, relational operators are allowed. Additionally, the enumerated types can be a loop variable. However, the enumeration type cannot be input or output directly. Output of the enumeration type results in the value assigned to the enumerator being displayed.

The enumeration type can be a value and reference parameter to functions as well as a return type. When used as a value or reference parameter, the formal parameter must be an integer data type. The enumeration type that is defined without a type name, called an anonymous type, cannot be a function parameter.

Values can be assigned to the constants at definition. The syntax is:

```
enum typeName (value1, value2, ...) variable1, variable2, ...;
```

An **anonymous type** occurs when you directly specify values in a variable declaration with no type name. The syntax is:

```
enum (value1, value2, ...) variable1, variable2, ...;
```

Objectives

In this lab, you define your own enumeration type and write a program using that type.

After completing this lab, you will be able to:

- Define your own enumeration type.
- Use the `static_cast` operator to increment and decrement an enumeration type.
- Use the enumeration type in a `switch` statement.

Estimated completion time: **45–60 minutes**

Creating and Manipulating Enumerated Data Types

In the following exercises, you determine whether each statement is true or false. You then design and create a program that converts a date entered by the user to another format (e.g., convert 2/9/2008 to February 9, 2008).

Question	Answer (Circle the correct answer)	
1. The relational operators can be used with the enumeration type.	**True**	**False**
2. The enumeration type is a character type.	**True**	**False**
3. The enumeration type can be neither input nor output (directly).	**True**	**False**
4. If you try to output the value of an enumerator directly, the computer will output the value assigned to the enumerator.	**True**	**False**
5. In C++, enumeration types are passed to a function by reference, not by value.	**True**	**False**
6. Values used in one anonymous type can be used in another anonymous type, but variables of those types are treated differently.	**True**	**False**
7. In C++, you cannot declare variables of an enumeration type when you define an enumeration type.	**True**	**False**

8a. In this exercise, you design a program to convert a date entered by the user to another format. For example, if the user enters the date `2/9/2008`, your program should display: `February 9, 2008`. You must create an enumeration type called `monthType` to hold the month entered by the user (e.g., `JANUARY, FEBRUARY`, etc.). In your enumeration type, by default, `JANUARY` would be assigned the number 0, `FEBRUARY` the number 1, etc. In order to avoid having to add one and subtract one each time you want to convert to and from the month integer value to your month enumeration type, you can declare your enumeration type so that `JANUARY` is assigned the number 1, `FEBRUARY` the number 2, and so on. To do this, you can use the following syntax:

```
enum typeName (value1 = initialValue, value2, ...);
```

in which `initialValue` is the integer value you want to assign to the first enumerator in your enumeration type. The values increase by one for each succeeding enumerator.

In this particular program, since there is a direct correlation between the value of a month and of the enumerator corresponding to that month, you can assign the value entered by the user to a `monthType` variable by using a static cast:

```
monthTypeVariable = static_cast<monthType>(intVariable);
```

in which `intVariable` holds a number between 1 and 12.

Include comments to identify the program author, to describe the program, and to describe program statements. Additionally, remember to include all necessary preprocessor directives. Write your design in the following space. Your design should consist of a list of C++ comments without any code.

8b. Write a C++ program based on the design you created in Exercise 8a, and name it **ConvertDate.cpp**. Step through the code by hand.

In the following space, show what is displayed on the screen after executing the program.

8c. Enter, compile, link, and execute **ConvertDate.cpp**. Then copy the output and save it in a block comment at the end of your program. Save **ConvertDate.cpp** in the Chap08 folder of your Student Disk.

The following is a copy of the screen results that might display after running your program, depending on the data entered. The input entered by the user is shown in bold.

```
Enter a date in the format MM/DD/YYYY (e.g., 2/9/2008): 2/9/2008
You entered: February 9, 2008
```

9a. *Critical Thinking Exercise*: You will now test your program with invalid input. Did you include code to perform input validation on the data entered by the user for the month? What might happen if you enter a number that is less than 1 or greater than 12?

9b. Now test your program with invalid input. For example, enter `33/9/2008`. What happens when you enter invalid input? Copy the output of your program in the following space. You should also copy the output and save it in a block comment at the end of your program. Don't forget to save **ConvertDate.cpp**.

9c. How can you avoid invalid input?

LAB 8.2 USING THE `typedef` STATEMENT

In C++, the `typedef` statement creates an alias to an existing data type. It does not create a new data type. The syntax of the `typedef` statement is:

`typedef` existingTypeName newTypeName;

For example:

```
typedef int integer;
```

creates an alias, `integer`, for the data type `int`.

When you change your program from one computer to another, the data types can have different sizes. If you are writing code for different machines, it can be difficult to use the default sizes. You can write directives at the beginning of the code to define the `typedef`. It is easier to change only the beginning `typedef` to use the data type than to change the entire program.

Objectives

In this lab, you use `typedef` statements to redefine data types of a particular size.

After completing this lab, you will be able to:

- Write `typedef` statements for `integer` declarations for byte sizes 1, 2, and 4.

Estimated completion time: **30–40 minutes**

Using the `typedef` Statement

In the following exercises, you determine whether statements are true or false. You also design and create a program that finds the sizes of data types on your computer. Recall that `typedef` statements are statements that redefine existing data types. Therefore, you might need to find out the sizes of different data types before writing a program that uses `typedef` statements to define `integer` types with the byte sizes of 1, 2, and 4.

Question	Answer (Enter or circle the correct answer)	
1. The `typedef` statement does not create any new data type; it creates only an alias to an existing data type.	**True**	**False**
2. The following statement creates an alias, Boolean, for the data type `int`: `typedef int Boolean;`	**True**	**False**
3. The `typedef` statement allows you to create new data types.	**True**	**False**

4a. Design a program that uses the `sizeof` operator to find the size of `char`, `short`, `int`, and `long` on your computer. Display your results.

Write your design in the following space. Your design should be a list of C++ comments without any code.

4b. Write a C++ program based on the design you created in Lab 8.2, Exercise 4a and name it **sizeOf.cpp**. Step through the code by hand.

In the following space, show what is displayed on the screen after executing the output message.

4c. Enter, compile, link, and execute **sizeOf.cpp**. Then copy the output and save it in a block comment at the end of your program. Save **sizeOf.cpp** in the Chap08 folder of your Student Disk.

The following is a copy of the screen results that might display after running your program, depending on your computer.

```
The size of char on this computer is 1
The size of short on this computer is 2
The size of int on this computer is 4
The size of long on this computer is 4
```

5a. After you run **sizeOf.cpp** and determine the number of bytes used on your computer for the data types `char`, `short`, `int`, and `long`, design a program that uses typedef statements to define the following identifiers:

- `shortInt` with a size of 1 byte
- `integer` with a size of 2 bytes
- `longInt` with a size of 4 bytes

Then use the `sizeof` operator to find the size of `shortInt`, `integer`, and `longInt`. Display your results.

5b. Write a C++ program based on the design you created in Exercise 5a and name it **sizeOf2.cpp**. Step through the code by hand.

In the following space, show what is displayed on the screen after executing the output message.

5c. Enter, compile, link, and execute **sizeOf2.cpp**. Then copy the output and save it in a block comment at the end of your program. Save **sizeOf2.cpp** in the Chap08 folder of your Student Disk.

The following is a copy of the screen results that might appear display after running your program.

```
The size of shortint on this computer is 1
The size of integer on this computer is 2
The size of longint on this computer is 4
```

LAB 8.3 USING THE namespace MECHANISM

Some additional features of C++ are available for ANSI/ISO Standard C++ that are not available for Standard C++. When including header files with global identifiers, those global identifiers are recognized in your C++ program. If you define your own global identifiers with the same name as global identifiers in the header files, you receive a syntax error such as "identifier redefined." To avoid this problem, global identifiers from libraries generally start with the underline (_) character, as in _xxx.

ANSI/ISO Standard C++ uses the `namespace` mechanism to solve the problem of overlapping global identifier names. The syntax of the statement `namespace` is:

```
namespace namespace_name

{

    members

}
```

The scope of a namespace member is local to the namespace and uses the scope resolution operator. The syntax for accessing a namespace is:

```
namespace_name::identifier
```

The statement `using` simplifies accessing a namespace member. The syntax is:

```
using namespace namespace_name;
```

To access a specific namespace member, the syntax is:

```
using namespace_name::identifier;
```

Objectives

In this lab, you use ANSI/ISO Standard C++ header files. Additionally, you use the predefined `namespace std`, use the scope resolution operator for global identifiers that are part of the header files, and write your own namespace definition.

After completing this lab, you will be able to:

- Use ANSI/ISO Standard C++ header files with the scope resolution operator.
- Define a namespace.

Estimated completion time: **20–30 minutes**

Using the namespace Mechanism

In the following exercises, you determine whether statements are true or false. You also design and create a program that displays a message.

Question	Answer (Circle the correct answer)
1. When a header file is included in a program, the global identifiers for the header file become global identifiers in the program.	**True** **False**
2. To avoid overlapping global identifiers, you should make it a practice to name your global identifiers beginning with an underline (_) character.	**True** **False**
3. The scope of a namespace member is local to the namespace.	**True** **False**
4. You access a namespace member by using the dot operator, for example: `namespace_name.identifier`	**True** **False**
5. To simplify the accessing of identifiers in `iostream`, `cmath`, and `iomanip`, use the following statement: `using namespace std;`	**True** **False**

6a. Create the design for a program that displays the message "Hello World" and do not define it using `namespace std`.

Write your design in the following space. Your design should be a list of C++ comments without any code.

6b. Write a C++ program based on the design you created in Exercise 6a and name it **Hello.cpp**. Step through the code by hand.

In the following space, show what is displayed on the screen after executing the output message.

6c. Enter, compile, link, and execute **Hello.cpp**. Then copy the output and save it in a block comment at the end of your program. Save **Hello.cpp** in the Chap08 folder of your Student Disk.

The following is a copy of the screen results that might display after running your program.

```
Hello World
```

7a. Design a program that declares a namespace named `message`. The namespace should declare a `string` variable greeting. In your `main` function, assign "Hello World" to the `string` greeting. Then display the `string` greeting.

7b. Write a C++ program based on the design you created in Exercise 7a and name it **Hello2.cpp**. Step through the code by hand.

In the following space, show what is displayed on the screen after executing the output message.

7c. Enter, compile, link, and execute **Hello2.cpp**. Then copy the output and save it in a block comment at the end of your program. Save **Hello2.cpp** in the Chap08 folder of your Student Disk.

The following is a copy of the screen results that might display after running your program.

```
Hello World
```

LAB 8.4 USING THE `string` DATA TYPE AND `string` FUNCTIONS

Several predefined functions are included for the string data type when using the compiler directive `#include <string>`. Among those predefined functions are length, size, find, substr, and swap. In addition, the + operator has been overloaded in the string class so that it will function as a concatenation operator when used with string operands. In order to use these string functions and the concatenation operator (+) in a program, the header file string, `#include<string>`, must be included as a compiler directive at the beginning of the code.

Objectives

In this lab, you will use the ANSI/ISO Standard C++ header file functions for string manipulations.

After completing this lab, you will be able to:

- Use the binary + operator to concatenate `strings`.
- Use the `length` or `size` function to find the number of characters in a `string`.
- Use the find function to search a `string` for the first occurrence of a particular substring.
- Use the `substr` function to search a `string` beginning at a specified position in the `string` and return a substring of a specified `length`.
- Use the `swap` function to interchange the contents of two `string` variables.
- Design and write a program that uses one or more of the `string` functions and the + operator for concatenation.

Estimated completion time: **50–60 minutes**

What will the following C++ statements display?

1.
```
string lastName = "Smith", firstName = "Ted";
      cout << firstName + " F." + lastName;
```

2.
```
string ssn = "529-25-9861";
      cout << ssn.length();
```

3.
```
string name = "John L. Lewis";
      cout << name.find(".");
```

4.
```
string quote= "All that glitters is not gold.";
      cout << quote.substr(25, 10);
```

5.
```
string date1 = "May 15, 2008", date2 = "15 May 2006";
      cout << date1.swap(date2);
```

6. Design a program that will check the format for telephone numbers. Telephone numbers should be entered as a string with the first three characters followed by a dash and the last four numbers, e.g., 000-0000. The program will check that a number entered contains eight characters and has a dash after the first three characters. Use string functions to do the validation. Output a message that states whether the telephone number is or is not in the proper format.

   Write your design in the following space. For your design, write an algorithm (an English language description of the steps required to successfully solve the problem).

7. Write a C++ program based on the design you created in the previous exercise and name it **ValidatePhone.cpp**.

8. Enter, compile, link and execute **ValidatePhone.cpp**. Copy the output and save it in a block comment at the end of the source code. Save **ValidatePhone.cpp** in the Chap08 folder of your student disk.

   The following is a copy of the screen results that might display after running your program depending on the data entered.

```
Enter a seven-digit phone number with a dash
between the first three and last four characters: 5558888
The number is not in proper format.

Enter a seven-digit phone number with a dash
between the first three and last four characters: 555-773
The number is not in proper format.

Enter a seven-digit phone number with a dash
between the first three and last four characters: 722-8891
The number is in proper format.
```

9. Modify the program you designed in the previous exercise. If the telephone number input was in the proper format, convert the telephone number input to a toll-free 800 number. The string 800 and a dash should be added to the telephone number input so that the format of the telephone number will be 800-000-0000. Output the new 800 telephone number.

   Write your design in the following space. For your design, write an algorithm (an English language description of the steps required to successfully solve the problem).

Table 8-1 Data type and named constant for the strings

Data type	Description
string:: size_type	An unsigned integer (data) type related to the characters in the string
string::npos	The maximum value of the (data) type string::size_type, a number such as 4294967295 on many machines

10. Write a C++ program based on the design you created in the previous exercise and name it **Validate800Phone.cpp**.

Estimated completion time: **50–60 minutes**

11. Enter, compile, link and execute **ValidatePhone.cpp**. Copy the output and save it in a block comment at the end of the source code. Save **ValidatePhone.cpp** in the Chap08 folder of your student disk.

    The following is a copy of the screen results that might display after running your program depending on the data entered.

```
Enter a seven-digit phone number with a dash
between the first three and last four characters: 559_1123
The number is not in proper format

Enter a seven-digit phone number with a dash
between the first three and last four characters: 436-9257
The number is in proper format
The new phone number is 800-436-9257
```

LAB 8.5 CHALLENGE PROGRAMMING USING string MANIPULATIONS

The data type `string` is associated with a data type (`string`::size_type) and a named constant (`string`::npos), which are defined in Table 8-1.

Objectives

In this lab, you combine the use of various `string` manipulations, testing when a search is not successful.

After completing this lab, you will be able to:

- Combine various `string` manipulations to solve a problem.
- Test for a successful search of a `string`.

1a. *Critical Thinking Exercise:* Design a program that prompts the user to enter a sentence. Count the number of vowels in the sentence. Display the length of the sentence and the number of each vowel in the sentence.

    Write your design in the following space. Your design should be a list of C++ comments without any code.

1b. Write a C++ program based on the design you created in Exercise 1a and name it **Vowel.cpp**. Step through the code by hand.

    In the following space, show what is displayed on the screen after executing the output message.

9 Arrays and Strings

In this chapter, you will:

- Learn about arrays
- Explore how to declare and manipulate data into arrays
- Understand the meaning of "array index out of bounds"
- Become familiar with the restrictions on array processing
- Discover how to pass an array as a parameter to a function
- Learn about C-strings
- Examine the use of string functions to process C-strings
- Discover how to input data into—and output data from—a C-string
- Learn about parallel arrays
- Discover how to manipulate data in a two-dimensional array
- Learn about multidimensional arrays

Chapter 9: Assignment Cover Sheet

Name ______________________________ Date ______________________________

Section ______________________________

Lab Assignments	Assigned	Grade
Lab 9.1 Declaring and Manipulating Data into Arrays		
Lab 9.2 Checking Index Bounds and Initializing Arrays (Critical Thinking Exercise)		
Lab 9.3 Passing Arrays as Parameters to Functions (Critical Thinking Exercise)		
Lab 9.4 Coding with C-strings		
Lab 9.5 Inputting and Outputting Data Using C-strings		
Lab 9.6 Coding with Parallel Arrays		
Lab 9.7 Manipulating Data in a Two-Dimensional Array		
Lab 9.8 Using a Multidimensional Array (Critical Thinking Exercise)		
Total Grade		

See your instructor or the introduction to this book for instructions on submitting your assignments.

LAB 9.1 DECLARING AND MANIPULATING DATA INTO ARRAYS

Structured data types are collections of other data types. Simple data types are the building blocks of structured data types. An array is a structured data type that is a collection of a fixed number of components. A one-dimensional array is an array in which the components are arranged in a list. Arrays are declared using square brackets with the number of components shown inside of the brackets, as in `int num[5]`. The syntax for declaring a one-dimensional array is:

```
dataType arrayName[intExp];
```

To access a component of the array, you also use the square bracket with an integer inside of the brackets indicating the position from the beginning of the array. The position of the start of the array is position 0. The syntax for accessing an array's component is:

```
arrayName[indexExp];
```

To access a component of the array, you also use an expression that evaluates to a nonnegative integer that appears inside of the brackets and indicates the position from the beginning of the array. Do not confuse the size at declaration with the position from the beginning of the array. Additionally, when you declare an array, its size must be known.

Working with arrays almost always requires iteration. Like all variables, an array and its size must be declared when the program is compiled. An individual array component is treated the same as any individual variable. Operations for individual components are the same as operations for any variable.

For example, the following code would assign the fourth variable of an array to the variable **num**.

```
int array[5] = {5, 8, 9, 6, 4};
int num;
num = array[3];
```

Objectives

In this lab, you process individual array components. Write the code for the design given.

After completing this lab, you will be able to:

- Declare arrays and process each array element individually.

Estimated completion time: **40–50 minutes**

Declaring and Manipulating Data into Arrays

In the following exercises, enter or select the correct answer for each question. Then provide the array-processing code missing from a C++ program.

Question	Answer (Enter or circle the correct answer)
1. How many components are contained in the following array declarations? `double values [14];`	a. 14 b. 15
2. Write a **for** loop that sums the numbers in an array with five components.	

3. An array ______________ .

a. is a simple data type

b. is a structured data type

4. Simple data types are building blocks for arrays. **True** **False**

5. An array index starts at 1. **True** **False**

6. In C++, `array` is a reserved word. **True** **False**

7. The following code allows the size of an array to be determined at execution. **True** **False**

```
int n;
cout << "Enter the size of the array: ";
cin >> n;
int array[n];
```

8a. The following C++ program is missing the code that is designed for array processing. In this exercise, you write a program from a design that prompts a user to enter 10 numbers. This program reads the numbers into an array and finds the smallest number in the list, the largest number in the list, the sum of the 10 numbers, and the average of the 10 numbers. Using the comments, add the missing code.

// Enter your name as a comment for program identification

// Program assignment List.cpp

// Enter your class section and time

/* The program List.cpp prompts the user for 10 numbers. */

/* The numbers are input into an array. Then the
smallest, largest, and average of the numbers in the
list are found. */

// The user inputs 10 values.

/* The largest, smallest, and average of the number is
displayed. */

// header files

// use the correct preprocessor directives for input/output

// function prototypes

/* The function instruct describes the use
and purpose of the program. */

/* The function getNumber reads in a value
one at a time. */

/* The function findLargest returns the
largest of two numbers. */

/* The function findSmallest returns the
smallest of two numbers. */

/* The function display reports the

```
  largest, smallest, and average of the
  numbers in the list. */

// main function
        // declare variables
        /* an integer variable smallest initialized
          to INT_MAX to hold the smallest number in
          the list, an integer variable largest
          initialized to INT_MIN to hold the largest
          number in the list, an integer array number
          to hold the 10 values in a list, an integer
          variable sum to sum all of the numbers, an
          integer variable count initialized to 0 to
          count the values in the list, a double variable
          average to hold the average of the numbers */

        // call the function instruct

        // loop for all values in the list
                /* assign to an array element the value
                  returned from getNumber */
                /* assign to largest the value returned
                  from findLargest that has arguments largest
                  and the current array element */

                /* assign to smallest the value returned
                  from findSmallest that has arguments
                  smallest and the current array element */

                /* increment sum by the current array element */


        // display a message identifying the values
        // write a for loop to display the array of numbers

        // calculate the average
        // call the display function to display the results
```

/* The function instruct describes the use
and purpose of the program. */

/* The function getNumber reads in a value
one at a time. */
/* declare an integer variable value
to read in each array component */
// read in data value
// return data value

/* The function findLargest returns the
largest of two numbers. */
// test for largest value
// return largest value

/* The function findSmallest returns the
smallest of two numbers. */
// test for smallest value
// return smallest value

/* The function display reports the
smallest, largest, sum, and average of the
numbers in the list. */
// display the smallest, largest, sum, and average

8b. In the following space, show what is displayed on the screen after executing the output message.

8c. Enter, compile, link, and execute **List.cpp**. Then copy the output and save it in a block comment at the end of your program. Save **List.cpp** in the Chap09 folder of your Student Disk.

The following is a copy of the screen results that might display after running your program, depending on the data entered. The input entered by the user is shown in bold.

```
This program asks the user to enter 10 numbers, each separated by a space.
The program will find the smallest, largest, sum, and average of the numbers.

Enter your list of numbers: 10 5 3 -5 9 14 -8 0 2 -6
```

Your array has these values:

```
10 5 3 -5 9 14 -8 0 2 -6

From your list of 10 numbers:
        smallest: -8
        largest:  14
        sum:      24
        average:  2.4
```

LAB 9.2 CHECKING INDEX BOUNDS AND INITIALIZING ARRAYS

An array can be initialized at declaration by placing the values between braces separated by commas. If the size of the array is not indicated at declaration, it defaults to the number of values in the initialization block. If partial initialization of an array occurs at declaration, the size of the array must be indicated and all remaining values are initialized to 0.

For example, an array with no initialization is defined as follows:

```
dataType[size] arrayName;
```

An array with initialization can be defined as follows:

```
dataType[] arrayName = {value1, value2, value3, …, valuen};
dataType[5] arrayName = { value1, value2, value3, value4, value5};
dataType[5] arrayName = {0};
```

The C++ compiler does not check whether an array index is out of bounds. The programmer must do this. Because the index position starts counting with the number 0, there is no array position that is the same number as the size of the array.

Arrays do not accept aggregate operations. Operations must be done one component at a time, called component-wise in programming. To copy the values of one array into another, you need to copy each value.

```
for (int index = 0; index < 5; index++)
        arrayA[index] = arrayB[index];
```

Objectives

In this lab, you check to see that an index value is in bounds and initialize an array at declaration.

After completing this lab, you will be able to:

- Check for an array index that is out of bounds.
- Initialize arrays at declaration.
- Process data in an array.

Estimated completion time: **60–75 minutes**

Checking Index Bounds and Initializing Arrays

In the following exercises, select the correct answer for each question. Then design and write a program that checks index bounds and initializes arrays.

Question	**Answer (Circle the correct answer)**
1. How many components are contained in the following array declarations? `double values [14];`	a. 14 b. 15

2. The following statements assign 5 to the last value in the array.
`int array [10];`
`array [10] = 5;`
	True **False**

3. Given:

```
int array[5] =  { 1, 2, 3};
```

What are the values of each array component?

4. The following code correctly initializes each component to 0. **True** **False**

```
int array[3];
array[3] = {0};
```

5. The following code correctly initializes each component to 0. **True** **False**

```
int array[3] = {0};
```

6. The following code correctly initializes each component to 0. **True** **False**

```
int array[3];
for (int count = 0; count <= 3; count++)
     array[count] = 0;
```

7. The following code correctly initializes each component to 0. **True** **False**

```
int array[3];
for (int count = 1; count <= 3; count++)
     array[count] = 0;
```

8a. *Critical Thinking Exercise*: Design a program for a trucking company that has seven trucks in its fleet. Each truck is identified by a number from one to seven and has a maximum weight allowance, which has already been determined. Assign the maximum weight limit to each truck at initialization. Before a truck can begin its route, it must be weighed to see if it falls within its weight allowance. Ask the user for the truck number and the loaded weight. Display a message indicating whether the truck falls in the allowable weight limit. Use the following values as maximum weight limits, and enter the weigh-in values for each truck.

Truck Number	Maximum Weight Limit (in lbs)	Truck Weigh-In (in lbs)
1	50,000	45,000
2	25,000	30,000
3	20,000	20,000
4	35,000	30,000
5	40,000	35,000
6	25,000	27,000
7	30,000	20,000

Write your design in the following space. Your design should be a list of C++ comments without any code.

8b. Write a C++ program based on the design you created in Exercise 8a and name it **Trucks.cpp**. Step through the code by hand.

In the following space, show what is displayed on the screen after executing the output message.

8c. Enter, compile, link, and execute **Trucks.cpp**. Then copy the output and save it in a block comment at the end of your program. Save Trucks.cpp in the Chap09 folder of your Student Disk.

The following is a copy of the screen results that might display after running your program, depending on the data entered. The input entered by the user is shown in bold.

```
This program asks the user for the truck number
and the weigh-in value for each truck in a fleet.

The weigh-in value is compared to the established maximum weight limit.
A message is displayed to tell the user whether the truck is within
weight limits.


Please enter the truck number and weight: 1 45000
Your truck is ready to roll.

Please enter the truck number and weight: 2 30000
You have exceeded your allowable weight allowance.

Please enter the truck number and weight: 3 20000
Your truck is ready to roll.

Please enter the truck number and weight: 0 40000
Your entered an invalid truck number or weight.

Please enter the truck number and weight: 4 33000
Your truck is ready to roll.

Please enter the truck number and weight: 5 41000
You have exceeded your allowable weight allowance.
```

```
Please enter the truck number and weight: 6 18000
Your truck is ready to roll.

Please enter the truck number and weight: 7 28000
Your truck is ready to roll.

All trucks have weighed in.
```

9a. Design a program for a shoe distribution company that has five salespersons. Each salesperson has an ID number of one to five. An array is used to accumulate total sales for each salesperson. Sales can be entered multiple times for multiple sales by each salesperson. The user enters –1 to complete the input step. After all of the input has been entered, a table is printed with each salesperson's ID in the first row and the total sales in the second row.

Write your design in the following space. Your design should be a list of C++ comments without any code.

9b. Write a C++ program based on the design you created in Exercise 9a and name it **Sales.cpp**. Step through the code by hand.

In the following space, show what is displayed on the screen after executing the output message.

9c. Enter, compile, link, and execute **Sales.cpp**. Then copy the output and save it in a block comment at the end of your program. Save **Sales.cpp** in the Chap09 folder of your Student Disk.

The following is a copy of the screen results that might display after running your program, depending on the data entered. The input entered by the user is shown in bold.

```
Five salespersons work for the Comfort Shoe Company.
The sales for each salesperson are called in to the company to be entered.
```

The salesperson's ID (a number one through five) is entered first.

```
        If a valid ID is entered, the amount of sale is then entered.
Multiple sales for the same salesperson can be entered,
but each time the ID must also be entered.
Enter -1 to end the program.

Enter sales ID number: 1
Enter sales amount: 1000
Enter sales ID number: 2
Enter sales amount: 2000
Enter sales ID number: 3
Enter sales amount: 3000
Enter sales ID number: 9
Invalid ID entered.
Enter sales ID number: 4
Enter sales amount: 350
Enter sales ID number: 5
Enter sales amount: -700
```

```
Invalid amount entered.
Enter sales amount: 120
Enter sales ID number: 1
Enter sales amount: 300
Enter sales ID number: 2
Enter sales amount: 800
Enter sales ID number: -1

The sales total for each of the salespersons is:
          1          2          3          4          5
    1300.00    2800.00    3000.00     350.00     120.00
```

LAB 9.3 PASSING ARRAYS AS PARAMETERS TO FUNCTIONS

Function parameters and arguments are not limited to individual array components; they can also be entire arrays. When an entire array is passed, it is passed by reference. You do not use the address of "&" operator. Because arrays are passed by reference, use the reserved word `const` in the declaration of the formal parameter to prevent the function from changing the actual parameters.

The name used to identify the array is a reference to the array. Used by itself, it is the memory address of the first component of the array. In other words, the value contained in the reference of the array is the memory address of the first component of the array. When you pass an array as a parameter, the base address of the actual array is passed to the formal parameter. Although you may pass an entire array, functions cannot return a value of the type array. You can use any integral type as an array index. The size of an array must be defined with a constant or constant expression. The size must be declared before the array is declared and cannot be initialized interactively.

The syntax to call a function with an array argument is:

```
funcArrayAsParam(list);
```

The syntax for the function head is:

```
void funcArrayAsParam(dataType list[])
{
      .
      .
      .
}
```

If you put a size in the function head, it is treated only as a comment. It does not indicate the actual size of the array. To indicate the size of the array, the syntax of the call is:

```
funcArrayAsParam(list, listSize);
```

The syntax of the function head with the array size indicated is:

```
void funcArrayAsParam(dataType list[], int listSize)
{
      .
      .
      .
}
```

If you wish for the array to be treated as pass by value, you would need to change only the function head, not the call. The syntax is:

```
void funcArrayAsParam(const dataType list[], int listSize)
{
      .
      .
      .
}
```

Objectives

In this lab, you initialize an array at declaration, use an array as arguments to a function, and use a constant array as a formal parameter.

After completing this lab, you will be able to:

- Partially initialize an array at declaration.
- Use arrays as actual arguments to functions.
- Use constant arrays as formal parameters.

Estimated completion time: **50–60 minutes**

Passing Arrays as Parameters to Functions

In the following exercises, select the correct answer for each question. Then design and write a program that passes arrays as parameters to functions.

Question	Answer (Circle the correct answer)
1. Given the prototype: `void function(int array[5]);` The formal parameter is an array of five elements.	True False
2. When passing an array to a function, the size of the array is automatically passed.	True False

3. Given the declaration:
`int array[5];`
and the prototype:
`void function(int []);`
Which code calls a function with `array` as the argument?
	a. `function (array);`
	b. `function (array[]);`
	c. `function (array[5]);`

4. Which prototype for a function reads in an integer array and returns the array to the calling function?	a. `int function();` b. `int[] function();` c. `void function(int array[]);` d. `void function(int &array[]);`

5a. *Critical Thinking Exercise*: Design a program that prompts the user for a word and then prompts the user for a letter. Your program should count the number of times the letters entered appear in the word and then continue prompting for new letters. The program should list the letters found. *Hint*: Declare a Boolean array of size 26 to track whether a letter has been found.

Write your design in the following space. Your design should be a list of C++ comments without any code.

5b. Write a C++ program based on the design you created in Exercise 5a and name it **HangMan.cpp**. Step through the code by hand.

In the following space, show what is displayed on the screen after executing the output message.

5c. Enter, compile, link, and execute **HangMan.cpp**. Then copy the output and save it in a block comment at the end of your program. Save **HangMan.cpp** in the Chap09 folder of your Student Disk.

The following is a copy of the screen results that might display after running your program, depending on the data entered. The input entered by the user is shown in bold.

```
Please enter a word: howdy
The word contains 5 characters.

What letter would you like to guess? (Enter zero to quit.) a
There are 0 a's.
What letter would you like to guess? (Enter zero to quit.) e
There are 0 e's.
What letter would you like to guess? (Enter zero to quit.) d
There are 1 d's.
```

```
What letter would you like to guess? (Enter zero to quit.) o
There are 1 o's.
What letter would you like to guess? (Enter zero to quit.) y
There are 1 y's.
What letter would you like to guess? (Enter zero to quit.) b
There are 0 b's.
What letter would you like to guess? (Enter zero to quit.) 0
You found these letters
d       o       y
```

Lab 9.4 Coding with C-strings

A character array is an array whose components are of the type char. A string is a sequence of zero or more characters enclosed in double quotation marks. In C++, C-strings (or strings) are always terminated with the null character. A character array may or may not end with a null character. The character 'A' differs from the C-string "A" in that the C-string "A" consists of two characters, 'A' and the null character '\0'. The size of the C-string is one greater than the number of characters to provide for the null character '\0'. The default size of the character array `char greeting[] = "Hello";` is 6 because the C-string adds the null character. However, the size of the character array `char greeting[] = {"H', 'e', 'l', 'l', 'o'}` is 5 because it is not a C-string.

Most rules that apply to other arrays also apply to character arrays. C++ provides a set of functions that can be used for string manipulation. The header file cstring describes these functions. The function `strcpy(s1, s2)` copies string s2 into string variable s1. The function `strcmp(s1,s2)` returns a value < 0 if s1 is less than s2, 0 if s1 and s2 are the same, and a value >0 if s1 is greater than s2. The function `strlen(s)` returns the length of the string s, excluding the null character.

Objectives

In this lab, you use `char` arrays that end with the null terminator. You also use the string function `strlen` to determine the length of the string contained in the char array.

After completing this lab, you will be able to:

- Use `char` arrays that end with the null terminator.
- Use the string function `strlen`.

Estimated completion time: **40–50 minutes**

Coding with C-strings

In the following exercises, enter the correct answer for each question. Then redesign a program you already wrote to use the c-string class instead of the string class.

Question	Answer (Enter the correct answer)

1. The null character is represented as:
2. How many bytes does it take to represent the character 'A'?
3. How many bytes does it take to represent the c-string "A"?
4. How many characters are in the string

   "Hello World"?
5. How many characters are in the array str1?

   ```
   char str1[] = "Hello";
   ```
6. Given the following:

   ```
   char str1[] = "Hello";
   char str2[] = "Hello";
   cout << strcmp(str1, str2) << endl/
   ```

   What is displayed?

7. Given the following:

```
char greeting[15];
```

What occurs with the following code?

```
greeting = "Hello World";
```

8a. Redesign your **HangMan.cpp** program to omit the use of the string class. Instead, use the c-string class.

Write your design in the following space. Your design should be a list of C++ comments without any code.

8b. Write a C++ program based on the design you created in Exercise 8a and name it **HangMan2.cpp**. Step through the code by hand.

In the following space, show what is displayed on the screen after executing the output message.

8c. Enter, compile, link, and execute **HangMan2.cpp**. Then copy the output and save it in a block comment at the end of your program. Save **HangMan2.cpp** in the Chap09 folder of your Student Disk. Compare the output of HangMan2 to the output of HangMan.

The following is a copy of the screen results that might display after running your program, depending on the data entered. The input entered by the user is shown in bold.

```
Please enter a word: howdy
The word contains 5 characters.

What letter would you like to guess? (Enter zero to quit.) a
There are 0 a's.
What letter would you like to guess? (Enter zero to quit.) e
There are 0 e's.
What letter would you like to guess? (Enter zero to quit.) d
There are 1 d's.
What letter would you like to guess? (Enter zero to quit.) o
There are 1 o's.
What letter would you like to guess? (Enter zero to quit.) y
There are 1 y's.
What letter would you like to guess? (Enter zero to quit.) b
There are 0 b's.
What letter would you like to guess? (Enter zero to quit.) 0
You found these letters
d      o      y
```

Lab 9.5 Inputting and Outputting Data Using C-strings

Aggregate operations such as assignment and comparison are not allowed on arrays. However, the one place where C++ allows aggregate operations on arrays is in input and output of strings (that is, character arrays). However, because there is no check on array index bounds, strings longer than the declared array size store the entire string, extending into and corrupting adjacent memory cells if necessary.

Strings containing blanks cannot be read in using the extraction operator (>>). To read in a string with blanks and to limit the number of characters read into the string, use the function `cin.get`(str,m+1), in which str is the name of the character array or string and m+1 is the length of the string. Input stops either at the indicated length or when the newline character is found. If the string is shorter than the length specified, the newline character needs to be discarded. However, if the length is longer than the length specified, the remainder of the string remains in the buffer.

C++ allows an aggregate operation for output until the null character is found. Additionally, C++ allows the name of a file to be entered at execution. However, the string type does not contain the null terminator. In the string header file in ANSI/ISO Standard C++, the function `c_str()` converts the type string to a null-terminated character array.

The syntax to use the function `c_str` is:

```
strVar.c_str()
```

The syntax to open a file with a variable filename that has been entered by the user is:

```
infile.open(fileName.c_str());
```

Objectives

In this lab, you use the `cin.get` function to input strings of a specified length, specify filenames at execution time, and use the string type as the data type for a variable filename.

After completing this lab, you will be able to:

- Use the `cin.get()` function to input strings of a specified length.
- Specify the name of a file at execution time.
- Use the string type as the data type for a variable filename.

Estimated completion time: **40–50 minutes**

Inputting and Outputting Data Using C-strings

In the following exercises, enter or select the correct answer for each question. Then design and write a program that prompts the user to enter names and output the names to a file.

Question	Answer (Enter or circle the correct answer)

1. Given:
`char name[20];`
`cin >> name;`
What does name contain if the user enters "George Washington"?	

2. Using the code in Question 1, what value is returned from the following? `cout << strlen(name) << endl;`	a. 6 b. 20 c. 17 d. 18

3. Aggregate operations are allowed on strings for input and output. **True** **False**

4. Given:

```
char name[5] = {'H', 'e', 'l', 'l', 'o'};
cout << name << endl;
```

What is output?

a. Hello

b. Hello???????...???

5. Given:

```
int name[5];
cout << "Enter a name: ";
cin >> name;
```

If the user enters "Washington", what occurs?

6. To avoid corrupting adjacent memory cells when reading in a string, use the `cin.get` function with a maximum length to be read. **True** **False**

7. The `cin.get` function reads in input and clears the buffer after the read. **True** **False**

8a. Design a program that prompts the user to enter names and output the names to a file. The lengths of the strings to be output are limited to 20 characters. When the name is greater than 20 characters, the output file will be multiple lines. The user should enter the string "stop" to quit. The filename should be declared as a string and entered by the user.

Write your design in the following space. Your design should be a list of C++ comments without any code.

8b. Write a C++ program based on the design you created in Exercise 8a and name it **Names.cpp**. Step through the code by hand.

8c. Enter, compile, link, and execute **Names.cpp**. Save **Names.cpp** in the Chap09 folder of your Student Disk. Print your output file and submit it with your program.

The following is a copy of the screen results that might display after running your program, depending on the data entered. The input entered by the user is shown in bold.

```
Enter the name of the output file to be created: (Do not use spaces.)
names.txt

Enter a list of names to create a file. Enter stop to end the list.
George Washington Carver
Thomas Alva Edison
Dwight David Eisenhower
John Quincy Adams
stop
```

Following is the output of names.txt. Because the character arrays are limited to 20 characters, some names require more than one line.

```
George Washington C
arver
Thomas Alva Edison
Dwight David Eisenh
ower
John Quincy Adams
```

LAB 9.6 CODING WITH PARALLEL ARRAYS

Parallel arrays consist of two or more arrays with the same number of elements, in which the corresponding elements in each of the arrays contain values that are related. The arrays do not have to be of the same data type nor do they have to be of the same size (when declared) as long as every element in each array has a value that is associated with a value in the same element of the other arrays.

Objectives

In this lab, you use parallel arrays.

After completing this lab, you will be able to:

- Process two parallel arrays.
- Process three parallel arrays.
- Pass parallel arrays to functions.

Estimated completion time: **60–90 minutes**

Coding with Parallel Arrays

1a. Design a program that will initialize two parallel arrays, one with the name of a college in the Big Twelve Conference and the other with the conference ranking of the college's football team.

Use the following data to initialize the arrays:

College	Conference Ranking
Baylor	12
Colorado	11
Iowa State	10
Kansas	9
Kansas State	5
Missouri	8
Nebraska	3
Oklahoma	2
Oklahoma State	7
Texas	1
Texas A&M	6
Texas Tech	4

When a user inputs the college name, the program will output the ranking of that college. If the user inputs an incorrect name, the program should output a message that an incorrect name has been entered.

Write your design in the following space. For your design, write an algorithm (an English language description of the steps required to successfully write the program).

1b. Write a C++ program based upon the design you created in Exercise 1a and name it **BigTwelve.cpp**.

1c. Enter, compile, link, and execute **BigTwelve.cpp**. Copy the output and save it in a block comment at the end of your program. Save **BigTwelve.cpp** in the Chap09 folder of your Student Disk.

The following is a copy of the screen results that might display after running your program:

```
Enter the name of a Big Twelve College: Nebraska
Nebraska's ranking is 3

Enter the name of a Big Twelve College: Texas A&M
Texas A&M's ranking is 6

Enter the name of a Big Twelve College: Baylor Tech
You did not correctly enter the name of a Big Twelve College.
```

2a. Design a program for the World Bowling Competition. An input file, **Scores.txt**, contains the name of each player, the name of the player's team, and each player's individual score. There will only be two two teams (Blue and White). Read the data from the input file into three parallel arrays. The program must accumulate the total score for each team and then output the name of the winning team and the players' names and scores of the winning team. Assume there is no chance of a tie. Use functions to: 1) read in the data from the input file into parallel arrays, 2) determine the winning team, and 3) display the winning team players' names and scores.

Write your design in the following space. For your design, write an algorithm (an English language description of the steps required to successfully write the program).

2b. Write a C++ program based upon the design you created in Exercise 2a and name it **BowlingScores.cpp**.

Create an input file named **Scores.txt** with the following data:

```
Fred  Blue  20
Harry  Blue  35
Tony  White  43
Hilda  Blue  32
Paul  White  34
Tom  White  20
```

2c. Enter, compile, link, and execute **BowlingScores.cpp**. Copy the output and save it in a block comment at the end of your program. Save **BowlingScores.cpp** and **Scores.txt** in the Chap09 folder of your Student Disk.

Your output should look like this:

```
Winning Team: White
Player Score
Tony   43
Paul   34
Tom    20
```

Lab 9.7 Manipulating Data in a Two-Dimensional Array

Sometimes data is provided in a table form called a two-dimensional array, a collection of a fixed number of components arranged in rows and columns, in which all components are of the same type. To access the components of a two-dimensional array, you need a pair of indices—one for the row position and one for the column position. However, two-dimensional arrays are stored in row order in memory. The syntax for declaring a two-dimensional array is:

```
dataType arrayName[intExp1][intExp2];
```

The expression `intExp1` specifies the number of rows, and the expression `intExp2` specifies the number of columns.

You can initialize two-dimensional arrays at declaration. Use braces for the initialization values. You can use additional braces separated by commas to subdivide each row for initialization. To initialize a two-dimensional array when it is declared:

1. The elements of each row are enclosed within braces and separated by commas.
2. All rows are enclosed within braces.
3. For number arrays, if all components of a row are not specified, the unspecified components are initialized to 0.

Two-dimensional arrays are also passed by reference. The name of the array by itself is the base address of the first component. The syntax to call a function with a two-dimensional array argument is:

```
funcTwoArrayAsParam(list);
```

The syntax for the function head is:

```
void funcTwoArrayAsParam(dataType list[][NUMBER_OF_COLUMNS])
{
      .
      .
      .
}
```

The number of rows is required because arrays are stored in row order form and the location where one row ends and the next row begins is computed.

You also can use enumeration types to enhance readability. However, be sure to use the default starting value of zero (0) for the enumerated value.

Objectives

In this lab, you become acquainted with the two-dimensional array, including processing by row and column, initializing at declaration, printing, inputting, summing by column, and finding the largest element in a column.

After completing this lab, you will be able to:

- Search the first column of a two-dimensional array for a particular value.
- Use the second column of a two-dimensional array to hold data that is related to the first column.
- Initialize a two-dimensional array to zero (0) at declaration.
- Process a two-dimensional array by row.
- Process column elements of a two-dimensional array.
- Print all elements of a two-dimensional array.

- Pass a two-dimensional array to a function.
- Input values into a column of a two-dimensional array.
- Sum the values of a column of a two-dimensional array.
- Find the largest element in a column of a two-dimensional array.

Estimated completion time: **50–60 minutes**

Manipulating Data in a Two-Dimensional Array

In the following exercises, select the correct answer for each question. Then redesign a program to use two-dimensional arrays.

Question	Answer (Enter or circle the correct answer)
1. In a two-dimensional array, the actual parameter and the formal parameter must have the same number of columns.	True False
2. Two-dimensional arrays are stored in column order in memory.	True False

3. Given:

```
int stats[25][3];
```

How many components are in the array stats?

4. Given:

```
int stats[2][3] = {4, 4, 4, 3, 12, 15};
int totalHits = 0;
for (int row = 0; row < 2; row++)
     totalHits += stats[row][0];
```

What is the value of `totalHits`?

5. Given:

```
int stats[2][3] = {4, 4, 4, 3, 12, 15};
int atBats[2] = {0};
for (int row = 0; row < 2; row++)
{
     for (int column = 0; column < 3; column++)
          atBats[row] += stats[row][column];
cout << "Player " << row + 1
       << " was up to bat " << atBats[row]
      << " times.\n";
}
```

What is output?

6a. Redesign your **PlayBall.cpp** program to use a two-dimensional array instead of parallel arrays. Add an additional column that keeps track of the number of times a player was up to bat. When printing the report, add a totals line that totals the number of hits, walks, and outs for the team. Find the player(s) with the greatest number of hits, the player(s) with the greatest number of walks, and the player(s) with the greatest number of outs.

Write your design in the following space. Your design should be a list of C++ comments without any code.

6b. Write a C++ program based on the design you created in Lab 9.7, Exercise 6a and name it **PlayBall2**. Step through the code by hand.

In the following space, show what is displayed on the screen after executing the output message.

6c. Enter, compile, link, and execute **PlayBall2.cpp**. Then copy the output and save it in a block comment at the end of your program. Save **PlayBall2.cpp** in the Chap09 folder of your Student Disk.

The following is a copy of the screen results that might display after running your program, depending on the data entered.

```
This program keeps track of the hits, walks, outs, at bats, and team totals
of a baseball team.

        Player  Hits    Walks   Outs    At Bats

        1       4       4       4       12
        2       3       12      15      30
        3       6       8       10      24
        4       5       5       8       18
        5       2       2       2       6
        6       6       0       0       6
        7       0       0       6       6
        8       6       10      2       18
        9       6       4       2       12
        10      6       6       6       18
        11      14      2       2       18
        12      0       0       0       0
        13      8       1       3       12
        14      2       4       6       12
        15      0       0       0       0
        16      0       0       0       0
        17      4       2       6       12
        18      9       8       1       18
        19      3       2       1       6
        20      0       10      14      24
------------------------------------------
Totals:         84      80      88      252

Player 11 had the most hits
Player 2 had the most walks
Player 2 had the most outs
Player 2 had the most at bats
Press any key to continue
```

Lab 9.8 Using a Multidimensional Array

In C++, there is no limit on the dimension of arrays. An array is a collection of a fixed number of elements arranged in n dimensions (n >=1), called an n-dimensional array. The base address of an array of any dimension is the address of the first array component. The first dimension of an array does not need to be declared as a formal parameter, but you must declare all other dimensions. The syntax to declare an n-dimensional array is:

```
dataType arrayName[intExp1][intExp2] … [intExpn];
```

Objectives

In this lab, you become acquainted with processing three-dimensional arrays. You will initialize the array to zero (0) at declaration, sum components from each dimension, and sum all components in the array. Then you display the sums computed. Additionally, you will find the component of the array with the largest value.

After completing this lab, you will be able to:

- Initialize a three-dimensional array to zero (0) at declaration.
- Process individual components of a three-dimensional array.
- Print all elements of a three-dimensional array.
- Pass a three-dimensional array to a function.
- Sum the values of a three-dimensional array by the first dimension, second dimension, third dimension, and by all components.
- Find the largest element in a three-dimensional array.

Estimated completion time: **60–75 minutes**

Using a Multidimensional Array

In the following exercise, you design and write a program using a three-dimensional array.

1a. *Critical Thinking Exercise*: Design a program that keeps track of ticket sales for an auditorium. A concert will be performed over three days in an auditorium with three levels of seating—floor, balcony, and upper balcony. There are 20 seats for each type of seating. Write a program that initializes all seats to the '*' character. Allow a user to request a seat for a particular seat assignment area on a specific day. Use a three-dimensional array to keep track of the ticket sales. The first dimension indicates the performance day: T for Thursday, F for Friday, and S for Saturday. The second dimension indicates the type of seating: F for floor, B for balcony, and U for upper balcony. The third dimension indicates if a seat is sold, using S for sold.

The floor seats sell for $30, the balcony seats sell for $20, and the upper balcony seats sell for $10 each. The program must allow input of ticket requests until an X is entered to indicate that no more sales will be made. After the close of sales, calculate the amount of ticket sales for each performance for each day. Calculate the number of each type of seat sold for each day. Calculate the sales amount for each performance for each day. Calculate the total number of seats sold for all performances.

Write your design in the following space. Your design should be a list of C++ comments without any code.

1b. Write a C++ program based on the design you created in Exercise 1a and name it **Concert.cpp**. Step through the code by hand.

1c. Enter, compile, link, and execute **Concert.cpp**. Then copy the output and save it in a block comment at the end of your program. Save **Concert.cpp** in the Chap09 folder of your Student Disk.

The following is a copy of the screen results that might display after running your program, depending on the data entered. The input entered by the user is shown in bold.

```
This program keeps track of ticket sales for an auditorium. Tickets are
available for three days--Thursday, Friday, and Saturday--for 20 seats
in each of three levels: the floor, balcony, and upper balcony.

Enter day, (T)hursday, (F)riday, (S)aturday for concert, (X)closed
Enter level, (F)loor, (B)alcony, (U)pper Balcony
TF
Enter day, (T)hursday, (F)riday, (S)aturday for concert, (X)closed
Enter level, (F)loor, (B)alcony, (U)pper Balcony
TF
Enter day, (T)hursday, (F)riday, (S)aturday for concert, (X)closed
Enter level, (F)loor, (B)alcony, (U)pper Balcony
FU
Enter day, (T)hursday, (F)riday, (S)aturday for concert, (X)closed
Enter level, (F)loor, (B)alcony, (U)pper Balcony
FU
Enter day, (T)hursday, (F)riday, (S)aturday for concert, (X)closed
Enter level, (F)loor, (B)alcony, (U)pper Balcony
FU
Enter day, (T)hursday, (F)riday, (S)aturday for concert, (X)closed
Enter level, (F)loor, (B)alcony, (U)pper Balcony
SB
Enter day, (T)hursday, (F)riday, (S)aturday for concert, (X)closed
Enter level, (F)loor, (B)alcony, (U)pper Balcony
SB
Enter day, (T)hursday, (F)riday, (S)aturday for concert, (X)closed
Enter level, (F)loor, (B)alcony, (U)pper Balcony
SB
Enter day, (T)hursday, (F)riday, (S)aturday for concert, (X)closed
Enter level, (F)loor, (B)alcony, (U)pper Balcony
FB
Enter day, (T)hursday, (F)riday, (S)aturday for concert, (X)closed
Enter level, (F)loor, (B)alcony, (U)pper Balcony
FB
Enter day, (T)hursday, (F)riday, (S)aturday for concert, (X)closed
Enter level, (F)loor, (B)alcony, (U)pper Balcony
TB
Enter day, (T)hursday, (F)riday, (S)aturday for concert, (X)closed
Enter level, (F)loor, (B)alcony, (U)pper Balcony
TB
Enter day, (T)hursday, (F)riday, (S)aturday for concert, (X)closed
Enter level, (F)loor, (B)alcony, (U)pper Balcony
x
Thursday Floor         Tickets sold: 2 $60
         Balcony       Tickets sold: 2 $40
         Upper Balcony Tickets sold: 0 $0
Friday   Floor         Tickets sold: 0 $0
         Balcony       Tickets sold: 2 $40
         Upper Balcony Tickets sold: 3 $30
Saturday Floor         Tickets sold: 0 $0
         Balcony       Tickets sold: 3 $60
         Upper Balcony Tickets sold: 0 $0

Total tickets sold for all concerts: 12 $ 230
```

```
Total Floor         tickets sold for all concerts: 2 $60

Total  Balcony        tickets sold for all concerts: 7 $140

Total  Upper Balcony  tickets sold for all concerts: 3 $30

Total tickets sold for Thursday  concerts: 4 $100
Total tickets sold for Friday    concerts: 5 $70
Total tickets sold for Saturday  concerts: 3 $60
```

10 Applications of Arrays (Searching and Sorting) and the `vector` Type

In this chapter, you will:

- Learn how to implement the sequential search algorithm
- Discover how to sort an array using the bubble sort, selection sort, and insertion sort algorithms
- Learn how to implement the binary search algorithm
- Become familiar with the `vector` type

Chapter 10: Assignment Cover Sheet

Name ______________________________ Date ______________________________

Section ______________________________

Lab Assignments	Assigned	Grade
Lab 10.1 Implementing the Sequential Search Algorithm		
Lab 10.2 Sorting an Array Using Selection Sort		
Lab 10.3 Implementing the Binary Search Algorithm		
Lab 10.4 Implementing the Insertion Sort (Critical Thinking Exercise)		
Lab 10.5 Using the `vector` Data Type		

See your instructor or the introduction to this book for instructions on submitting your assignments.

LAB 10.1 IMPLEMENTING THE SEQUENTIAL SEARCH ALGORITHM

A list is a set of values of the same type. Because all values are of the same type in a list, lists can be stored in arrays. Because lists may be of varying sizes, the size of the array should be declared as the maximum size of the list. You can perform the following basic operations on a list:

- Input a list.
- Output a list.
- Search the list for a given item.
- Sort the list.
- Insert an item in the list.
- Delete an item from the list.

To search a list, you need to know the length of the list and the item for which you are searching. At the conclusion of the search, you need to determine whether the item was found. If the item was found, you need to know where it was found.

Searching each location of a list until an item is found is called a sequential search or a binary search.

Objectives

In this lab, you search a list of a particular size for a value and then indicate whether the item is found. If it is, indicate the location where the item was found.

After completing this lab, you will be able to:

- Search a list of a given size for a particular value.
- Report whether an item is found in the list.
- Report where an item is found in the list.

Estimated completion time: **60–90 minutes**

Implementing the Sequential Search Algorithm

Question	**Answer (Circle the correct answer)**
1. The average number of comparisons in an unordered sequential search is one-half the number of items in the list.	**True** **False**
2. To search a list sequentially, you only need to know the array name and the search item.	**True** **False**
3. Given: `int list[6] = {93, 14, 3, 52, 44, 39};` In a sequential search, how many comparisons are needed to find the number 44?	a. 6 b. 3 c. 5 d. 4

4. Given:

```
int list[6] = {93, 14, 3, 52, 44, 39};
```

In a sequential search, how many comparisons are needed to find that the number 66 is not in the list?

a. 6
b. 3
c. 5
d. 4

5. Given:

```
int list[6] = {3, 14, 39, 44, 52, 93 };
```

In a sequential search, how many comparisons are needed to find the number 44?

a. 6
b. 3
c. 5
d. 4

6. Given:

```
int list[6] = {3, 14, 39, 44, 52, 93 };
```

In a sequential search, how many comparisons are needed to find that the number 66 is not in the list?

a. 6
b. 3
c. 5
d. 4

7. A sequential search requires an ordered list. **True** **False**

8a. Design a program that simulates a radio station's contest that awards a $10,000 prize to the first caller who correctly guesses a number in a list of randomly generated numbers. A caller can make one guess per call. The contest is held until a number has been matched or the user enters a value of –1. The code used to generate a random list between 1 and 500 is in **CreateList.cpp** in the Chap10 folder of your Student Disk. The list generated from running CreateList is **PrizeList.txt** in the Chap10 folder of your Student Disk.

The following list is the file **PrizeList.txt**.

```
42
468
335
1
170
225
479
359
463
465
206
146
282
329
462
492
496
443
328
437
```

Write your design in the following space. Your design should be a list of C++ comments without any code.

8b. Write a C++ program based on the design you created in Exercise 8a. Step through the code by hand.

In the following space, show what is displayed on the screen after executing the output message.

8c. Enter, compile, link, and execute **Prize.cpp**. Then copy the output and save it in a block comment at the end of your program. Save **Prize.cpp** in the Chap10 folder of your Student Disk.

The following is a copy of the screen results that might display after running your program, depending on the data entered. The input entered by the user is in bold.

```
This program simulates a radio station that asks the caller to guess a
number.
The number is compared against a list of 20 numbers between 1 and 500
inclusive.

The contest is held until a number has been matched or a value of
-1 is entered.

A message is displayed containing the winning number, the location
in the list of numbers, the number of calls made, and the amount of
the prize.
```

```
Hello Caller. What number between 1 and 500 are you guessing? 250
250 is not in the list. Call again.

Hello Caller. What number between 1 and 500 are you guessing? 625
Your guess must be between 1 and 500 inclusively.

Hello Caller. What number between 1 and 500 are you guessing? 423
423 is not in the list. Call again.

Hello Caller. What number between 1 and 500 are you guessing? 122
122 is not in the list. Call again.

Hello Caller. What number between 1 and 500 are you guessing? 42
Caller. Your number 42 was found at location 1 of the list.
Counting you, there were 4 callers. Your winnings are $10,000.
```

LAB 10.2 SORTING AN ARRAY USING SELECTION SORT

The selection sort algorithm rearranges a list by selecting an element in the list and moving it to its proper position. For example, first the smallest item in the list is moved to the first location. Starting with the second item in the list, the next smallest item is moved to the second location. You can also sort by placing the largest value in the first position, the second largest value in the second position, and so on.

Once a list has been sorted—also called ordered—the list can be sequentially searched. In a sequential search on an ordered list, once a value in the list is greater than the value being searched for, the search is complete and the item is not found. (In a descending list, once a value in the list is smaller than the value being searched for, the search is complete and the item is not found.)

Objectives

In this lab, you become acquainted with the selection sort. You also search an ordered list of a particular size for a value. Indicate whether the item is found; if it is, indicate the location where the item was found. If the number is not in the search list, discontinue the search once a list value exceeds the search value.

After completing this lab, you will be able to:

- Sort an unordered list using the selection sort.
- Search an ordered list of a given size for a particular value.
- Report whether an item is found in the list.
- If the item is found, report the location in the list where it is found.
- If the item is not found, stop the search once a list value exceeds the search value and then indicate that the value is not found.

Estimated completion time: **60–90 minutes**

Sorting an Array Using Selection Sort

1a. Design for a program that reads the file **PrizeList.txt** in the Chap10 folder of your Student Disk that you used in Lab 10.1. Sort the array using the selection sort algorithm.

1b. Write a C++ program based on the design you created in Exercise 1a. Step through the code by hand.

In the following space, show what is displayed on the screen after executing the output message.

1c. Enter, compile, link, and execute **SortList.cpp**. Then copy the output and save it in a block comment at the end of your program. Save **SortList.cpp** in the Chap10 folder of your Student Disk.

The following is a copy of the screen results that might display after running your program.

```
The program SortList.cpp reads the file PrizeList.txt into an array and
sorts the array using the selection sort algorithm.
The sorted array is written to a file named PrizeList.srt.

Your list has been sorted.
```

The following is the file PrizeList.txt.

```
1
42
146
170
206
225
282
328
329
335
359
437
443
462
463
465
468
479
492
496
```

2a. Redesign your program **Prize.cpp** to sequentially search the ordered list **PrizeList.srt** created in Exercise 1. Because the list is ordered, you can make your search a "smart search" by first checking to see if the value is less than the first element in the list or greater than the first element in the list. If the value falls in the range of the list, then the list should be searched. You may start searching the list at the beginning of the list or at the end of the list. Include an output line that shows how many comparisons it takes to search for each guess.

Write your design in the following space. Your design should be a list of C++ comments without any code.

2b. Write a C++ program based on the design you created in Exercise 2a. Step through the code by hand.

In the following space, show what is displayed on the screen after executing the output message.

2c. Enter, compile, link, and execute **Prize2.cpp**. Then copy the output and save it in a block comment at the end of your program. Save **Prize2.cpp** in the Chap10 folder of your Student Disk.

The following is a copy of the screen results that might display after running your program, depending on the data entered. The input entered by the user is in bold.

```
This program simulates a radio station
that asks the caller to guess a number.
The number is compared against an ordered
list of 20 numbers between 1 and 500 inclusive.
The contest is held until a number has been
matched or a value of -1 is entered.
```

```
A message is displayed containing the winning
number, the location in the list of numbers,
the number of calls made, the number of
comparisons, and the amount of the prize.

Hello Caller. What number between 1 and 500 are you guessing? 500
It took 0 comparisons to check the list.
Your number is not in the list.

Hello Caller. What number between 1 and 500 are you guessing? 25
It took 20 comparisons to check the list.
Your number is not in the list.

Hello Caller. What number between 1 and 500 are you guessing? 1
Caller. Your number 1 was found at location 1 of the list.
Counting you, there were 3 callers.
Your winnings are $10,000.
It took 20 comparisons to check the list.
```

LAB 10.3 IMPLEMENTING THE BINARY SEARCH ALGORITHM

A sequential search on an ordered list usually requires searching about half of the list. For long lists, the binary search is much faster than the sequential search. The first search item is compared with the middle element of the list. Then, the search item is compared either with the middle of the first half of the list or the middle of the second half of the list. This process is repeated until the search item is found or there are no more list items.

Each time the item is searched, the list is cut in half. Because every iteration of the loop makes two item comparisons, the binary search will make at most $2 \star \log_2 n + 2$ item comparisons. In non-mathematical turns, the number of comparisons can be calculated by the size of the list. This example has a list size of 20. The number 2 raised to the power of 4 is 16. The number 2 raised to the power of 5 is 32. The list size of 20 is greater than 2 to the power of 4 and less than 2 to the power of 5. It should take four or five comparisons to search the list because the list is cut in half each time.

Objectives

In this lab, you use a binary search on an ordered list of a given size to find a particular value. Indicate whether the item is found. If it is, indicate the location where the item is found.

After completing this lab, you will be able to:

- Use a binary search on an ordered list of a given size for a particular value.
- Report whether an item is found in the ordered list.
- If the item is found, report the location in the list where it is found.

Estimated completion time: **40–50 minutes**

Implementing the Binary Search Algorithm

Question

Answer (Enter or circle the correct answer)

1. A binary search is usually a faster alternative to search an unordered list.

   True **False**

2. Suppose a list has 32 components. What is the greatest number of comparisons needed in a binary search to determine if a particular value is in the list?

   a. 5
   b. 32
   c. it depends on the location of the value in the list
   d. 31

3. Suppose you have a list:

   ```
   int list[8] = {1, 2, 3, 4, 5, 6, 7, 8};
   ```

   Using a binary search, what is the greatest number of comparisons needed to find the number 5?

   a. 3
   b. 4
   c. 5
   d. 8

4. Suppose you have a list:

   ```
   int list[8] = {1, 2, 3, 4, 5, 6, 7, 8};
   ```

   Using a sequential search, what is the greatest number of comparisons needed to find the number 5?

   a. 3
   b. 4
   c. 5
   d. 8

5. Suppose you have a list:

```
int list[8] = {1, 3, 5, 7, 9, 11, 13, 15};
```

Using a binary search, what is the greatest number of comparisons needed to see if the number 14 is in the list?

6. Suppose you have a list:

```
int list[8] = {1, 3, 5, 7, 9, 11, 13, 15};
```

Using a sequential search, what is the greatest number of comparisons needed to see if the number 14 is in the list?

7. A binary search is always preferable to a sequential search. **True** **False**

8a. Redesign your program Prize2.cpp to use a binary search on the ordered list PrizeList.srt created in Exercise 1.

Write your design in the following space. Your design should be a list of C++ comments without any code.

8b. Write a C++ program based on the design you created in Exercise 8a. Step through the code by hand.

In the following space, show what is displayed on the screen after executing the output message.

8c. Enter, compile, link, and execute **Prize3.cpp**. Then copy the output and save it in a block comment at the end of your program. Save **Prize3.cpp** in the Chap10 folder of your Student Disk.

The following is a copy of the screen results that might display after running your program, depending on the data entered. Compare your output with the output for your program **Prize2.cpp**. The input entered by the user is in bold.

```
This program simulates a radio station
that asks the caller to guess a number.
The number is compared against an ordered
list of 20 numbers between 1 and 500 inclusive.
The contest is held until a number has been
matched or a value of -1 is entered.

A message is displayed containing the winning
number, the location in the list of numbers,
the number of calls made, the number of
comparisons, and the amount of the prize.

Hello Caller. What number between 1 and 500 are you guessing? 500
It took 0 comparisons to check the list.
Your number is not in the list.

Hello Caller. What number between 1 and 500 are you guessing? 25
It took 4 comparisons to check the list.
Your number is not in the list.

Hello Caller. What number between 1 and 500 are you guessing? 1
Caller. Your number 1 was found at location 1 of the list.
Counting you, there were 3 callers.
Your winnings are $10,000.
It took 4 comparisons to check the list.
```

LAB 10.4 IMPLEMENTING THE INSERTION SORT

The insertion sort tries to reduce the number of key comparisons of a sort. The insertion sort algorithm sorts the list by moving each element to its proper place.

An array containing the list is divided into two sublists, upper and lower. Elements in the upper sublist are sorted; elements in the lower sublist are to be moved to the upper sublist into their proper places one at a time. Use an index to point to the first element in the lower sublist; that is, the index of the first element in the unsorted portion of the array. Initially, that index is initialized to 1. The following C++ function implements the insertion algorithm.

```
void insertionSort(int list[], int listLength)
{
     int firstOutOfOrder, location, temp;

     for(firstOutOfOrder =1; firstOutOfOrder < listLength;
 firstOutOfOrder++)
     if(list[firstOutOfOrder] < list[firstOutOfOrder-1])
     {
          temp = list[firstOutOfOrder];
          location = firstOutOfOrder;

          do
          {
               list[location] = list[location - 1];
               location–;
          }
          while(location > 0 && list[location - 1] > temp);
          list[location] = temp;
     }
}
```

Objectives

In this lab, you use the insertion sort.

After completing this lab, you will be able to:

- Sort an unordered string array using the insertion sort.

Estimated completion time: **40–50 minutes**

Implementing the Insertion Sort

1a. *Critical Thinking Exercise*: Design a program that reads a file of names into a one-dimensional string array, sorts the array, and writes the names to an output file.

Write your design in the following space. Your design should be a list of C++ comments without any code.

1b. Write a C++ program based on the design you created in Exercise 1a. Step through the code by hand.

In the following space, show what is displayed on the screen after executing the output message.

1c. Enter, compile, link, and execute **insertSort.cpp** using **cardList.txt** as the input file. Then copy the output and save it in a block comment at the end of your program. Save **insertSort.cpp** in the Chap10 folder of your Student Disk.

The following is a copy of the screen results that might display after running your program, the file **cardList.txt**, and the file **cardList.srt**.

```
The program insertSort.cpp reads the file cardList.txt into an array
and sorts the array using the insertion sort algorithm.
The sorted array is written to a file named cardList.srt.
```

```
Your list is sorted.
cardList.txt
Schmidt, Helga
Alvarez, Ruben
Zowkowski, Aaron
Huang, Sun Lee
Einstein, Beverly

cardList.srt

Alvarez, Ruben
Einstein, Beverly
Huang, Sun Lee
Schmidt, Helga
Zowkowski, Aaron
```

LAB 10.5 USING THE `vector` DATA TYPE

Instead of using an array, one can create and use an object of the vector class, often referred to as a `vector` data type. Its use requires placing the `#include<vector>` compiler directive in a program. Like an array, its elements or values must be of the same data type, are stored contiguously in memory, and can be accessed using the subscript operator ([ ]). Also, vectors can be passed as parameters to functions.

Unlike arrays, vector variables do not have to be declared with a specified number of elements. The number of elements can be dynamically expanded or contracted by adding new or deleting existing values. Another difference is the manner in which vector variables are passed versus arrays. Whereas arrays are passed by reference by default, a vector variable *must* be passed by reference. The data type (`vector`), the data type of the elements, and the reference operator (&) must be included in the parameter list, e.g., `vector<int>&`.

Objectives

In this lab, you become acquainted with the vector class and the functions used to implement and manipulate it.

After completing this lab, you will be able to:

- Create vector variables.
- Use functions of the vector class.
- Sort a vector using a sorting algorithm.
- Pass a vector to a function.

Estimated completion time: **60–90 minutes**

Using the `vector` Type

1. Write the code to declare a `vector` variable named list and insert the following values into the variable: 46 13 9 4.

2. Using the values that you placed in the variable list in Exercise 1, what will the following statements output?

    A. `cout << list.length();`

    B. `cout << list[3];`

    C. `cout << list.front();`

    D. `cout << list.empty();`

    E. `cout << list.back();`

3. Using the variable list that you created in Exercise 1, write the code so that the list variable will contain only the following values: 46 13 9.

4. Declare a **`vector`** variable named numbers and initialize it with the values that are currently in the list variable.

5. Write a code statement that will delete all of the values in the list variable.

6. Write a code statement to declare a **`vector`** variable named collection with ten elements all initialized to 0.

7a. Design a program to use a **vector** variable that adds a name to a list or drops a name from a list. After a name is added or dropped, use a function to sort the list in ascending order (alphabetically) with a sort algorithm of your choice. For simplicity, have the user enter only a one-word last name and indicate whether it is an add or a drop operation. Initialize the list with four last names (use the **push_back** function).

Hints: You will need a selection structure to process the add or drop operation and a loop to search for the name if it is a drop operation. If a drop operation, exchange the element containing the name to be dropped with the name in the last element of the list and the use the **pop_back** function to drop the name, and then sort the list.

Write your design in the following space. For your design, write an algorithm (an English language description of the steps required to successfully write the program).

7b. Write a C++ program based on the design you created in Exercise 7a and name it **ClassRoster.cpp**. In your code, use the following data to initialize the `vector` variable using the `push_back` function.

```
Smith
Jones
Zack
Wilson
```

7c. Enter, compile, link, and execute **ClassRoster.cpp**. Copy the output and save it in a block comment at the end of your program. Save **ClassRoster.cpp** in the Chap10 folder of your Student Disk.

The following is a copy of the screen results that might display after running your program, assuming you initialized the list with the following names:

```
Enter the name of the person to add or drop: Roth
Enter an A for an add or a D for a drop: A
This is the new sorted list
Jones
Roth
Smith
Wilson
Zack

Enter the name of the person to add or drop: Smith
Enter an A for an add or a D for a drop: D
This is the new sorted list
Jones
Wilson
Zack
```

11 Records (`structs`)

In this chapter, you will:

- Learn about records (`structs`)
- Examine various operations on a `struct`
- Explore ways to manipulate data using a `struct`
- Learn about the relationship between a `struct` and functions
- Discover how arrays are used in a `struct`
- Learn how to create a vector of `struct` items

Chapter 11: Assignment Cover Sheet

Name ______________________________ Date ______________________________

Section ______________________________

Lab Assignments	Assigned	Grade
Lab 11.1 Defining `structs` and Declaring `struct` Variables		
Lab 11.2 Manipulating Data Using a `struct` (Critical Thinking Exercise)		
Lab 11.3 Using Arrays in `structs`		
Lab 11.4 Using `structs` in Arrays (Critical Thinking Exercise)		
Group Project: The EmployeePay program written in Lab 11.4 can be used as a Group Project. The group should work together to establish the menu options, and then group members can be assigned different options. Some options can be further subdivided among group members.		
Total Grade		

See your instructor or the introduction to this book for instructions on submitting your assignments.

LAB 11.1 DEFINING structs AND DECLARING struct VARIABLES

Data structures contain multiple data items structured in a defined manner. An array is a data structure containing multiple data items of the same data type stored contiguously in memory. A struct is a data structure designed to hold a record, i.e., a group of related data items. These related data items are called members. Unlike an array, the data items in a struct need not be of the same data type. Arrays and other structs may be members of a struct. A struct must be defined before it can be declared.

Structs are defined with the reserved word struct followed by an open brace ({) and declaration statements with data types for each of the members of the struct. The declaration ends with a closing brace (}) and a semicolon (;). The struct definitions usually are made before the function definitions or prototypes in a program. No memory is reserved when the struct is defined, only when struct variables are declared.

Struct variables are commonly declared along with the other variables in the main function. While it is permissible to declare a variable of the struct type within the struct definition, this can be problematic when a struct is defined outside of the main function before the function definitions or prototypes. A variable declaration here would make the variable global, which is not considered good programming practice.

The syntax for defining a struct is as follows:

```
struct structName
{
    datatype identifier1;
    datatype identifier2;
    .
    .
    datatype identifiern;
};
```

and the syntax for declaring a struct variable is:

```
structName variableName;
```

The syntax for including a variable declaration along with the struct definition is:

```
struct structName
{
    datatype identifier1;
    .
    .
    .
    datatype identifiern;
} variableName;
```

Objectives

Defining structs and declaring struct variables.

After completing this lab, you will be able to:

- Write struct definitions.
- Declare struct variables.
- Know the differences among struct definitions, declarations, and members.

Estimated completion time: **20–30 minutes**

Defining srtucts and Declaring struct Variables

Questions

Choose whether the following definitions are valid or invalid and specify the error if invalid.

1. struct address
```
{
   string number;
   string street;
   string city;
   string state;
   string zip;
};
```

2. struct square
```
{
   double dimension;
   double area;
}
```

3. struct cube
```
{
   square object;
   double volume;
};
```

4. struct
```
{
   int month;
   int date;
   int year;
} birthDate;
```

5. struct family
```
{
   string father;
   string mother;
   string sibling[5];
};
```

6. `struct` basketballTeam

```
{
   string leftForward;
   string rightForward;
   string center;
   string leftGuard;
   string rightGuard;
   int gamesPlayed;
}Celtics;
```

For questions 7 through 10, choose whether the following variable declarations are valid or invalid and, if invalid, specify the error. Assume the above `struct` definitions are all valid.

7. `struct basketballTeam;`
8. `family TimJohnson;`
9. `address local, vacation, temporary, permanent;`
10. `birthDate JimSmith;`

11. Write the definition for a `struct` named box with members named length, width, height, weight, thickness, color, and constructionMaterial. Choose an appropriate data type for the members.

12. Declare three variables of the `struct` basketballTeam.

LAB 11.2 MANIPULATING DATA USING A `struct`

To access a `struct` member, you use the `struct` variable name together with the member name; these names are separated by a dot called the dot operator, member access operator, or member selection operator. For example, in `familyCar.type`, the `struct` variable name is `familyCar`, and `type` is the member name.

Unlike arrays, you can assign the value of one `struct` variable to another `struct` variable. One advantage of grouping components that are related, but of different types, is that a single variable can pass all components as parameters to a function. When using `struct`s, parameters can be passed either by value or by reference. The proper syntax for the prototype, call, and function heading for a function, `func1` with the reference parameter `familyCar` of the `struct` type `cars`, is:

```
Prototype
void func1(cars&);
Call
func1(familyCar);
Function heading
void func1(cars& familyCar)
```

However, like arrays, you cannot use relational operators or aggregate input/output operations on `struct` variables. This must be done member by member, also called member-wise.

Objectives

In this lab, you become acquainted with manipulating data using a `struct`.

After completing this lab, you will be able to:

- Access `struct` members.
- Pass `struct`s to functions.
- Use `struct`s in file processing.

Estimated completion time: **90–100 minutes**

Manipulating Data Using a `struct`

Question	**Answer (Circle the correct answer)**	
1. The order in which `struct` members are defined does not affect the order in which they are accessed.	**True**	**False**
2. A `struct` is accessed by the `struct` variable name, the name of the `struct`, and the `struct` member name.	**True**	**False**

3. Given:

```
struct animal
{
    bool mammalian;
    string habitat;
    int longevity;
};
animal cat;
```

Which of the following correctly initializes cat?

a.
```
mammalian = true;
habitat = "house";
longevity = 12;
```

b.
```
cat.mammalian = true;
cat.habitat = "house"
cat.longevity = 12;
```

c.
```
animal.cat.mammalian = true;
animal.cat.habitat = "house";
animal.cat.longevity = 12;
```

d. all of the above may be used

4. Use the `struct animal` previously defined and the statements:

```
animal cat;
animal dog;
```

Which of the following statements are valid in C++?

a. `cat = dog;`

b.
```
cat.mammalian = dog.mammalian;
cat.habitat = dog.habitat;
cat.longevity = dog.longevity;
```

c. both a and b

Critical Thinking

5a. *Critical Thinking Exercise*: Design a program for a car lot. The program will prompt the user for the specifications of a car and check your inventory to see if the car is on the car lot. The inventory is found in the file **CarLot.txt** in the Chap11 folder of your Student Disk. Define a struct named Cars with the following data members: type, seatingCapacity, price, mpg, and color. You will read in the inventory using the struct Cars. You will read data from CarLot.txt into a `struct` variable and the user's specifications into a `struct`. Because you do not want to lose the customer, ask the customer if he wants a list of all vehicles that match some specifications or only the exact car for which he is searching. *Hint*: Because you are only reading a record at a time and you loop until the end of file flag, if you need to go through the file again, you must clear all file flags using the `clear` function. The following specifications apply to the cars in the lot.

- Valid car types include (C)oupe, (M)inivan, or (S)UV.
- The coupe gets 25 mpg at a base cost of $15,000 and seats 4.
- The minivan gets 20 mpg at a base cost of $18,000 and seats 7.
- The SUV gets 18 mpg at a base cost of $22,000 and seats 5.

Write your design in the following space. Your design should be a list of C++ comments without any code.

5b. Write a C++ program based on the design you created in Exercise 5a. Step through the code by hand.

In the following space, show what is displayed on the screen after executing the output message.

5c. Enter, compile, link, and execute **CarSales.cpp**. Then copy the output and save it in a block comment at the end of your program. Save **CarSales.cpp** in the Chap11 folder of your Student Disk.

The following is a copy of the screen results that might display after running your program, depending on the data entered. The input entered by the user is shown in bold.

```
This program prompts the user for specifications of a car.
These are then checked against a list of cars found in file CarLot.txt.
The user specifies if an exact match is required or if a list of cars
that meet some specifications is acceptable.
Enter type of car:(C)oupe, (M)inivan, or (S)UV: c
Enter the seating capacity that you want: 5
Warning: Coupes only seat 4 passengers.
Please make another selection.

Enter type of car:(C)oupe, (M)inivan, or (S)UV: s
Enter the seating capacity that you want: 5
An SUV gets 18 mpg and has a base price of $22,000.
Do you want to change your selection? (y)es/(n)o: y

Enter type of car:(C)oupe, (M)inivan, or (S)UV: m
Enter the seating capacity that you want: 7
A minivan gets 20 mpg and has a base price of $18,000.
Do you want to change your selection? (y)es/(n)o: n
Enter the color of your choice: gold
Are you only interested in an exact match? (y)es/(n)o y

I'm sorry, we do not have the exact car you want.
Do you want to try another selection? (y)es/(n)o y

Enter type of car:(C)oupe, (M)inivan, or (S)UV: m
Enter the seating capacity that you want: 7
A minivan gets 20 mpg and has a base price of $18,000.
Do you want to change your selection? (y)es/(n)o: n
Enter the color of your choice: silver
Are you only interested in an exact match? (y)es/(n)o y

Congratulations. We have the car you want in stock.


This program prompts the user for specifications of a car.
These are then checked against a list of cars found in file CarLot.txt.
The user specifies if an exact match is required or if a list of cars
that meet some specifications is acceptable.

Enter type of car:(C)oupe, (M)inivan, or (S)UV: s
Enter the seating capacity that you want: 5
An SUV gets 18 mpg and has a base price of $22,000.
Do you want to change your selection? (y)es/(n)o: n
Enter the color of your choice: any
Are you only interested in an exact match? (y)es/(n)o n

We have the following cars that you might want to consider.
A blue SUV.
A silver SUV.
A green SUV.
A black SUV.
```

LAB 11.3 USING ARRAYS IN structs

Any defined data type can be a member of a `struct`. Therefore, a defined struct data type can be contained within another `struct`. Additionally, you can use array as a member of a `struct`. The syntax for a `struct` with an array and a `struct` variable declaration is as follows:

```
struct structType
{
      dataType structMember[arraySize];
      dataType anotherMember;
};
structType var1;
```

The syntax to access a component in the array is as follows:

```
var1.structMember[location]
```

Objectives

In this lab, you define and use `struct`s containing data members that are `struct`s and arrays of `struct`s.

After completing this lab, you will be able to:

- Design and implement in C++ a program using `struct`s containing data members that are `struct`s.
- Design and implement in C++ a `struct` containing array elements.

Estimated completion time: **90–120 minutes**

Using Arrays in structs

Answer (Circle the correct answer)

1. Given the following structures and variables:

```
struct date
{
   int month;
   int day;
   int year;
};
struct birthStatistics
{
   date birthday;
   string citizenship;
   };
   birthStatistics student;
```

Which of the following statements are valid in C++?

a. `student.birthday.month = 12;`
`student.birthday.day = 14;`
`student.birthday.year = 1984;`
`student.citizenship = "US";`

b. `student.birthday = {12, 14, 1984);`
`student.citizenship = "US";`

c. `student.month = 12;`
`student.day = 14;`
`student.year = 1984;`
`student.citizenship = "US";`

d. None. You cannot use a `struct` as a data type of another `struct`.

2. Using the structures and variables defined above, what is the data type of `student.birthday`?

a. `int`

b. `date`

c. None. You cannot use a `struct` as a data type of another `struct`.

3a. Your instructor wants to create a **struct** to keep track of student grades. The information the instructor needs includes the student's first name, last name, a six-digit ID number, ten programming assignment grades, three exam grades, and a final exam grade. Define a **struct** named **grades** that will contain all of these members.

3b. Declare a **struct** variable named **student** of the data type **grades**.

4a. Design a program that prepares a grade book for an instructor. Use **struct grades** and the variable **students** of data type **grades** declared in Exercise 3. Input the student information (first name, last name, six-digit ID number, ten programs, three exam grades, and final exam grade) from the file **GradeBook.txt**. Calculate the grade as follows: programs 30% total, exams 15% each, and final exam 25%. Students with 90 and above averages earn an A, 80 to 89 earn a B, 70 to 79 earn a C, 60 to 69 earn a D, and all grades below 60 earn an F. Display each student's name and final grade.

Write your design in the following space. Your design should be a list of C++ comments without any code.

4b. Write a C++ program based on the design you created in Exercise 4a. Step through the code by hand. The following is a copy of the file **GradeBook.txt** found in the Chap11 folder of your Student Disk.

```
George Smith 589308    100 90 80 95 85 99 98 97 89 100     90 95 85     85
Elaine Sanders 455436    85 90 80 95 89 99 100 98 97 100     96 98 84     90
Jack Cunningham 235412    72 78 97 84 83 68 85 84 83 90     70 75 80     75
Susie Brown 902568    68 85 84 83 90 80 95 85 99 98     75 92 85     87
Marvella Garcia 345432    92 78 97 98 97 89 80 95 85 99     98 89 88     95
Tony Peterson 256436    85 84 83 90 72 78 97 98 97 99     88 87 88     88
John Jones 165435    75 75 80 80 90 90 75 70 87 84     78 82 84     75
Mary Evans 879778    60 89 86 65 89 88 77 60 87 65     65 69 66     60
Nancy Drew 234234    80 75 50 60 79 89 50 45 70 50     60 58 65     45
Lola Zapeta 458741    89 98 79 97 90 96 94 100 99 98     83 78 89     88
```

In the following space, show what is displayed on the screen after executing the output message.

4c. Enter, compile, link, and execute **CalcGrades.cpp**. Then copy the output and save it in a block comment at the end of your program. Save **CalcGrades.cpp** in the Chap11 folder of your Student Disk.

The following is a copy of the screen results that might display after running your program, depending on the data entered.

```
This program reads a data file of student grades, calculates the final
grade, and displays the student's name and final grade.

        Final Grades
George Smith              B
Elaine Sanders            A
Jack Cunningham           C
Susie Brown               B
Marvella Garcia           A
Tony Peterson             B
John Jones                C
Mary Evans                D
Nancy Drew                F
Lola Zapeta               B
```

Lab 11.4 Using structs in vectors

The struct and array data structures can be combined to organize information. Basically, when you need multiple struct variables, you can use a struct variable as an array. For example, in the Sales Data Analysis Programming Example provided in the book, you practice creating an array whose elements are of the type struct salesPersonRec.

Another useful alternative is to use a struct variable as an element of a vector. The syntax for creating a vector of structs is as follows:

```
struct structType
{
       dataType aMember;
       dataType structMember;
       dataType enumType;
};

vector<structType> vectorName;
```

You can also declare the vector variable using any of the following formats:

```
vector<structType> vectorName(otherVectorList);
vector<structType> vectorName(size);
vector<structType> vectorName(n, elem);
```

Finally, the syntax to access the aMember component in the vector is as follows:

```
vectorName.at(loc).aMember //or
vectorName[loc].aMember
```

Objectives

In this lab, you create a program using a vector of structs, a struct that contains another struct as a data member, and a struct that contains an enumeration type as a data member.

After completing this lab, you will be able to:

- Design and implement in C++ a program using a struct that contains another struct as a data member.
- Design and implement in C++ a vector of structs.
- Design and implement in C++ a program using a struct that contains an enumeration type as a data member.

Estimated completion time: **50–60 minutes**

structs in vectors

1a. You would like to maintain a list with the birthdays of your friends. You decide to create a C++ program for this purpose. Because you need to store the first and last names of each friend and the month, day, and year of their birth dates, defining a struct with the appropriate members makes sense.

Define a `struct` named `date` that has `year`, `month`, and `day` as members. The `year` and `day` members should be of type `int`. The `month` member should be of the `enum monthType` you defined in Lab 8.1 (alternatively, you could create an appropriate enumerator for this purpose).

1b. Design a `struct` named `birthdateRecord` that has `firstName`, `lastName`, and `birthDate` as members.

1c. Declare a `vector` named `friendList` that holds data of type `birthdateRecord`.

2a. *Critical Thinking Exercise*: Design a program that allows you to maintain a list (`vector`) with the birth dates of your friends. The program displays a menu for the user to select a task. The choices on the menu are the following:

1. Show an alphabetized listing of your friends' birth dates
2. Show the birth date of one of your friends
3. Add a new friend to the list
4. End the program

Option 1 requires the `struct vector` to be sorted alphabetically (you may use the function you created in Lab 8.1). Option 2 requires the `struct vector` to be searched for a name match (first and last). Option 3 requires the user to enter the information of a new friend. Option 9 ends the program.

Write your design in the following space. Your design should be a list of C++ comments without any code.

2b. Write a C++ program based on the design you created in Exercise 2a. Step through the code by hand. Use your program (Option 3) to add the following information to the list:

```
Casey Smith 09/13/1977
John Miller 11/19/1977
Rose Peterson 10/05/1975
```

Once the information has been stored in the `vector`, display its contents on the screen (Option 1). In the following space, show what is displayed on the screen after executing the program.

2c. Enter, compile, link, and execute **BirthDates.cpp**. Then copy the output and save it in a block comment at the end of your program. Save **BirthDates.cpp** in the Chap11 folder of your Student Disk.

The following is a copy of the screen results that might display after running your program. The input entered by the user is shown in bold.

```
Please enter
    <1> to display an alphabetized listing of your friends and their
        birthdates
    <2> to search for a person
    <3> to add a friend to your list
 or <9> to exit this program: 3

Please enter the name of your friend (e.g., casey smith): casey smith
Enter his/her birthdate in the format mm/dd/yyyy (e.g., 09/13/1977):
09/13/1977
This person was successfully added to your list.
Please enter
    <1> to display an alphabetized listing of your friends and their
        birthdates
    <2> to search for a person
    <3> to add a friend to your list
 or <9> to exit this program: 3

Please enter the name of your friend (e.g., casey smith): john miller
Enter his/her birthdate in the format mm/dd/yyyy (e.g., 09/13/1977):
11/19/1977
This person was successfully added to your list.
Please enter
    <1> to display an alphabetized listing of your friends and their
        birthdates
    <2> to search for a person
    <3> to add a friend to your list
 or <9> to exit this program: 3
```

```
Please enter the name of your friend (e.g., casey smith): rose peterson
Enter his/her birthdate in the format mm/dd/yyyy (e.g., 09/13/1977):
10/05/1975
This person was successfully added to your list.
Please enter
    <1> to display an alphabetized listing of your friends and their
        birthdates
    <2> to search for a person
    <3> to add a friend to your list
 or <9> to exit this program: 1

Your list:
miller, john November 19, 1977
peterson, rose October 5, 1975
smith, casey September 13, 1977

Please enter
    <1> to display an alphabetized listing of your friends and their
        birthdates
    <2> to search for a person
    <3> to add a friend to your list
 or <9> to exit this program: 9
Thank you!
```

12 Classes and Data Abstraction

In this chapter, you will:

- Learn about classes
- Learn about `private`, `protected`, and `public` members of a class
- Explore how classes are implemented
- Examine constructors and destructors
- Learn about the abstract data type (ADT)
- Explore how classes are used to implement ADTs
- Learn about information hiding
- Explore how information hiding is implemented in C++
- Learn about the `static` members of a class

CHAPTER 12: ASSIGNMENT COVER SHEET

Name ______________________ Date ______________________

Section ______________________

Lab Assignments	Assigned	Grade
Lab 12.1 Describing Classes Using the Unified Modeling Language (UML) Notation and Declaring Objects		
Lab 12.2 Manipulating and Accessing Data within the Class		
Lab 12.3 Designing Driver Programs (Critical Thinking Exercise)		
Lab 12.4 Invoking Default Constructors, Constructors with Parameters, and Constructors with Default Parameters		
Lab 12.5 Invoking Destructors		
Lab 12.6 Using the Abstract Data Type (ADT) and Information Hiding (Critical Thinking Exercise)		
Lab 12.7 Using `static` Members of a Class		
Group Projects: Labs 12.1, 12.2, 12.3, and Lab 12.6, Exercises 1 and 2 can be used together as a Group Project. Labs 12.4, 12.5, and Lab 12.6, Exercise 3 can be used together as a Group Project.		
Total Grade		

See your instructor or the introduction to this book for instructions on submitting your assignments.

LAB 12.1 DESCRIBING CLASSES USING THE UNIFIED MODELING LANGUAGE (UML) NOTATION AND DECLARING OBJECTS

Recall that two structured data types are arrays, which have elements of the same type, and structures, which have elements of differing types. Another structured data type is a class, which is specifically designed to combine data and functions in a single unit. A class is a collection of a fixed number of components. The components of a class are called the members of the class.

The general syntax for defining a class is:

```
class classIdentifier
{
        classMembersList
};
```

The classMembersList consists of variable declarations and/or functions.

- If a member of a class is a variable, you define it just like any other variable, but you cannot initialize it at definition.
- If a member of a class is a function, you typically use the function prototype to define that member.
- Member functions can directly access any data member of the class without passing that data member as an argument.

No memory is allocated in a class definition. Instead, memory is allocated when the class is instantiated (an object is created). Additionally, the semicolon (;) is part of the syntax. The members of a class are classified into three categories: private, public, and protected. By default, all members of a class are private. Private members cannot be accessed outside of the class. A public member is accessible outside of the class. A class and its members can be described graphically using Unified Modeling Language (UML) notation. A UML diagram contains three boxes stacked vertically. The top box contains the name of the class; the middle box contains the data members and their data types; and the bottom box contains the member method names, parameter list, and return types. The + (plus) sign indicates that it is a public member; the – (minus) sign indicates that it is a private member. The # (pound) symbol indicates that it is a protected member.

Objectives

In this lab, you define a class and declare objects.

After completing this lab, you will be able to:

- Use UML notation.
- Create an instantiation of the class (declare objects).
- Recognize the difference among class definitions, objects, and members of the class.

Estimated completion time: **50–60 minutes**

Describing Classes Using the Unified Modeling Language (UML) Notation and Declaring Objects

Question	Answer (Circle the correct answer)	
1. A class is __________________.	a. a structured data type b. a homogenous data type c. a simple data type	
2. All data members of a class must be of the same data type.	**True**	**False**
3. You define an object of a class in the same way that you define a variable of a data type.	**True**	**False**
4. It is optional to initialize an object at declaration.	**True**	**False**
5. A data member is another term for an object.	**True**	**False**

6a. There is no standard library for a date class. Create a UML diagram for a class named `Date` that will contain data members and member functions to allow a user to enter a date, validate the date entered, and display the date entered. Your class should meet the criteria in the following list:

- The data members named `month`, `day`, and `year` should be private members so that they cannot be directly manipulated outside of the class.
- The Boolean data member named `good` should be a public member so that it can be accessed outside of the class.
- The public `void` member method `getData` has no parameters.
- The private `void` member method `checkFormat` has an integer reference variable parameter.
- The private `void` member method `validate` has no parameters.
- The public `void` member method `display` has no parameters.

Write the class definition in the space provided.

6b. Implement your diagram in C++ and save your code in a file named **testDate.cpp** in the Chap12 folder of your Student Disk.

6c. Define an object named `today` of the class `Date`. Write the object definition in the space provided.

7a. Create a UML diagram for a `struct` (if you skipped Chapter 11, define a class instead) named `Money` that will contain data members. Your `struct` (or class) should contain a `char` data member named `type` and a `double` data member named `amount` as public members.

7b. Implement your diagram in C++ and save your code in a file named **Money.h** in the Chap12 folder of your Student Disk.

8a. Create a UML diagram for a class named `Exchange` that will contain data members and member functions to allow a user to input, validate, and convert pesos, Euro dollars, and Swiss francs to U. S. dollars. Your class should meet the criteria in the following list:

- The data members `US` and those the user enters will be of the type `Money` that you defined in Exercise 7 and should be private members. (In Chapter 11, you learned that a `struct` is a user-defined data type and can be used in the data type of an array, a data member of a `struct`, and as a variable of that `struct` type. A `struct` and a class can also be a data type of a member of a class.)
- The Boolean function `getData` and the `void` functions `convert` and `displayExchange` have no formal parameters and should be public members.
- The `void` function `outputType` has no formal parameters and is a private member.

8b. Implement your diagram in C++ and save your code in a file named **testExchange.cpp** in the Chap12 folder of your Student Disk. Open your **Money.h** file and copy and paste your `struct` (or class) definition in your **testExchange.cpp** program above your `Exchange` class definition.

8c. Define an object named `amount` of the class `Exchange`. Write the object definition in the space provided.

LAB 12.2 MANIPULATING AND ACCESSING DATA WITHIN THE CLASS

To access another class member from a member function of the class, you use the class variable name or function name. It is not necessary to pass a class data member between the class member functions. However, if it is passed, the formal parameter is a local variable to that member function. In this case, if the change is to be reflected in the class, then the formal parameter must be passed by reference.

To access a public class member outside of the class, you use the class variable name together with the member name. The syntax is to separate the name of the class and the class variable name by a dot, called the dot operator or member access operator (.). The general syntax for an object to access a member of a class is:

```
classObjectName.memberName
```

There are two built-in operations that are valid for class objects, the member access (.) operator and the assignment (=) operator. If you have variables of the same type, you can assign one variable to the other and each component of the variable will be assigned member-wise. A class variable (object), like other variables, can be automatic or static and has the same scope as other variables. When you access a class member outside of the class, you use the member access operator (.).

The relationship between functions and classes is as follows:

- Class objects can be passed as parameters to functions and returned as function values.
- As parameters to functions, classes can be passed either by value or by reference.
- If a class object is passed by value, the contents of the data members of the actual parameter are copied into the corresponding data members of the formal parameter.

Using value parameters creates a large amount of overhead when passing class variables. However, passing values by reference may cause unwanted side effects. In C++, you can pass a variable by reference and still prevent the function from changing its value by using the keyword `const` in the formal parameter declaration. The general syntax to declare a `const` argument is:

```
returnType functionName(const class& classObject)
{
    class variableName;
    .
    .
    .
}
```

When you include only the function prototype in the class definition, you must later define the function. When the function is defined, you must reference the identifiers to the class by using the scope resolution operator :: (double colon). The general syntax for the function definition is:

```
returnType className::functionName(dataType parameter1, …, dataType
     parametern)
{
    statement;
    .
    .
    .
}
```

Member functions of a class are categorized as member functions that modify the data members, called mutator functions, and member functions that only access the data members, called accessor functions. Mutator functions typically include the word **const** at the end of the headings. The general syntax for an accessor function prototype is:

```
dataType functionName(parameter list) const;
```

Objectives

In this lab, you become acquainted with accessing data members and member functions within a class.

After completing this lab, you will be able to:

- Access class members from member functions of the class.

Estimated completion time: **60–90 minutes**

Manipulating and Accessing Data within the Class

1a. Using the `Date` class design you created in Lab 12.1, Exercise 6a, design the member functions so they meet the following criteria:

- The member function `getData` should call the member function `checkFormat` to read in the integer data member month. If `month` is formatted correctly, `getData` calls `checkFormat` again to read in the integer data member `day`. If `day` is formatted correctly, `getData` calls `checkFormat` again to read in the integer data member `year`. If `year` has been entered in the proper format, `checkData` calls the member function `validate`.
- The member function named `checkFormat` should check to see if the value to be read in is a number between 0 and 9 inclusively or is a blank. If it is a number, then the value is read in and the data member `good` is set to true. If it is not a number, then a message "You used the wrong format to enter the date." is displayed and the data member `good` is set to false.
- The member function `validate` should check that the month is within the limits of 1 to 12 and that the days are within the limits associated with each month. The year should be a positive integer value. If a valid date is entered, the data member `good` should be set to true; if invalid, `good` should be set to false, and a message that an invalid date has been entered should be displayed.
- The member function `displayDate` should display the date entered.

1b. Implement in C++ the design of your member functions. Open your **testDate.cpp** file and add the new code below your `Date` class definition. Save your **testDate.cpp** with the changes in the Chap12 folder of your Student Disk. Compile. Because there is no `main` function defined, you will not be able to link or execute this code. Print the source code.

2a. Using the `Exchange` class created in Lab 12.1, Exercise 8a, design the member functions so that they meet the following criteria:

- The member function named `getData` should prompt the user for the type of currency: (p) for Mexican pesos, (d) for U. S. dollars, (f) for Swiss francs, (e) for Euro dollars, and (q) for quit, and then input the character into the data member `entered.type`. If a 'q' is entered, the value false is returned. If a valid character is entered, the program prompts the user for an amount and inputs that amount into the data member `entered.amount`. Use a loop in the function until the user enters q to quit or enters a valid type.

- The member function named `displayExchange` displays the type of currency and the beginning amount and the amount in U. S. dollars. The amounts are displayed in six decimal places. The member function `outputType` is called from `displayExchange`.
- The member function named `outputType` displays a description for the character type of currency; for example, 'd' would display "U. S. dollars".
- The member function named `convert` assigns the exchange amount of the value entered in U. S. dollars to `US.amount` and assigns the character type of `entered.type` to `US.type`. The conversions are:

  1 U. S. dollar = 0.9553 Euro dollars = 1.4054 Swiss francs = 9.815 Mexican pesos

2b. Implement in C++ the design of your member functions. Open your **testExchange.cpp** file and add the new code below your `Exchange` class definition. Save your **testExchange.cpp** with the changes in the Chap12 folder of your Student Disk. Compile. Because there is no `main` function defined, you will not be able to link or execute this code. Print the source code.

LAB 12.3 DESIGNING DRIVER PROGRAMS

All C++ programs must have a `main` function. The class does not have a `main` function. To test a class, you must write a driver program (one that has a `main` function) that contains the class definition and instantiates an object of the class.

Objectives

In this lab, you become acquainted with using a class in a driver program.

After completing this lab, you will be able to:

- Write a driver program that contains a class definition.
- Instantiate an object of a class.
- Access public class members through objects of the class.

Estimated completion time: **40–50 minutes**

Designing Driver Programs

1a. *Critical Thinking Exercise*: Create the design for a driver program that implements the `Date` class you implemented in **testDate.cpp**. Your `main` function should call a function `instruct` that describes the purpose and use of the program; instantiate the `today` object that you created in Lab 12.1, Exercise 6c; prompt the user with the message "Please enter today's date, month, day, and year separated by spaces:"; and call the class function `getData` using the `today` object.

Write your design in the following space. Your design should be a list of C++ comments without any code.

1b. Write a C++ program based on the design you created in Exercise 1a. Step through the code by hand.

In the following space, show what is displayed on the screen after executing the output message.

1c. Enter, compile, link, and execute **testDate.cpp**. Then copy the output and save it in a block comment at the end of your program. Save **testDate.cpp** in the Chap12 folder of your Student Disk.

The following is a copy of the screen results that might display after running your program, depending on the data entered. The input entered by the user is shown in bold.

```
This program prompts the user to enter a date and validates the date
entered.

Please enter today's date (month, day, and year separated by spaces):
12/23/2006
```

With that input, the output displayed should resemble:

```
You used the wrong format to enter the date.
```

Run the program again with the following input:

```
12 23 2006
```

With that input, the output displayed should resemble:

```
You entered: 12-23-2006
```

2a. Design a driver program that implements the Exchange class you used in **testExchange.cpp**. Your main function should call the function instruct to show the purpose and use of the program, prompt the user to enter a currency type and amount, and loop until the user enters q. Your loop control should be the return value from the class function getData using the amount object that you created in Lab 12.1, Exercise 8c. The loop should continue until the returned value is false. Within the loop, the data member functions convert and displayExchange should be called.

Write your design in the following space. Your design should be a list of C++ comments without any code.

2b. Write a C++ program based on the design you created in Exercise 2a. Step through the code by hand.

In the following space, show what is displayed on the screen after executing the output message.

2c. Enter, compile, link, and execute **testExchange.cpp**. Then copy the output and save it in a block comment at the end of your program. Save **testExchange.cpp** in the Chap12 folder of your Student Disk.

The following is a copy of the screen results that might display after running your program, depending on the data entered. The input entered by the user is shown in bold.

```
This program prompts the user to enter
a character to designate the type of
currency to be exchanged and the amount of money
to be exchanged.

Enter a character for currency type and an amount.
(P)esos, Swiss (f)rancs, (E)uro dollars or (q)uit: x 123.543
You entered an invalid type, please re-enter.

p 123.543
You entered 123.54 in Pesos, which is $12.59 in U.S. dollars.

Enter a character for currency type and an amount.
(P)esos, Swiss (f)francs, (E)uro dollars or (q)uit: f 500
You entered 500.00 in Swiss francs, which is $355.77 in U.S. dollars.

Enter a character for currency type and an amount.
(P)esos, Swiss (f)francs, (E)uro dollars or (q)uit: e 987
You entered 987.00 in Euro dollars, which is $1033.18 in U.S. dollars.

Enter a character for currency type and an amount.
(P)esos, Swiss (f)francs, (E)uro dollars or (q)uit: q
```

LAB 12.4 INVOKING DEFAULT CONSTRUCTORS, CONSTRUCTORS WITH PARAMETERS, AND CONSTRUCTORS WITH DEFAULT PARAMETERS

C++ does not automatically initialize variables. To guarantee that the data members of a class are initialized, you use constructors. The constructor without parameters is called the default constructor.

Constructor functions have the same names as the class, have no type, and are automatically executed when a class object enters its scope. (They cannot be called directly.) When there are multiple constructors, the names are the same, but the parameter lists must differ. All constructors must be public data members.

If there is more than one constructor, the constructor called when an object is instantiated is decided by the formal parameter list and arguments. If the type of argument does not match the formal parameters of any constructor, C++ does a type conversion and looks for the best match. Any ambiguity will result in a compile-time error.

A constructor with all default parameters is the default constructor. You should not have multiple default constructors. However, a constructor with no parameters will be ignored when a constructor with default parameters is part of the class.

If a class has constructors and you declare an array of class objects, the class must have the default constructor. It is not possible to specify different constructors for each component.

Objectives

In this lab, you define a constructor with parameters.

After completing this lab, you will be able to:

- Write a default constructor function.
- Write a constructor function with parameters.
- Write a constructor function with default parameters.
- Create an array of objects that uses the default constructor.

Estimated completion time: **60–75 minutes**

Invoking Default Constructors, Constructors with Parameters, and Constructors with Default Parameters

The Information Technology (IT) Department of a company wants to maintain consistency in the different areas dealing with employee information. To do this, they need a class to keep track of employee information. In addition, their Equal Employment Opportunity (EEO) Department needs to report ethnicity statistics to the federal government. You will need to use the `Date` class you created in Lab 12-3, Exercise 1a.

1a. Create a UML diagram for a class named `Employee` that will contain data members and member functions to allow consistency in the company programs. Your class should meet the criteria in the following list:

- The private string data members named `lastName` and `firstName`
- A private character data member named `ethnicity`
- The private double data member `rateOfPay`

- The private `Date` (created in Lab 12.1) data member `startDate`
- The default constructor `Employee` to set the base pay rate
- The constructor `Employee` with parameters to assign the pay rate
- The public member method `pay` to calculate the employee pay
- The public member method `eeo` to report the ethnic diversity
- The private member method `newHire` to add employees

Write the class definition in the space provided.

1b. Using the `Employee` class design you created in Exercise 1a, design the member functions so that they meet the following criteria:

- The default constructor `Employee` sets `rateOfPay` to 7.25 and calls the private member method `newHire`.
- The constructor `Employee` has a double parameter `rate` that assigns `rate` to `rateOfPay` and calls the private member method `newHire`.

- The member method **newHire** prompts the user for the starting date in the format mm dd yyyy; calls the `Date` member method `getData` with the `startDate` data member; prompts the user for first and last name; inputs the values entered into the data members `firstName` and `lastName`; prompts the user for ethnicity using the following characters (C)aucasian, (A)frican American, (N)ative American, (H)ispanic, A(s)ian, (O)ther; enters the value entered into the data member `ethnicity`; and converts the value entered to uppercase.
- The member method `pay` prompts the user by name for the number of hours worked during the week, calculates `payAmount`, and displays the weekly salary. Overtime of 1.5 should be paid for all hours worked greater than 40.
- The member method `eeo` should display the employee's ethnicity according to the value of the data member `ethnicity`.

1c. Implement in C++ the design of your class and class member functions. Save your code in a file named **testEmployee.cpp** in the Chap12 folder of your Student Disk. Compile and correct any syntax errors.

1d. Define an object named `worker` of the class `Employee` and an object named `suit` with a parameter 25.0. Write the object definitions in the space provided.

1e. Write a driver program that implements the `Exchange` and `Date` classes. Using the objects created in Exercise 1d, call the member methods `pay` and `eeo`. Enter compile, link, and execute **testEmployee.cpp**. Then copy the output and save it in a block comment at the end of your program. Save **testEmployee.cpp** in the Chap12 folder of your Student Disk.

The following is a copy of the screen results that might display after running your program, depending on the data entered. The input entered by the user is shown in bold.

```
The program testEmployee.cpp is a driver program to test the class
Employee.

Enter first name and last name separated by a space: Juanita Gonzalez
Please enter starting date mm dd yyyy for Juanita Gonzalez: 11 02 2004
Please enter your ethnicity: (C)aucasian, (A)frican American,
(N)ative American, (H)ispanic, A(s)ian, (O)ther: H

Enter first name and last name separated by a space: Gordon Chang
Please enter starting date mm dd yyyy for Gordon Chang: 09 02 1984
Please enter your ethnicity: (C)aucasian, (A)frican American,
(N)ative American, (H)ispanic, A(s)ian, (O)ther: s

How many hours did Juanita Gonzalez work this week? 42

Weekly pay for Juanita Gonzalez is $311.75
The employee ethnicity is Hispanic.

How many hours did Gordon Chang work this week? 54

Weekly pay for Gordon Chang is $1525.00
The employee ethnicity is Asian.
```

2a. Redesign your class Employee to have one constructor with a default parameter rather than two constructors. The redesigned program will be named **testEmployee2.cpp**.

2b. Enter, compile, link, and execute **testEmployee2.cpp**. Then copy the output and save it in a block comment at the end of your program. Save **testEmployee2.cpp** in the Chap12 folder of your Student Disk. Your output should be the same for both testEmployee.cpp and testEmployee2.cpp.

3a. Change your **testEmployee2.cpp** program to create an array object `hourly` of the class `Employee` of size 5. Change your program to call the member method for each array element. Save the new program as **testEmployee3.cpp** in the Chap12 folder of your Student Disk.

3b. Enter, compile, link, and execute **testEmployee3.cpp**. Then copy the output and save it in a block comment at the end of your program.

The following is a copy of the screen results that might display after running your program depending on the data entered. The input entered by the user is shown in bold.

```
The program testEmployee.cpp is a driver program to test the class
Employee.

Enter first name and last name separated by a space: Angela Vito
Please enter starting date mm dd yyyy for Angela Vito: 1 14 2002
Please enter your ethnicity: (C)aucasian, (A)frican American,
(N)ative American, (H)ispanic, A(s)ian, (O)ther: C

Enter first name and last name separated by a space: Boubacar Zimba
Please enter starting date mm dd yyyy for Boubacar Zimba: 3 5 2003
Please enter your ethnicity: (C)aucasian, (A)frican American,
(N)ative American, (H)ispanic, A(s)ian, (O)ther: A

Enter first name and last name separated by a space: Charles Casey
Please enter starting date mm dd yyyy for Charles Casey: 5 8 2001
Please enter your ethnicity: (C)aucasian, (A)frican American,
(N)ative American, (H)ispanic, A(s)ian, (O)ther: C

Enter first name and last name separated by a space: Wanda Torres
Please enter starting date mm dd yyyy for Wanda Torres: 12 14 2000
Please enter your ethnicity: (C)aucasian, (A)frican American,
(N)ative American, (H)ispanic, A(s)ian, (O)ther: H

Enter first name and last name separated by a space: Huy Wuan
Please enter starting date mm dd yyyy for Huy Wuan: 3 22 1999
Please enter your ethnicity: (C)aucasian, (A)frican American,
(N)ative American, (H)ispanic, A(s)ian, (O)ther: s

Enter first name and last name separated by a space: Jack Smith
Please enter starting date mm dd yyyy for Jack Smith: 8 12 1998
Please enter your ethnicity: (C)aucasian, (A)frican American,
(N)ative American, (H)ispanic, A(s)ian, (O)ther: O

How many hours did Angela Vito work this week? 37

Weekly pay for Angela Vito is $268.25
The employee ethnicity is Caucasian.

How many hours did Boubacar Zimba work this week? 42

Weekly pay for Boubacar Zimba is $311.75
The employee ethnicity is African American.

How many hours did Charles Casey work this week? 14
```

```
Weekly pay for Charles Casey is $101.50
The employee ethnicity is Caucasian.

How many hours did Wanda Torres work this week? 47

Weekly pay for Wanda Torres is $366.13
The employee ethnicity is Hispanic.

How many hours did Huy Wuan work this week? 28

Weekly pay for Huy Wuan is $203.00
The employee ethnicity is Asian.

How many hours did Jack Smith work this week? 56

Weekly pay for Jack Smith is $1600.00
The employee ethnicity is not listed.
```

LAB 12.5 INVOKING DESTRUCTORS

A destructor is another type of function used in a class. It is not typed and has no parameters, and there can be only one destructor per class. The name of the destructor is the same as the name of the class, but it is differentiated from the constructor by the tilde character (~). The destructor automatically executes when the class object goes out of scope. The general syntax for a destructor is:

```
~className();
```

Objectives

In this lab, you define a destructor of a class.

After completing this lab, you will be able to:

- Write a destructor for a class.

Estimated completion time: **10–15 minutes**

Invoking Destructors

1a. Modify your `Employee` class to include a destructor. Design a destructor function that outputs the message "Employment for `Employee` has been terminated."

1b. Revise your **testEmployee3.cpp** program, saving it as **testEmployee4.cpp**. Compile, link, and execute **testEmployee4.cpp**. Then copy the output and save it in a block comment at the end of your program. Save **testEmployee4.cpp** in the Chap12 folder of your Student Disk.

The following is a copy of the screen results that might display after running your program, depending on the data entered. The input entered by the user is shown in bold.

```
The program testEmployee.cpp is a driver program to test the class
Employee.

Enter first name and last name separated by a space: Juanita Gonzalez
Please enter starting date mm dd yyyy for Juanita Gonzalez: 11 2 2004
Please enter your ethnicity: (C)aucasian, (A)frican American,
(N)ative American, (H)ispanic, A(s)ian, (O)ther: H

Enter first name and last name separated by a space: Gordon Chang
Please enter starting date mm dd yyyy for Gordon Chang: 9 2 1984
Please enter your ethnicity: (C)aucasian, (A)frican American,
(N)ative American, (H)ispanic, A(s)ian, (O)ther: s

How many hours did Juanita Gonzalez work this week? 42

Weekly pay for Juanita Gonzalez is $311.75
The employee ethnicity is Hispanic.

How many hours did Gordon Chang work this week? 54

Weekly pay for Gordon Chang is $1525.00
The employee ethnicity is Asian.

Employment for Gordon Chang has been terminated.
Employment for Juanita Gonzalez has been terminated.
```

Lab 12.6 Using the Abstract Data Type (ADT) and Information Hiding

Separating the design details from their use is called abstraction. An abstract data type (ADT) is a data type that specifies the logical properties without the implementation details. Hiding the implementation details ensures that an object will be used in exactly the same way throughout the project. The implementation details are placed in a separate file called an implementation file. The specifications are kept in a file called a header file that has the extension .h.

The implementation file contains the definitions of the functions to implement the operations of an object. There is no `main` function in the implementation file. The object code of the implementation file is linked with the object code of the program using the class (the source file). The implementation file has an extension of .cpp.

The implementation file must include the specification file (the .h file enclosed in double quotation marks) so that it will compile. When using an SDK, all files are put in the same project to be compiled, linked, and executed.

Objectives

In this lab, you create a specification file, an implementation file, and a file with a program that includes the class.

After completing this lab, you will be able to:

- Create a specification file.
- Create an implementation file.
- Create a file that uses the class specified and implemented in the specification and implementation files.

Estimated completion time: **40–50 minutes**

Using the Abstract Data Type and Information Hiding

1a. *Critical Thinking Exercise*: Using the program **testDate.cpp**, place the class `Date` definition in the header file **Date.h**, the implementation of the class functions in the file **Date.cpp**, and the rest of the program in **testDateAB.cpp**. Save the files in the Chap12 folder of your Student Disk.

1b. Enter, compile, link, and execute **testDateAB.cpp** and **Date.cpp**. Copy the output for each and save it in a block comment at the end of your program. Save **testDateAB.cpp** and **Date.cpp** in the Chap12 folder of your Student Disk. Your output should be the same as your output for testDate.cpp.

2a. Using the program **testExchange.cpp**, place the `struct Money` definition in the header file **Money.h**, the class `Exchange` definition in the header file **Money.h**, and the implementation of the `Money` class functions in the file **Money.h**; delete the `Date` class definition and functions, and save the rest of the program in **testExchangeAB.cpp**. Save the files in the Chap12 folder of your Student Disk.

2b. Enter, compile, link, and execute **testExchangeAB.cpp** and **Money.h**. Copy the output for each and save it in a block comment at the end of your program. Save **testExchangeAB.cpp** and **Money.h** in the Chap12 folder of your Student Disk. Your output should be the same as your output for **testExchange.cpp**.

3a. Using the program **testEmployee2.cpp**, place the class `Employee` definition in the header file **Employee.h**, and the implementation of the `Employee` class functions in the file **Employee.cpp**; delete the `Date` class definition and functions, and save the rest of the program in **testEmployeeAB.cpp**. Save the files in the Chap12 folder of your Student Disk.

3b. Enter, compile, link, and execute **testEmployeeAB.cpp** and **Employee.cpp**. Copy the output for each and save it in a block comment at the end of your program. Save **testEmployeeAB.cpp** and **Employee.cpp** in the Chap12 folder of your Student Disk. Your output should be the same as your output for **testEmployee.cpp**.

LAB 12.7 USING STATIC MEMBERS OF A CLASS

Member variables of a class can be static or automatic, just as they can when declared in a function. In addition, member functions can also be static. Static members of a class can be used both with and without a class object (class variable). When utilized with the class object, dot notation is used to access the static data member and to call the static member function. Static public data members and functions can be accessed and called directly using the class name and the scope resolution operator (::).

The syntax for using a static public data member named count and a function named showCount( ) of a class named book would be as follows:

```
cout << book::count << endl;
book::showCount( );
```

Use of a static data member variable requires an additional separate definition of that variable outside of the class and before the main function. The variable will exist even though a class object may not exist; this is an example:

```
int book::count;
```

The syntax for declaring a data member of a class to be static is simply to begin the declaration statement with the keyword static. The syntax for defining a function is to begin the prototype or heading of the function with the keyword static.

Objectives

In this lab you will become acquainted with static data members and static functions of a class.

After completing this lab, you will be able to:

- Declare static member variables of a class.
- Define and implement static member functions of a class.
- Use class static member variables and static member functions in a program.

Estimated completion time: **30–45 minutes**

Given the following program, answer questions 1 through 6.

```
#include<iostream>
#include<string>
using namespace std;
class group
{
    public:
       static int number;
       group();
       group(string nam, string maj){name = nam; major = maj;
       number++;}
       void getNumber() {cout << number << endl;}
       void getStudent() {cout << name << "'s major is " << major
       << endl;}
       static void addNumber() {number++;}
    private:
       string name;
       string major;
};
int group::number = 0;
int main()
{
    group Jim("Jim","Sports");
    cout << group::number << endl;
    Jim.addNumber();
    group Sue("Sue", "CIS");
    Jim.getStudent();
    cout << group::number << endl;
    group::addNumber();
    Sue.getNumber();
    group::number++;
    cout << group::number << endl;
    return 0;
}
```

1. What is the output when the code in line 21 executes?

2. What is the output when the code in line 24 executes?

3. What is the output when the code in line 25 executes?

4. What is the output when the code in line 27 executes?

5. What is the output when the code in line 29 executes?

6. Write the definition for a class named package with the following members:
   a. static public integer variable named weight;
   b. static public function named addWeight that will take one integer parameter and add it to the member variable weight;
   c. one constructor that will take one integer parameter to initialize the value of the member variable weight; and
   d. one void function that will output the value of weight.

7. Write the code for a program to use the class package. Name the file **Package.cpp**. Include the following in the main function:

   a. instantiate one package class object;

   b. object call to the function to output the value of weight;

   c. call the addWeight function without using the object;

   d. have the object call the addWeight function;

   e. access the static member variable weight directly and increment its value; and

   f. object call to the function to output the value of weight.

8. Enter, compile, link and execute **Package.cpp**. Copy the output and save it in a block comment at the end of the source code. Save **Package.cpp** in the Chap12 folder of your student disk.

   The following is a copy of the screen results that might display after running your program, depending on the data entered.

```
5
22
```

13 Inheritance and Composition

In this chapter, you will:

- Learn about inheritance
- Learn about derived and base classes
- Explore how to redefine the member functions of a base class
- Examine how the constructors of base and derived classes work
- Learn how to construct the header file of a derived class
- Explore three types of inheritance: `public`, `protected`, and `private`
- Learn about composition
- Become familiar with the three basic principles of object-oriented design

Chapter 13: Assignment Cover Sheet

Name ______________________________ Date ______________________________

Section ______________________________

Lab Assignments	Assigned	Grade
Lab 13.1 Overriding Member Functions of the Base Class		
Lab 13.2 Using Constructors of Derived and Base Classes		
Lab 13.3 Creating Header Files for the Base Class and the Derived Classes (Critical Thinking Exercise)		
Lab 13.4 Using Protected Members of a Class in Inheritance		
Lab 13.5 Relating Classes through Composition (Critical Thinking Exercises)		
Lab 13.6 Defining Object-Oriented Design (OOD) and Object-Oriented Programming (OOP)		
Total Grade		

See your instructor or the introduction to this book for instructions on submitting your assignments.

LAB 13.1 OVERRIDING MEMBER FUNCTIONS OF THE BASE CLASS

Adding members extends the definition of a class. It is not necessary to do this by changing the class directly; instead, you can inherit members of a class when designing another class. In C++, you can relate two or more classes in more than one way. Two common ways to relate classes are inheritance and composition. Inheritance lets you create classes from existing classes. The new classes are called derived classes, and the existing classes are called base classes. The derived classes inherit the properties of the base classes.

Each derived class, in turn, could become a base class for a future derived class. In single inheritance, the derived class is derived from a single base class; in multiple inheritance, the derived class is derived from more than one base class.

The general syntax of a derived class is:

```
class className: memberAccessSpecifier baseClassName
{
     member list
};
```

in which `memberAccessSpecifier` is `public`, `protected`, or `private`. (The default is private.)

The public members of a class become public members of the derived class. The private members of a class become private members of the derived class. However, public members of a base class can be inherited either as public members or as private members of the derived class.

Objectives

In this lab, you define derived classes from base classes.

After completing this lab, you will be able to:

- Write a derived class when given the base class.
- Create an instantiation of the derived class (declare objects) and the base class.
- Recognize the difference between objects of the base class and objects of the derived class.

Estimated completion time: **50–60 minutes**

Overriding Member Functions of the Base Class

1a. Open the **Date.h** and **Date.cpp** class and implementation files from the Chap12 folder on your Student Disk. Change the private integer variables `month`, `day`, and `year` to be public members. Save them in the Chap13 folder of your Student Disk.

1b. Design a base class named `Animal` to allow the following public data members:

- Integer data members named `lifeExpectancy` and `weight`
- Character data member named `gender`
- String data members called `name` and `type`

The `Animal` class must also allow a public `void` function named `printValues` with no parameters.

1c. Design a derived class named `VetPatient` that inherits all of the properties of the base class `Animal` as public members and has the following additional private members:

- Date values named `dateIn` and `dateOut`
- Double named `charges`
- String named `procedure`

The class must also allow a `void` function named `printValues` with no parameters.

1d. Design a derived class named `Pet` that inherits all of the properties of the base class `Animal` as private members and has the following additional public members:

- String value named `home`
- Boolean value named `bites`
- Public `void` function named `printValues`

Because the base class data members are private for the derived class `Pet`, the function `printValues` needs parameters for the `Animal` class data members.

1e. Design three `printValues` functions—one for each class: `Animal`, `VetPatient`, and `Pet`—that will display all data members for the object of that class and then call the `print-Values` function of the `Animal` class when necessary to display private data members of the base class.

1f. Design a main function to test the classes that you created. Include all comments for documentation and identification of the program in your design. Create an object named `elephant` of the type `Animal`, an object named `horse` as the type `VetPatient`, and an object named `dog` as the type `Pet`. For gender, use 'm' for male, 'f' for female, 'n' for a neutered male, and 's' for a spayed female. You can expect a male elephant to live 65 years and weigh around 7 tons (13,000 pounds). Depending on the breed, you can expect a dog that has been spayed to live 12 years and weigh around 20 pounds. A dog can be an indoor or outdoor pet and may or may not bite. You can expect a female racehorse to live 25 years, weigh around 1,000 pounds, and have regular exams by a veterinarian. Using these facts, assign values to each data member in the class and call the `printValues` functions to output the values after they have been assigned.

1g. Write a C++ program based on the designs you created and name it **AnimalLife.cpp**. Step through the code by hand.

In the following space, show what is displayed on the screen after executing the output message using the following data with the following arguments:

- Animal elephant('M', 65, "Jumbo", 14000, "elephant")
- VetPatient horse('F', 25, "Pretty Filly", 1000, "horse", 8, 30, 2005, 8, 31, 2005, "check up", 58)
- Pet dog('S', 12, "Fifi", 20, "dog", false, "indoors")

Also call the `printValues` functions.

1h. Enter, compile, link, and execute **AnimalLife.cpp**. Then copy the output and save it in a block comment at the end of your program. Save **AnimalLife.cpp** in the Chap13 folder of your Student Disk.

The following is a copy of the screen results that display after running your program.

```
A male elephant named Jumbo should live to be 65 and weigh 13000 pounds.

A female horse named Pretty Filly should live to be 25 and weigh 1000
pounds.
The horse checked in 8/30/2006 and checked out 8/31/2006.
The procedure performed was a checkup at a cost of $58.00.

A spayed dog named Fifi should live to be 12 and weigh 20 pounds.
Your dog lives indoors and does not bite.
```

LAB 13.2 USING CONSTRUCTORS OF DERIVED AND BASE CLASSES

To redefine a public member function of a base class in the derived class, the corresponding function in the derived class must have the same name, number, and types of parameters. If the corresponding functions in the base class and the derived class have the same name but different sets of parameters, then this function is overloading in the derived class, which is also allowed.

If the derived class overrides a public member function of the base class, then to specify a call to that public member function of the base class, you use the name of the base class, followed by the scope resolution operator, (::), followed by the function name with the appropriate parameter list. For example, to call the member function of the base class, the syntax is:

```
baseClass::memberFunction();
```

If the derived class does not override a public member function of the base class, you may specify a call to that public member function by using the name of the function and the appropriate parameter list.

The constructor of a derived class cannot directly access the private member variables of the base class. If the base class has a constructor function, the derived class must also have a constructor function to reach the private members of the base class. Thus, when a derived class object is declared, it must also automatically execute one of the constructors of the base class. When a constructor of the base class has parameters, you specify the base class constructor name with the parameters in the heading of the derived class constructor definition.

Objectives

In this lab, you design constructor functions to initialize values sent at instantiation of the class objects.

After completing this lab, you will be able to:

- Use constructor functions in a base class.
- Use constructor functions in a derived class.

Estimated completion time: **30–40 minutes**

Using Constructors of Derived and Base Classes

1a. Using the classes `Animal`, `VetPatient`, and `Pet` that you created in Lab 13.1, design constructor functions to initialize values sent at instantiation of the class objects. Design a new source program that has a main function. Your main function should instantiate the same objects that you used in **AnimalLife.cpp** with the following arguments:

- Animal elephant('M', 65, "Jumbo", 14000, "elephant")
- VetPatient horse('F', 25, "Pretty Filly", 1000, "horse", 8, 30, 2005, 8, 31, 2005, "check up", 58)
- Pet dog('S', 12, "Fifi", 20, "dog", false, "indoors")

Also call the `printValues` functions. Name the revised program **AnimalLife2.cpp**.

1b. Enter, compile, link, and execute **AnimalLife2.cpp**. Then copy the output and save it in a block comment at the end of your program. Save **AnimalLife2.cpp** in the Chap13 folder of your Student Disk.

Compare your output to your output in **AnimalLife.cpp**. It should be the same.

Lab 13.3 Creating Header Files for the Base Class and the Derived Classes

Derived classes can be contained in header files, the same as a base class. When the derived class is in a separate file, the file containing the base class must be used in the file containing the derived class, using the preprocessor directive include.

If you try to compile a program that has more than one file that includes the same user-defined class, you will get compile errors because of the duplicated class definition. To avoid this duplication, the following preprocessor directives are used: `ifndef` (meaning if not defined), `define` (meaning define), and `endif` (meaning end of the if not defined).

The data items of a class should be private when at all possible. This is "information hiding" that protects the members of the class from being changed.

Objectives

In this lab, you become acquainted with using multiple header files of classes requiring the preprocessors `ifndef`, `define`, and `endif`.

After completing this lab, you will be able to:

- Write a base class and derived classes using the preprocessors `ifndef`, `define`, and `endif`.

Estimated completion time: **40–50 minutes**

Creating Header Files for the Base Class and the Derived Classes

1a. Using **AnimalLife2.cpp**, break the classes into individual header files.

Save your header files as **Date.h**, **Animal.h**, **VetPatient.h**, and **Pet.h** and the implementation in C++ of the class functions in the files **Date.cpp**, **Animal.cpp**, **VetPatient.cpp**, and **Pet.cpp**.

Include the header files in your program and save the program as **AnimalLife3.cpp** in the Chap13 folder of your Student Disk.

1b. Enter, compile, link, and execute **AnimalLife3.cpp**. Then copy the output and save it in a block comment at the end of your program. Save **AnimalLife3.cpp** in the Chap13 folder of your Student Disk.

Compare your output to the output in **AnimalLife.cpp** and **AnimalLife2.cpp**. All output should be the same.

2a. *Critical Thinking Exercise*: Design a program for a veterinarian's office. Use the **Date.h**, **Date.cpp**, **Animal.h**, and **Animal.cpp** files. Design a new header file named **VetOffice.h** and the member function implementation file **VetOffice.cpp** that is similar to the VetPatient.h header file you created in Exercise 1. Make the changes necessary to include the following requirements.

The veterinary practice is limited to dogs and cats. The procedures provided by the office include:

- Checkups for $40
- Spaying for $75
- Neutering for $50
- Anesthesia for $40

- Worming for $10
- Annual cat inoculations for $75
- Annual dog inoculations for $60
- Dog grooming for $75
- Declawing for $75
- Nail clipping for $8
- Surgery type 1 for $100
- Surgery type 2 for $200
- Surgery type 3 for $300
- Boarding for $18 per night
- Other (allows both the service and the amount to be entered)

You also need to total the charges for the day. Enter the data for each patient. Create a daily output report file named **patients.txt** with the day's procedures. Display information about the patient procedure and cost on the screen.

2b. Write a C++ program based on the designs you created in Exercise 2a, and name it **VetReport.cpp**. Step through the code by hand.

2c. Enter, compile, link, and execute **VetReport.cpp**. Then copy the output and save it in a block comment at the end of your program. Save **VetReport.cpp** in the Chap13 folder of your Student Disk. Print your patients.txt file and attach it to your program.

The instructions to the user should appear at execution and again when requested by the user. They should resemble the following:

```
The Healthy Pet Clinic offers services for your cats and dogs.

1       Anesthesia $40
2       Annual cat inoculations $75
3       Annual dog inoculations $60
4       Boarding per night $18
5       Checkups $40
6       Declawing $75
7       Dog grooming $75
8       Nail or claw clipping $8
9       Neutering $50
10      Spaying $75
11      Worming $10
12      Surgery type 1 $100
13      Surgery type 2 $200
14      Surgery type 3 $300
15      Other
0       Quit
```

The date prompt should occur after the first set of instructions. It should resemble the following code and continue until a valid date has been entered.

```
Please enter today's date (month, day, and year separated by spaces):
12 02 2006
```

The following prompts should appear until the user enters a 0 to end the program or until a valid procedure number has been entered.

```
Please enter the number of the service that you wish: 2
Please enter the name of your pet: Ferdinand
Please enter whether your pet is a cat or a dog: cat
Please enter the gender of your pet (m)ale, (f)emale, (s)payed, (n)eut
ered: n
Would you like to see the instructions (y)es or (n)o? n
```

If an invalid number for a service is entered, the following message and prompt should be displayed until a valid procedure number is entered.

```
You entered an invalid procedure.
Please enter the number of the service that you wish: 2
```

If a 15 is entered as the procedure number, the following prompt should appear.

```
Please enter the cost of this procedure: 85
```

If an invalid pet type is entered, the following message and prompt should be displayed until a valid pet type is entered.

```
This practice is limited to dogs and cats.
Please enter whether your pet is a cat or a dog: cat
```

If an invalid gender type is entered, the following message and prompt should be displayed until a valid gender type is entered.

```
You did not enter a valid gender.
Please enter the gender of your pet (m)ale, (f)emale, (s)payed,
(n)eutered: n
```

If procedure 4 (boarding per night $18) is chosen, the following prompt should appear.

```
How many days do you wish to board? 1
```

If a positive number is not entered, the following message and prompt should be displayed until a positive number is entered.

```
You entered an invalid number of days.
```

For each patient that visits the veterinary clinic, a message similar to the following one should appear, depending on the input data.

```
The following services were performed on your neutered cat Ferdinand:
12/02/2005      2       annual cat inoculations at a cost of $75.00.
```

The output file patients.txt should resemble the following report, depending on the data entered.

```
                The Healthy Pet Clinic Services for 12-2-2006

   Patient                   Service                              Fees

Bowser              1  anesthesia                                $ 40.00
Ferdinand           2  annual cat inoculations                   $ 75.00
Fifi                3  annual dog inoculations                   $ 60.00
Rover               4  boarding per night                        $ 54.00
```

```
Harvard        5  checkups                      $ 40.00
Sweetie        6  declawing                     $ 75.00
Isabel         7  dog grooming                  $ 75.00
Tia            8  nail or claw clipping         $  8.00
Spot           9  neutering                     $ 50.00
Fluffy         10 spaying                       $ 75.00
Gretchen       11 worming                       $ 10.00
Heinrich       12 surgery type 1                $100.00
Lucky          13 surgery type 2                $200.00
Zachery        14 surgery type 3                $300.00
Fido           15 other                         $ 20.00

Total                                          $1182.00
```

LAB 13.4 USING PROTECTED MEMBERS OF A CLASS IN INHERITANCE

A derivative class can inherit members of the base class. How objects of the derivative class can access members of the base class depends on two factors: 1) the access specifiers in the base class and 2) the access specifier of the inheritance. In addition to the access specifiers of public and private, a third access specifier of protected is allowed and is relevant for inheritance.

Protected members in a base class have the same characteristics as private members in the base class. Protected members of the base class may be inherited as protected members of the derived class and accessed by the functions of the derived class. If the access specifier of the inheritance is protected or public, the protected members of the base class are protected in the derived class. If the access specifier of the inheritance is private, the protected members of the base class are private in the derived class.

The private members of the base class are hidden and not accessible to the derived class except by the member functions of the derived class through the public or protected members of the base class.

Public members of the base class become protected members of the derived class when the inheritance is protected or private but become public members of the derived class in which the inheritance is public.

Objectives

- understand the differences among the public, protected, and private access specifiers in base and derived classes
- understand the differences of the access specifiers when used in inheritance

Estimated completion time: **30–40 minutes**

Using Protected Members of a Class in Inheritance

Given the following program code, answer Questions 1 through 4.

```
#include <iostream>
using namespace std;
 class sequence
 {
       public:
          void addValue();
          void showObject() const;
              sequence(int = 0, int = 1);
       protected:
                 int value;
                 int increment;
};
class counter : public sequence
{
      public:
         void setMaxValue(int);
         void showObject() const;
      private:
         int maxValue;
};
int main()
{
    sequence sq1(1,3);
    counter cnt1;
    cnt1.setMaxValue(100);
    cnt1.addValue();
    sq1.showObject();
    cnt1.showObject();
    system("pause");
    return 0;
}
void sequence::addValue()
{
     value += increment;
}
void sequence::showObject() const
{
     cout << "Value is: " << value << endl;
     cout << "Increment is: " << increment << endl;
}
sequence::sequence(int v, int i)
{
     value = v;
     increment = i;
}
void counter::setMaxValue(int x)
{
     maxValue = x;
}
void counter::showObject() const
{
     cout << "Value is: " << value << endl;
     cout << "Increment is: " << increment << endl;
     cout << "Max Value is : " << maxValue << endl;
}
```

Questions

1. What is the output when line 27 executes?

2. What is the output when line 28 executes?

3. What will happen to the program if the access specifier in line 13 is changed from public to protected?

4. If the access specifier in line 13 is changed from public to private, what line of code in the main function can be eliminated that would allow the program to compile and run?

   Choose an answer from among the following choices for questions 5 through 10.

   a) directly

   b) by the member functions of the derived class

   c) by the member functions of the derived class through the protected or public members of the base class

   d) they cannot be accessed

5. If the inheritance of the base class is private, how can the public members of the base class be accessed in the derived class?

6. If the inheritance of the base class is private, how can the private members of the base class be accessed in the derived class?

7. If the inheritance of the base class is protected, how can the public members of the base class be accessed in the derived class?

8. If the inheritance of the base class is protected, how can the private members of the base class be accessed in the derived class?

9. If the inheritance of the base class is public, how can the private members of the base class be accessed in the derived class?

10. If the inheritance of the base class is public, how can the protected members of the base class be accessed in the derived class?

LAB 13.5 RELATING CLASSES THROUGH COMPOSITION

Composition allows a class to be composed of objects of another class. When you include the `string` data type in your class, then you are using composition. Similarly, the first three labs of this chapter used the `Date` header file to allow `Date` data types. This, too, is composition.

When an object of a class is a data member of another class, the private data members of that class must be accessed through public or protected members of the class. When constructor functions are used for initialization, you invoke the constructor function of the class object in the class by associating that class using the colon, the class name, and arguments to the constructor function of the class object.

Objectives

In this lab, you become acquainted with accessing the constructor function of a class that has an object of that class as a data member.

After completing this lab, you will be able to:

- Access the constructor function of a class that has an object of that class as a data member.

Estimated completion time: **50–60 minutes**

Relating Classes through Composition

In the following exercises, you redesign header files, and then create a program based on your designs. After running a program, copy the output and then paste it in a comment block at the end of your program. Submit your program with the output in the comment block.

Critical Thinking

1a. *Critical Thinking Exercise*: Redesign the Date class in the **Date.h** header file in the Chap13 folder of your Student Disk to have a constructor function that has three integer formal parameters that initialize the private data members `month`, `day`, and `year`. Because `month`, `day`, and `year` are now private, create a `getDate2` function that has three integer values that are passed by reference. The function `getDate2` should assign those parameters the values of the private data members `month`, `day`, and `year`. Rename your new Date.h file **Date2.h**.

1b. Redesign the `VetPatient` class in the **VetPatient.h** header file in the Chap13 folder of your Student Disk to conform to the changes in the **Date2.h** file. Your constructor function should add six additional integer values that are passed by reference to access the private data members of the new `Date` class to return to the main function. You will need to create two objects, `dateIn` and `dateOut`, of the type `Date2` with arguments to initialize the `Date2` private data members. You need to call the `getDate2` function with both objects to access the private data members. You need to change your `printValues` function to have six integer formal parameters for the `month`, `day`, and `year` values for both `dateIn` and `dateOut`.

1c. Redesign **AnimalLife3.cpp** in the Chap13 folder of your Student Disk to use the new **Date2.h** and **VetPatient2.h** header files. You need to declare six local integer variables `inMonth`, `inDay`, `inYear`, `outMonth`, `outDay`, `outYear` to set with the dates of the private data members `month`, `day`, and `year` from the objects `dateIn` and `dateOut` that are created in the **VetPatient2.h** class. Include these as arguments in the list of arguments for the VetPatient2 constructor function and as arguments for the VetPatient2 `printValues` function.

1d. Revise VetPatient.cpp to use the new VetPatient2.h and save the program as **VetPatient2.cpp**. Revise Date.cpp to use the new Date.h and save the program as **Date2.cpp**. Be sure to include the same versions of Pet.h, Pet.cpp, Animal.h, and Animal.cpp from previous labs.

2. *Critical Thinking Exercise*: Save the new Date.h header file as **Date2.h** in the Chap13 folder of your Student Disk. Save the new VetPatient.h as **VetPatient2.h** in the Chap13 folder of your Student Disk. Save your program as **AnimalLife4.cpp** in the Chap13 file of your Student Disk. Compile, run, and test the program. Copy the output that is displayed, and then paste it in a block comment at the end of your program. Compare your output to your output from **AnimalLife2.cpp** and **AnimalLife3.cpp**. All of the output should be the same.

Lab 13.6 Defining Object-Oriented Design (OOD) and Object-Oriented Programming (OOP)

This lab is designed to reinforce the principles of object-oriented design that you have used in the previous labs of this chapter. Object-oriented design has three basic principles:

- Encapsulation—The ability to combine data, and operations on that data, in a single unit
- Inheritance—The ability to create objects from existing objects
- Polymorphism—The ability to use the same expression to denote different operations

OOD encourages code reuse. Once an object becomes error-free, it can be reused in many programs because it is a self-contained entity. Object-oriented programming implements OOD.

Objects are created when class variables are declared. Objects interact with each other via function calls. The private members form the internal state of an object. The public members form the external state of an object.

Objectives

In this lab, you recognize the principles of object-oriented design and become acquainted with the differences between structured programming and object-oriented programming.

After completing this lab, you will be able to:

- Recognize the principles of object-oriented design.
- Differentiate between structured programming and object-oriented programming.

Estimated completion time: **15–20 minutes**

Defining Object-Oriented Design (OOD) and Object-Oriented Programming (OOP)

These questions reinforce the principles that you have applied in previous labs in this chapter.

1. What is the basic unit of encapsulation?

2. What OOD property supports the concept of hierarchical classification?

3. What OOD property allows multiple operations when using the same expression?

4. What unit allows information hiding?

5. What type of programming is also called the top-down approach to programming?

6. What type of programming separates functions and data?

7. What type of programming encapsulates functions and data?

8. Which type of programming, structured or OOP, is easier to reuse?

9. How do objects interact?

10. What is the difference between an internal state and an external state of an object?

14 Pointers, Classes, and Virtual Functions

In this chapter, you will:

- Learn about the pointer data type and pointer variables
- Explore how to declare and manipulate pointer variables
- Learn about the address of operator and the dereferencing operator
- Discover dynamic variables
- Explore how to use the `new` and `delete` operators to manipulate dynamic variables
- Learn about pointer arithmetic
- Discover dynamic arrays
- Become aware of the shallow and deep copies of data
- Discover the peculiarities of classes with pointer data member variables
- Learn about virtual functions
- Examine the relationship between the address of operator and classes
- Become aware of abstract classes

Chapter 14: Assignment Cover Sheet

Name ______________________ Date ______________________

Section ______________________

Lab Assignments	Assigned	Grade
Lab 14.1 Declaring Pointer Variables, the Address Of Operator (&), and the Dereferencing Operator (*)		
Lab 14.2 Accessing Pointers to Classes and Structs		
Lab 14.3 Using Dynamic Variables and Dynamic Arrays (Critical Thinking Exercise)		
Lab 14.4 Understanding Shallow versus Deep Copy and Pointers		
Lab 14.5 Understanding Peculiarities of Classes with Pointer Data Members		
Lab 14.6 Using Inheritance, Pointers, and Virtual Functions (Critical Thinking Exercise)		
Total Grade		

See your instructor or the introduction to this book for instructions on submitting your assignments.

LAB 14.1 DECLARING POINTER VARIABLES, THE ADDRESS OF OPERATOR (&), AND THE DEREFERENCING OPERATOR (*)

A pointer is a variable that contains a memory address for its value. This memory address in the pointer is the address of another variable, that is, it points to the address of another variable. The declaration of a pointer specifies the data type of the other variable that is being pointed to. The syntax for declaring a pointer variable is: dataType *identifier;. For example, int *p; creates a pointer variable named `p` that points to a memory space of type int. The value of `p` needs to be initialized, that is, assigned an address of an integer variable. See the following paragraphs.

The address of operator (&) takes one variable as an operand and returns the memory address of that variable. The address of that variable can then be assigned to an integer pointer. In the following example, `x` is declared to be an integer variable and initialized to 25. The address of `x` is then assigned to the integer pointer variable `p`. `p` now points to the variable `x`.

Example:
```
int x = 25;
p = &x;
```

A pointer can also be initialized to point to nothing, that is, a NULL value.

Example:
```
p = NULL;
P = 0;
```

The dereferencing operator (*), when used with a pointer variable as an operand, returns the value of the variable that is pointed to by the pointer variable. Incorporating the statements used in the previous example, *p returns the value 25 and p returns the address of x.

Example:
```
cout << "The value of x is " << *p << "and the
address of x is " << p;
```

Objectives

After completing this lab, you will be able to:

- Use pointer variables.
- Use the address of operator (&).
- Use the dereferencing operator (*).

Estimated completion time: **20–30 minutes**

In the following exercises, design and code a program that uses pointers, the address of operator (&), and the dereferencing operator (*) for all input, calculations, and output.

1a. Design a program that will convert the value of US dollars to Euro dollars. Use the conversion rate of .0.6681; that is, one US dollar is worth 0.6681 Euro dollars. Prompt a user to input the number of US dollars, and the program will output the value in Euro dollars.

Write your design in the following space. For your design, write an algorithm (an English language description of the steps required to successfully write the program).

1b. In the following space, write a C++ program based on the design you created in Exercise 1a and name it **DollarsToEuros.cpp**.

1c. Enter, compile, link, and execute DollarsToEuros.cpp. Copy the output and save it in a block comment at the end of the source code file. Save DollarsToEuros.cpp in the Chapter 14 folder of your Student Disk.

The following is a copy of the screen results that might appear after running your program. The input entered by the user is shown in bold.

```
Enter the amount of money in US dollars: 10.5
10.50 US dollars will buy 7.02 Euro dollars
```

LAB 14.2 ACCESSING POINTERS TO CLASSES AND STRUCTS

Pointers can also be used to point to classes and structs. The dot operator (.) has a higher precedence than the dereferencing operator, thus requiring the use of parentheses. To assign a value to a component of an object using a pointer type, use the following syntax:

```
(*ptrVariableName).classMemberName = value;
```

C++ provides another operator, the member access operator arrow (->). To assign a value to a component of an object using the -> operator, use the following syntax:

```
ptrVariableName->classMemberName = value;
```

If you want to initialize a pointer variable, the only number that can be directly assigned to a pointer variable is 0 or NULL, called the null pointer.

Objectives

In this lab, you declare a pointer to a class, initialize the pointer to NULL, and use pointer notation to call member methods of a class.

After completing this lab, you will be able to:

- Declare a pointer to a class.
- Initialize a pointer to NULL.
- Use pointer notation to call member methods of a class.

Estimated completion time: **30–45 minutes**

Accessing Pointers to Classes and Structs

In the following exercises, you create a UML diagram and implementation file and then write a program that uses pointer notation.

1a. Design a UML diagram for a class named **Grade.h** with the following private data members:

- `char letterGrade;`
- `int numericGrade;`
- `string student;`

The `Grade` class includes the following private member method:

- `void calcLetterGrade()` to calculate a letter grade depending on the numeric grade

The `Grade` class includes the following public member methods:

- `char getLetterGrade()` to return the `letterGrade`
- `int getNumericGrade()` to return the `numericGrade`
- `string getStudent()` to return the `string student`
- a constructor to prompt the user for a student name and a numeric grade and to call `calcLetterGrade()`

Implement your design in C++ and save the class as **Grade.h** in the Chap14 folder of your Student Disk.

1b. Write the implementation file **Grade.cpp** for the class `Grade`, and then compile and save the files in the Chap14 folder of your Student Disk.

1c. Write a C++ program to test your class that uses pointer notation to the class `Grade`, and name the program **TestGrade.cpp**. Step through the code by hand.

In the following space, show what is displayed on the screen after executing the output message.

1d. Enter, compile, link, and execute **TestGrade.cpp**. Then copy the output and save it in a block comment at the end of your program. Save **TestGrade.cpp** in the Chap14 folder of your Student Disk.

The following is a copy of the screen results that might appear after running your program. The input entered by the user is shown in bold.

```
This program uses pointer notation to the class Grade.

Enter student's name: Zelda Goldstein
Enter numeric score: 86

Zelda Goldstein has a score of 86 for a letter grade of B
```

LAB 14.3 USING DYNAMIC VARIABLES AND DYNAMIC ARRAYS

Variables that are created during program execution are called dynamic variables. C++ provides two operators, new and delete, to create and destroy dynamic variables, respectively. The operator new is used to allocate a single variable and to allocate an array of variables.

Consider the following statements:

```
int  *p;
int  *q;
p  = new int;
```

These statements create a variable during program execution somewhere in memory and store the address of the allocated memory in p.

The operator delete is used to deallocate the variable when it is no longer needed; however, this only marks the memory spaces as deallocated. Depending on a particular system, these pointer variables may still contain the addresses of the deallocated memory spaces, called dangling pointers. This could result in accessing a wrong memory space or in terminating with an error message. One way to avoid this is to set these pointers to NULL after the delete operation.

The operations that are allowed on pointer variables are the assignment and relational operations and some limited arithmetic operations. The increment operator increments the value of a pointer variable by the size of the memory to which it is pointing. If p is an integer pointer variable, then the statement:

```
p++; or p = p + 1;
```

increments the value of p by 4 bytes because p is a pointer of type int. Pointer arithmetic requires extra care.

An array created during the execution of a program is called a dynamic array.

The following statement creates an array of 16 components and stores the base address of the array in q.

```
q = new char[16]
```

You can use the increment and decrement operation to access the components of the array. You can also use array notation to access these memory locations. An array name is a constant pointer. You need to copy the value of the array name to another pointer variable to perform increment and decrement operations.

A pointer variable can be passed as a parameter to a function either by value or by reference. To make a formal parameter be a reference parameter, you use the (&) when you declare the formal parameter in the function heading. Meaning, (*) appears before the (&) and between the data type name and the identifier. For example:

```
void func (dataType* &var1, dataType *var2)
{
}
```

The parameter var1 is a reference parameter, and the parameter var2 is a value parameter. Additionally, a function can return a value of the type pointer. For example:

```
dataType * func (...)
{
}
```

You can also create a pointer to a pointer. For example:

```
dateType **var;
```

Objectives

In this lab, you create dynamic array variables and pass pointer reference variables.

After completing this lab, you will be able to:

- Call a `void` function with pointer reference parameters from the `main` function.
- Create dynamic array variables.

Estimated completion time: **20–30 minutes**

Using Dynamic Variables and Dynamic Arrays

In the following exercises, you create a UML diagram and then design and write a program that uses dynamic variables and dynamic arrays.

1a. *Critical Thinking Exercise:* Design a UML diagram for a class named **Vote.h** that has the following elements:

- A constructor to prompt the user for a candidate's name
- A private string data member `candidate`

Implement your design in C++ and save it as **Vote.h** in the Chap14 folder of your Student Disk.

1b. Design the member method described in Exercise 1a. Your design should be a list of C++ comments without any code.

Implement your design in C++ and name it **Vote.cpp**. Step through the code by hand. Compile and correct any syntax errors.

1c. Design a program named **declareCandidacy.cpp** that includes the following elements:

- Four pointer variables: `democrat`, `independent`, `libertarian`, and `republican` of type `Vote`
- Function `setArray` with a pointer reference variable of type `Vote` and a `char` variable to identify the party

The `setArray` function should prompt the user for the number of candidates for the appropriate party and create a dynamic array of type `Vote` of that size.

In the following space, show what is displayed on the screen after executing the output message.

1d. Enter, compile, link, and execute **declareCandidacy.cpp**. Then copy the output and save it in a block comment at the end of your program. Save **declareCandidacy.cpp** in the Chap14 folder of your Student Disk.

The following is a copy of the screen results that might appear after running your program, depending on the data entered. The input entered by the user is shown in bold.

```
How many Democratic candidates are there? 2
Enter name of candidate: Lawrence Liberal
Enter name of candidate: Lucille Left
How many Independent candidates are there? 1
Enter name of candidate: Gertrude Hopper
How many Libertarian candidates are there? 0
How many Republican candidates are there? 3
Enter name of candidate: Richard Right
Enter name of candidate: Constance Conservative
Enter name of candidate: Hector Rodriquez
```

LAB 14.4 UNDERSTANDING SHALLOW VERSUS DEEP COPY AND POINTERS

In a shallow copy, two or more pointers of the same type point to the same memory; that is, they point to the same data. If the memory is deallocated by deleting the pointer that points to that location, any other pointer that points to that location subsequently becomes invalid. Consider the following statements:

```
int *first;
int *second;
first = new int[10];
second = first;
delete [] second;
```

In this example, `first` becomes invalid, and `first` and second are now dangling pointers.

In a deep copy, two or more pointers have their own data.

Objectives

In this lab, you learn the difference between shallow versus deep copying and pointers.

After completing this lab, you will be able to:

- Differentiate between shallow versus deep copying and pointers.

Estimated completion time: **5 minutes**

Understanding Shallow versus Deep Copy and Pointers

In the following exercises, you answer multiple-choice questions.

Question	**Answer (Circle the correct answer.)**

1. The following statements:
`int *num, *value;`
`num = new int;`
`*num = 10;`
`value = num;`
are an example of what?
	a. shallow copying
	b. deep copying
	c. a compiler error

2. The following statements:
`nt *num, *value;`
`num = new int;`
`value = new int;`
`*num = 10;`
`*value = *num;`
are an example of what?
	a. shallow copying
	b. deep copying
	c. a compiler error

Lab 14.5 Understanding Peculiarities of Classes with Pointer Data Members

When an object goes out of scope, all data members of the object are destroyed. However, if a data member of that object is a pointer used to create a dynamic array, that dynamic memory must be deallocated using the operator `delete`. If the pointer `p` does not use the `delete` operator to deallocate dynamic memory, the memory space stays marked and cannot be accessed. A destructor can be used to ensure that all memory created by a pointer is deallocated when an object goes out of scope.

To avoid shallow copying of data for classes with a pointer data member, C++ allows the programmer to extend the definition of the assignment operator. This process is called overloading the assignment operator.

When declaring a class object, you can initialize it by using the value of an existing object of the same type. This initialization is called the default member-wise initialization. The default member-wise initialization is due to the constructor, called the copy constructor (provided by the compiler). This would result in shallow copying. For example:

```
pointerDataClass objectThree(objectOne);
```

To force each object to have its own copy of the data, you must override the definition of the copy constructor provided by the compiler; that is, you must provide your own definition of the copy constructor. The general syntax to include the copy constructor in the definition of a class is:

```
className (const className& otherObject);
```

For classes with pointer member variables, three things are normally done:

1. Include the destructor in the class.
2. Overload the assignment operator for the class.
3. Include the copy constructor.

Objectives

In this lab, you learn the coding peculiarities of classes with pointer data members.

After completing this lab, you will be able to:

- Understand the coding peculiarities of classes with pointer data members.

Estimated completion time: **5 minutes**

Understanding Peculiarities of Classes with Pointer Data Members

In the following exercises, you answer a series of True or False questions.

Question	Answer (Circle the correct answer.)	
1. Because objects are deallocated when the object is out of scope, there is no concern regarding deallocation of dynamic memory when the object goes out of scope.	**True**	**False**
2. If a class has a destructor, that destructor is automatically called when the object goes out of scope.	**True**	**False**
3. C++ allows overloading of the assignment operator.	**True**	**False**
4. A `copy` constructor is automatically executed when an object is declared and initialized to the value of another object.	**True**	**False**
5. A `copy` constructor cannot automatically be executed when, as a parameter, an object is passed by value.	**True**	**False**

LAB 14.6 USING INHERITANCE, POINTERS, AND VIRTUAL FUNCTIONS

In the case of classes, C++ allows the user to pass an object of a derived class to a formal parameter of the base class type.

The binding of a member function in a user program (client code) that has a formal reference parameter of the base class occurs at compile time. In compile-time binding, also known as static binding, the necessary code to call a specific function is generated by the compiler.

C++ corrects this problem by providing the mechanism of virtual functions. The binding of virtual functions occurs at program execution time, not at compile time. This kind of binding is called run-time binding. More formally, in run-time binding, the compiler does not generate the code to call a specific function; instead, it generates enough information to enable the run-time system to generate the specific code for the appropriate function call. Run-time binding is also known as dynamic binding. In C++, virtual functions are declared using the reserved word `virtual`.

It is recommended that classes with pointer data members have destructors. The virtual destructor of a base class automatically makes the destructor of a derived class virtual.

The base class can contain functions that you would want each derived class to implement. One way to handle this is to make the body of these functions empty. However, you want to prevent the user from creating objects of that class. Those functions should be converted to pure virtual functions. The syntax for the prototypes is:

```
virtual dataType func1() = ;
```

or

```
virtual dataType func2(dataType var1, ..., dataType varn) = 0;
```

Once a class contains one or more virtual functions, then that class is called an abstract class. Because an abstract class is not a complete class, you cannot create objects of that class. An abstract class can contain instance variables, constructors, and functions that are not pure virtual. However, the abstract class must provide the definitions of constructors and functions that are not pure virtual.

The address of operator (&) is also used to create aliases to an object. Consider the following statements:

```
int x;
int &y = x;
```

The second statement declares **y** to be an alias of **x**. That is, both **x** and **y** refer to the same memory location. Thus, **y** is like a constant pointer variable.

The address of operator can also be used to return the address of a private member variable of a class, but must be used carefully. To prevent a program from directly manipulating the private member, use the word **const** before the return type of the function. The syntax is:

```
const dataType& className::memberFunction()
{
      return privateMemberVariable;
}
```

This will cause the program to generate a compile-time error.

Objectives

In this lab, you use inheritance, pointers, and virtual functions.

After completing this lab, you will be able to:

- Write a program using inheritance and pointers.
- Understand the use of virtual functions.

Estimated completion time: **50–60 minutes**

Using Inheritance, Pointers, and Virtual Functions

In the following exercises, you design and write a program that uses inheritance, pointers, and virtual functions.

1a. *Critical Thinking Exercise:* Design a base class named `Worker` to allow the following private data members:

- A pointer to a character variable named `workerName`
- A string `SSN` in the format xxx-xx-xxxx

`Worker` should allow the following public member methods:

- A constructor to dynamically allocate enough memory to hold the employee's name setting `workerName` to 0 and `SSN` to `NULL`
- An overloaded constructor to dynamically allocate enough memory to hold the employee's name (the string length plus 1)
- A destructor to free the unused memory
- A member method `setWorkerName` to `set workerName` if `workerName` does not equal 0
- A member method `setSSN` to set the Social Security number
- A member method `getWorkerName` that returns the `workerName`
- A member method `getSSN` that returns the `SSN`
- A virtual void method `printValues` to print the data members

Write your design in the following space.

1b. Implement your design in C++ and save it as **Worker.h** in the Chap14 folder of your Student Disk. Implement the member methods, and then compile and save your program in a file named **Worker.cpp** in the Chap14 folder of your Student Disk.

1c. Design a derived class named `PayWorker` from the `Worker` class and allow the following private data members:

- An integer `dependents`
- A double `payRate`

`PayWorker` should allow the following public member methods:

- A member method `setPayRate` to set the pay rate
- A member method `setDependents` to set the number of dependents
- A member method `getPayRate` that returns the pay rate
- A member method `getDependents` that returns the dependents
- A member method `printValues` that displays the data members

1d. Implement your design in C++ and save it as **PayWorker.h** in the Chap14 folder of your Student Disk. Implement the member methods, and then compile and save your program in a file named **PayWorker.cpp** in the Chap14 folder of your Student Disk.

1e. Write a test program that creates a worker named Jesus Guerra, with a Social Security number 555-22-7788, a pay rate of $12.50, and 5 dependents.

1f. Enter, compile, link, and execute **TestPayWorker.cpp**. Then copy the output and save it in a block comment at the end of your program. Save **TestPayWorker.cpp** in the Chap14 folder of your Student Disk.

The following is a copy of the screen results that might appear after running your program, depending on the data entered.

```
In base class Worker workerName is Jesus Guerra
In base class Worker SSN is 555-22-7788

In derived class PayWorker payRate is 12.50
In derived class PayWorker dependents is 5

Worker Name: Jesus Guerra
Social Security Number: 555-22-7788
Pay Rate: $12.50
Number of Dependents: 5
```

15 Overloading and Templates

In this chapter, you will:

- Learn about overloading
- Become aware of the restrictions on operator overloading
- Examine the pointer `this`
- Learn about `friend` functions
- Explore the members and nonmembers of a class
- Discover how to overload various operators
- Learn about templates
- Explore how to construct function templates and class templates

Chapter 15: Assignment Cover Sheet

Name ______________________ Date ______________________

Section ______________________

Lab Assignments	Assigned	Grade
Lab 15.1 Using Operator Overloading		
Lab 15.2 Overloading Binary Operators (Critical Thinking Exercise)		
Lab 15.3 Overloading Unary Operators		
Lab 15.4 Understanding Templates (Critical Thinking Exercise)		
Total Grade		

See your instructor or the introduction to this book for instructions on submitting your assignments.

If you are using Visual Studio .NET to compile your C++ programs, you should disable precompiled headers before performing the exercises in the Chapter 15 labs. To do so, change the project properties so that your C++ projects do not use precompiled headers.

Lab 15.1 Using Operator Overloading

C++ allows you to extend the definitions of most of the operators so that they can be applied to classes; this practice is called operator overloading. However, while C++ allows you to overload operators, it does not allow you to create new operators. To overload an operator, you must write functions. The name of the function that overloads an operator is the reserved word `operator` followed by the operator to be overloaded.

The result of an operation is a value; therefore, the `operator` function is a value-returning function. The syntax of the heading for an operator function is:

```
returnType operator operatorSymbol (formal parameter list)
```

Keep the following restrictions in mind when overloading an operator:

- You cannot change the precedence of an operator.
- You cannot change the associativity of an operator.
- You cannot use default arguments with an overloaded operator.
- You cannot change the number of arguments an operator takes.
- You cannot create new operators. Only existing operators can be overloaded.
  - The operators that cannot be overloaded are: `.` `.*` `::` `?:` `sizeof`
- The meaning of how an operator works with built-in types, such as `int`, remains the same.
- Operators can be overloaded either for objects of the user-defined type or for a combination of objects of the user-defined type and objects of the built-in type.

Objectives

In this lab, you use operator overloading for the existing addition and subtraction operators.

After completing this lab, you will be able to:

- Write a class to extend the operators for – (subtraction) and + (addition).

Estimated completion time: **50–60 minutes**

Using Operator Overloading

1a. Design a UML diagram for a `TimeClock` class with the following private data members:

- `float days`
- `float hours`

The class should also have the following public member methods:

- Constructor with a default that sets the data values to 0
- `getDays` to return the private data member `days`
- `getHours` to return the private data member `hours`
- `setDays` to set the private data member `days`
- `setHours` to set the private data member `hours`
- An operator + function to add hours to the private data member `hours`
- An operator – function to subtract hours from the private data member `hours`

1b. Write the implementation file **TimeClock.cpp** for the class `TimeClock`. Compile the file, and save it in the Chap15 folder of your Student Disk.

1c. Write a C++ program named **WeeklyPay.cpp** to test your class `TimeClock`. Your program should ask the user how many hours the user worked each day of the week. An object should be created for each day of the week with the number of hours for each day worked and an object for the weekly total. Step through the code by hand, and then enter, compile, link, and execute **WeeklyPay.cpp**. Copy the output and save it in a block comment at the end of your program. Save **WeeklyPay.cpp** in the Chap15 folder of your Student Disk.

The following is a copy of the screen results that might appear after running your program, depending on the data entered. The input entered by the user is shown in bold.

```
This program asks the user for the number of hours worked each day of
the week, totals the hours, and shows the days and hours worked.

How many hours did you work Monday? 4
How many hours did you work Tuesday? 9
How many hours did you work Wednesday? 3
How many hours did you work Thursday? 12
How many hours did you work Friday? 3
How many hours did you work Saturday? 7
How many hours did you work Sunday? 0


This week you worked in days:    and in hours:
Monday:                 0.5              4
Tuesday:                1.125            9
Wednesday:              0.375            3
Thursday:               1.5              12
Friday:                 0.375            3
Saturday:               0.875            7
Sunday:                 0                0

Total for the week:     4.75             38
```

LAB 15.2 OVERLOADING BINARY OPERATORS

Every object of a class maintains a (hidden) pointer to itself, and the name of this pointer is `this`. In C++, `this` is a reserved word.

A `friend` function of a class is a nonmember function of the class but has access to all the members (public or non-public) of the class. To make a function be a `friend` to a class, the reserved word `friend` precedes the function prototype (in the class definition). The word `friend` appears only in the function prototype in the class definition, not in the definition of the `friend` function. When writing the definition of a `friend` function, the name of the class and the scope resolution operator do not precede the name of the `friend` function in the function heading. For example:

```
void two (/*parameters*/)
{
        .
        .
        .
}
```

To make an operator function be a member or nonmember function of a class, keep the following in mind:

1. The function that overloads any of the operators (), [], ->, or = for a class must be declared as a member of the class.
2. Suppose that an operator `op` is overloaded for a class—say, `OpOverClass`:
   a. If the leftmost operand of `op` is an object of a different type, the function that overloads the operator `op` for `OpOverClass` must be a nonmember—that is, a friend of the class `OpOverClass`.
   b. If the operator function that overloads the operator `op` for the class `OpOverClass` is a member of the class `OpOverClass`, then when applying `op` on objects of type `OpOverClass`, the leftmost operand of `op` must be of type `OpOverClass`.

To overload binary operators as member functions of a class, use the following syntax:

```
returnType operator op(const className&) const;
```

In this statement, `op` stands for the binary operator, arithmetic or relational, to be overloaded; `returnType` is the type of value returned by the function; and `className` is the name of the class for which the operator is being overloaded.

To overload binary operators as nonmember functions of a class, use the following syntax:

```
friend returnType operator op(const className&, const className&);
```

The operator function that overloads the insertion operator (<<) or the extraction operator (>>) for a class must be a nonmember of that class.

The assignment operator causes a member-wise copy of the data members of the class. To avoid the shallow copy of data for classes with pointer data members, you must explicitly overload the assignment operator.

Objectives

In this lab, you overload the `cin` and `cout` operator using a `friend` function.

After completing this lab, you will be able to:

- Write a `friend overload cin` operator function.
- Write a `friend overload cout` operator function.

Estimated completion time: **60–75 minutes**

Overloading Binary Operators

1a. *Critical Thinking Exercise*: Design a UML diagram for a `Date` class with the following private data members:

- `integer month`
- `integer day`
- `integer year`
- A two-dimensional 12-by-12 character array `names`

The class should also include the following public member methods:

- A default constructor to call the method `setNames` and to set the value `month` to 1, `day` to 1, and `year` to 2000
- A constructor to call the method `setNames` and to set the values `month`, `day`, and `year` to the parameter values
- A void method `setNames` to set the array `names` to the names of the month
- A void method `setMonth` to set the data member `month` to the value of the parameter
- A void method `setDay` to set the data member `day` to the value of the parameter
- A void method `setYear` to set the data member `year` to the value of the parameter
- A void method `displayDate()` to display the data members `month`, `day`, and `year` in the format of month dd, yyyy.
- A `friend` function with an overloaded operator for the `cout` operator
- A `friend` function with an overloaded operator for the `cin` operator

1b. Write the implementation file **Date.cpp** for the class `Date`. Compile the file, and save it in the Chap15 folder of your Student Disk.

1c. Write a C++ program named **OverloadDate.cpp** to test your class `Date`. Your program should create an object that will call the default constructor; an object with parameters 6, 10, and 2010; and another object with default parameters. The program should call the function DisplayDate after each object is created. Your program should then test the overloaded `cin` operator and the overloaded `cout` operator. Step through the code by hand, and then enter, compile, link, and execute **OverloadDate.cpp**. Copy the output and save it in a block comment at the end of your program. Save **OverloadDate.cpp** in the Chap15 folder of your Student Disk.

For testing purposes, your program should display the date. The default constructor should initialize the date to January 1, 2000. You should also have a constructor that accepts arguments to initialize the date. The following is a copy of the screen results that might appear after running your program, depending on the data entered. The input entered by the user is shown in bold.

```
January 1, 2000
June 10, 2010
January 1, 2000
Enter the month: 11
Enter the day: 27
Enter the year: 1492
November 27, 1492
January 1, 2000
January 1, 2000
```

LAB 15.3 OVERLOADING UNARY OPERATORS

Although the unary pre- and post-increment operators can be non-member functions, they are commonly overloaded as member functions. Even though member functions that overload unary operators normally have no parameters, the post-increment operator must take one parameter of type `int`. The syntax for the prototype of the pre-increment operator is:

```
className operator++();
```

and the function will return the dereferenced `this` pointer, for example:

```
className className::operator++()
{
        identifier++;
              .
              .
        return *this;
}
```

The syntax for the post-increment operator is:

```
className operator++(int);
```

and the function will return the pre-incremented object, for example:

```
className className::operator(int)
{
        className temp = *this;
        identifier++;
              .
              .
        return temp;
}
```

Objectives

In this lab, you create a class with overloaded pre- and post-increment operators.

After completing this lab, you will be able to:

- Design and implement a class with an overloaded pre-increment operator.
- Design and implement a class with an overloaded post-increment operator.

Estimated completion time: **40–50 minutes**

Overloading Unary Operators

1a. In the following space, design a UML diagram for a Worker class as follows:

- Three private data members: an `int`, age, an `int`, yrsService, and a `string`, jobTitle.
- Five public function members:
  - A constructor with three parameters to initiailize the object in lieu of the default constructor
  - A function to overload the pre-increment operator
  - A function to overload the post-increment operator
  - A function to change the jobTitle member's value
  - A function to print the values of the data members

1b. Write the implementation file **Worker.cpp** for the class `Worker`. Compile the file and save it in the Chap 15 folder of your Student Disk.

1c. Write a C++ program to test your class `Worker` and name it **testWorker.cpp**. Your program should create two objects, Jones and Smith, and initialize their data members to 25, 3, Sales and 37, 10, President, respectively. Print the values for each object. Test the overloaded pre- and post-increment operators for both objects and print the values for each object again. Copy the output and save it as a block comment at the end of the source code file. Save **testWorker.cpp** in the Chap 15 folder of your Student Disk.

The following is a copy of the screen results that should display after running your program.

```
Age: 25

Service: 3

Job: Sales

Age: 37

Service: 10

Job: President

Age: 26

Service: 4

Job: Sales

Age: 38

Service: 11

Job: President

Age: 27

Service: 5

Job: Sales

Age: 39

Service: 12

Job: President
```

Lab 15.4 Understanding Templates

Templates are a very powerful feature of C++. They allow you to write a single code segment for a set of related functions, called a function template, and for a set of related classes, called a class template. The syntax you use for templates is:

```
template <class Type>
declaration;
```

In these statements, **`Type`** is the name of a data type, and **`declaration`** is either a function declaration or a class declaration. In C++, **`template`** is a reserved word. The word **`class`** in the heading refers to any user-defined type or built-in type. **`Type`** is referred to as a formal parameter to the template.

Similar to variables being parameters to functions, types (that is, data types) are parameters to templates.

The syntax of a function template is:

```
template <class Type>
function definition;
```

in which **`Type`** is referred to as a formal parameter of the template. It is used to specify the type of parameters to the function and the return type of the function and to declare variables within the function.

The statements:

```
template <class Type>
Type larger(Type x, Type y)
{
     if (x >= y)
          return x;
     else
          return y;
}
```

define a function template `larger`, which returns the larger of two items. In the function heading, the type of the formal parameters `x` and `y` is **`Type`** which will be specified by the type of the actual parameters when the function is called.

If we omit the body of the function in the function template definition, the function template, as usual, is the prototype.

Objectives

In this lab, you create a function template and invoke it in various ways using two test programs.

After completing this lab, you will be able to:

- Define a function template to accept any data type.

Estimated completion time: **50–60 minutes**

Understanding Templates

1a. *Critical Thinking Exercise*: Design a function template called **`randomlySelect`** that receives two arguments of the same type **`Type`** and then randomly returns one of these values. For example, if the user calls `randomlySelect(3,9)`, then the function should return `3` or `9`. You may use the function `rand()`, defined in **`cstdlib`**, to return a random value between `0` and `RAND_MAX`. For more details on how to use this function, you may visit: www.cplusplus.com/reference/clibrary/cstdlib/rand.html.

Write the code of your function in the following space.

1b. Write a C++ program to test the function `randomlySelect` and name it **testRandomlySelect.cpp**. Your program should use the function to randomly select between two integers, two floating-point numbers, and two strings (all provided by the user). Additionally, it should print the results of the random selections on the screen. Write the `main` function of your program in the following space. Tip: Don't forget to initialize the random number generator with the following statement: `srand(time(NULL));`. Note that you will need to include the `<ctime>` header file in your program.

1c. Enter, compile, link, and execute **testRandomlySelect.cpp**. Run your program twice, with the following input values: `3 4 4.5 1.2 randomly select`. Use the same input values for both runs. Copy the output of your program in the following space.

1d. Was the output of your program the same for both runs? Why or why not?

1e. Copy the output of your program and save it in a block comment at the end of your program. Save **testRandomlySelect.cpp** in the Chap15 folder of your Student Disk.

The following is a copy of the screen results that might appear after running your program, depending on the data entered. The input entered by the user is shown in bold.

```
Enter two integers: 10 7
Selected integer: 7

Enter two floating point numbers: 1.33 8.37
Selected double: 1.33

Enter two words: a test
Selected word: a
```

2a. You will now explore different ways to invoke your function template. Make a copy of the **testRandomlySelect.cpp** source file and name it **testFunctionTemplate.cpp**. Replace the `main` function with the following code.

```
int main()
{
    srand(time(NULL));

    // explicitly specify template argument
     cout << randomlySelect<double>(65.5, 76.5) << endl;

    // template argument is implicitly deduced (in this case, double)
     cout << randomlySelect(65.5, 76.5) << endl;


    // the result has type int (explicitly specified)
     cout << randomlySelect<int>(65.5, 76.5) << endl;


    return 0;
}
```

2b. Enter, compile, link, and execute **testFunctionTemplate.cpp**. Run your program. Copy the output of your program in the following space.

2c. Now add the following line before the `return 0;` statement.

```
cout << randomlySelect<char>(65.5, 76.5) << endl;
```

What do you expect the output of the last line to be?

2d. Save, compile, link, and execute **testFunctionTemplate.cpp**. Run your program. What is the output of the line you just added to your program? Was the output what you expected?

Copy the output of your program in the following space.

16 Exception Handling

In this chapter, you will:

- Learn what an exception is
- Learn how to handle exceptions within a program
- See how a `try/catch` block is used to handle exceptions
- Become familiar with C++ exception classes
- Learn how to create your own exception classes

Chapter 16: Assignment Cover Sheet

Name ______________________ Date ______________________

Section ______________________

Lab Assignments	Assigned	Grade
Lab 16.1 Catching Exceptions and Processing Exceptions during Program Execution Using `try` and `catch` Blocks (Critical Thinking Exercise)		
Lab 16.2 Using C++ Exception Classes		
Lab 16.3 More About Exception Handling		
Lab 16.4 Creating Your Own Exception Classes		
Total Grade		

See your instructor or the introduction to this book for instructions on submitting your assignments.

If you are using Visual Studio .NET to compile your C++ programs, you should disable precompiled headers before performing the exercises in the Chapter 16 labs. To do so, change the project properties so that your C++ projects do not use precompiled headers.

Lab 16.1 Catching Exceptions and Processing Exceptions during Program Execution Using `try` and `catch` Blocks

Until now, you have dealt with exceptions by using an `if` statement or the `assert` function or by simply ignoring the exception. However, with some exceptions, you don't want the program to ignore the exception and terminate.

One common way to deal with exceptions is to provide exception-handling code at the point where an error might occur. You place statements that might generate an exception in a `try` block. The `try` block also contains statements that should not be executed if an exception occurs. The `try` block is followed by one or more `catch` blocks. A `catch` block specifies the type of exception it can catch and contains an exception handler.

Keep the following guidelines in mind when you use `try` and `catch` blocks.

- If no exception is thrown in a `try` block, all `catch` blocks associated with the `try` block are ignored, and program execution resumes after the last `catch` block.
- If an exception is thrown in a `try` block, the remaining statements in the `try` block are ignored. The program searches the `catch` blocks in the order they appear after the `try` block and looks for an appropriate exception handler. If the type of the thrown exception matches the parameter type in one of the `catch` blocks, the code of that `catch` block executes, and the remaining `catch` blocks are ignored.
- The last `catch` block that contains ellipses is designed to catch any type of exception.

The general syntax to throw an exception is:

```
throw expression;
```

in which expression is a constant value, variable, or object.

The order in which you list catch blocks is important because, once caught, the remaining catch blocks are ignored.

Objectives

In this lab, you catch exceptions that should be caught and process them during program execution.

After completing this lab, you will be able to:

- Catch exceptions that should be caught.
- Process caught exceptions during program execution.
- Use multiple `catch` blocks for multiple exceptions of different types in the same program.

Estimated completion time: **40–50 minutes**

Catching Exceptions and Processing Exceptions during Program Execution Using `try` and `catch` Blocks

Critical Thinking

1a. *Critical Thinking Exercise*: Design a program that surveys a customer to request the customer's age, state, and zip code. The program should meet the following criteria:

- Use a two-character abbreviation for the state.
- Compare the two-character abbreviation for the state to the data in a file named **states.txt** that is included in the Chap16 folder of your Student Disk.
- Display the user's age, state name, and zip code.

- Use `try` and `catch` blocks when the data does not match.
- If the user enters a character for the age, use a `catch` block to display an appropriate error message.
- Call a function to enter the state abbreviation and compare it against the file list. Return the state abbreviation and the state name from the function. Also use a `catch` block in the function for any error that occurs during the processing of the file.
- If the user enters an invalid state abbreviation, use a `catch` block in the main function to display a message that an invalid state abbreviation was entered.
- Call a function to enter the zip code. If the user enters a character for the zip code, use a `catch` block to display an appropriate error message.
- If the zip code is out of range, use a `catch` block to display an appropriate error message.
- Test your program by entering the data shown in Table 16-1.

Table 16-1 Data for Testing Exceptions.cpp

Data Entry Item	First Test	Second Test	Third Test	Fourth Test
Age	Character value	Integer value	Integer value	Integer value
State		Invalid two-character state abbreviation	Valid two-character state abbreviation	Valid two-character state abbreviation
Zip code			Zip code out of range	Zip code within the valid range

1b. Write a C++ program based on the design you created in Exercise 1a, and name it **Exceptions.cpp.** Step through the code by hand.

In the following space, show what is displayed on the screen after executing the output message.

1c. Enter, compile, link, and execute **Exceptions.cpp**. Then copy the output and save it in a block comment at the end of your program. Save **Exceptions.cpp** in the Chap16 folder of your Student Disk.

The following is a copy of the screen results that might appear after testing your program, depending on the data entered. The input entered by the user is shown in bold.

When the user enters a character for age:

```
Please enter your age: a
You entered a character for age: a
```

When the user enters a valid age and an invalid two-character state abbreviation:

```
Please enter your age: 20
Please enter your two-letter state abbreviation: WW
Your state abbreviation was invalid.
```

When the user enters a valid age, a valid two-character state abbreviation, and an invalid zip code:

```
Please enter your age: 20
Please enter your two-letter state abbreviation: TX
Please enter your zip code: 999999
Your zip code is out of range. 999999
```

When the user enters all valid data:

```
Please enter your age: 20
Please enter your two-letter state abbreviation: TX
Please enter your zip code: 78764

Thank you for participating in our survey.
Your data:
20       Age
Texas    State name
78764    Zip
```

LAB 16.2 USING C++ EXCEPTION CLASSES

C++ provides support to handle exceptions via a hierarchy of classes. Among others in the hierarchy, this class, named `exception`, contains the function what. All derived classes of the class `exception` override the function what to issue their own error messages.

C++ contains the following classes for handling exceptions.

- The class `invalid_argument` deals with illegal arguments used in a function call.
- The class `out_of_range` deals with string subscript out-of-range errors.
- The class `length_error` deals with the error that a length greater than the maximum size allowed for the object being manipulated is used.
- The class `runtime_error` deals with errors that can only be detected during program execution.
- The classes `overflow_error` and `underflow_error` are derived from the class `runtime_error`.

For exception classes that are used to handle exceptions thrown by functions of these classes, you do not include a `throw` statement in the `try` block.

C++ enables you to create your own exception classes. You use the same mechanism to process the exceptions that you define as for built-in exceptions. However, you must throw your own exceptions using the throw statement. What makes a class an exception is how you use it.

Objectives

In this lab, you handle exceptions using exception classes.

After completing this lab, you will be able to:

- Test the `out_of_range` and `bad_alloc` exception handlers.
- Use the `what` function within a `catch` block

Estimated completion time: **30–40 minutes**

Using C++ Exception Classes

In the following exercise, you design and write a program that uses exception-handling classes.

1a. Design a program to test the `out_of_range` and `bad_alloc` exception handlers. Prompt a user for a name, get the length of the name, and then try to get a substring of the name that is out of range. Use a `catch` block to display a message that the substring is out of range. Within the `catch` block, use the `what` function. Prompt the user for the beginning of the substring and the length of the substring to find. Run the program again with a valid substring to test for the memory allocation. Allocate an array that is too large for your computer. Make sure that you have nothing else running. Your operating system may warn you that you are running out of virtual memory and shut down before your program has a chance to handle the exception.

Write your design in the following space. Your design should be a list of C++ comments without any code.

1b. Write a C++ program based on the design you created in Exercise 1a, and name it **ExceptClass.cpp**. Step through the code by hand.

In the following space, show what is displayed on the screen after executing the output message.

1c. Enter, compile, link, and execute **ExceptClass.cpp**. Then copy the output and save it in a block comment at the end of your program. Save **ExceptClass.cpp** in the Chap16 folder of your Student Disk.

The following is a copy of the screen results that might appear after running your program, depending on the data entered. The input entered by the user is shown in bold.

```
Enter your first name, middle initial (no period), and last name:
Zelda A Goldstein
The length is 18
Enter the starting position and length of the substring: 20 5
In the out_of_range catch block: invalid string position


Enter your first name, middle initial (no period), and last name:
Zelda A Goldstein
The length is 18
Enter the starting position and length of the substring: 1 1
In the bad_alloc catch block: bad_alloc
```

LAB 16.3 MORE ABOUT EXCEPTION HANDLING

The code you develop to handle exceptions depends on the type of application. One common way to provide exception-handling code is to add the exception-handling code at the point where an error can occur. This technique allows the programmer to see the exception-handling code together with the actual code and to determine whether the error-checking code is properly implemented. The disadvantage of this approach is that the program can become cluttered with exception-handling code, which can make understanding and maintaining the program difficult. In some cases, it is best to let a program terminate when an exception occurs. However, there are many situations in which you will want to handle the exception and let the program continue.

If the program does not handle the exception, then the function `terminate` is called to terminate the program. C++ allows the programmer to indicate what a program should do before terminating by defining a customized handler and then installing it using the `set_terminate` function. To use this function, the program must include the `exception` header file.

For example, the statement:

```
set_terminate(my_handler);
```

indicates that the function `my_handler` should be called when an unhandled exception is thrown (before terminating the program). The signature of the handler function must be as follows:

```
void handler_function();
```

Objectives

In this lab, you handle exceptions, create your own handler function, and install the handler in a program.

After completing this lab, you will be able to:

- Handle exceptions.
- Create a handler function.
- Define a `catch` block that catches any type of exception.
- Use `set_terminate` to install a customized handler.

Estimated completion time: **60–90 minutes**

More About Exception Handling

1a. In this exercise, you will explore exception-handling issues. The following code (adapted from Example 16-8 in the book) handles the `out_of_range` exception.

```
// Handling an out_of_range exception.
#include <iostream>
#include <string>

using namespace std;

int main()
{
   string sentence;
   string str1, str2, str3;
```

```
    try
    {
          sentence = "Testing string exceptions!";
          cout << "Line 5: sentence = " << sentence
                << endl;
          cout << "Line 6: sentence.length() = "
                << static_cast<int>(sentence.length())
                << endl;

          str1 = sentence.substr(8, 20);
          cout << "Line 8: str1 = " << str1
                << endl;

          str2 = sentence.substr(28, 10);
          cout << "Line 10: str2 = " << str2
                << endl;

          str3 = "Exception handling. " + sentence;
          cout << "Line 12: str3 = " << str3
                << endl;
    }
    catch (out_of_range re)
    {
          cout << "Line 14: In the out_of_range "
                << "catch block: " << re.what()
                << endl;
    }
    return 0;
}
```

Enter, compile, link, and execute **testExceptions1.cpp**. Copy the output of your program in the following space.

1b. As you can see from the output of the program, the `catch` block correctly catches and handles the `out_of_range` exception. Note that you may use a `try/catch` block to handle an exception, but fail to handle all of the exceptions that may be thrown in the `try` block. This might occur if you forget or are unaware that a specific exception may be thrown. To illustrate this issue, make a copy of **testExceptions1.cpp** and name it **testExceptions2.cpp**. Edit the source code and make the following changes:

1) Comment or remove the `str2 = sentence.substr(28, 10);` statement and its accompanying output statement.

2) Add another string variable called `veryLongString`:
`string veryLongString = "";`

3) Add the following statement just before the end of the `try` block.

```
veryLongString.resize(veryLongString.max_size() + 1);
cout << "veryLongString.length() = "
     << veryLongString.length() << endl;
```

Save, compile, link, and execute **testExceptions2.cpp**. What happens when you run your program? Copy the output of your program in the following space.

1c. Save the output of your program in a block comment at the end of your program. Save **testExceptions2.cpp** in the Chap16 folder of your Student Disk.

The following is a copy of the screen results that might appear after running your program depending on the data entered.

```
Line 5: sentence = Testing string exceptions!
Line 6: sentence.length() = 26
Line 8: str1 = string exceptions!
Line 12: str3 = Exception handling. Testing string exceptions!

This application has requested the Runtime to terminate it in an
unusual way.
Please contact the application's support team for more information.
```

You may be wondering what caused this behavior. Essentially, your program tried to resize a string to a size greater than the maximum size allowed. The statement:

```
veryLongString.resize(veryLongString.max_size() + 1);
```

throws a `length_error` exception, which was not handled by your program and caused it to terminate with an error.

2a. Even though the error in the **testExceptions2.cpp** program can be avoided if you include a `catch` block to handle the `length_error` exception, sometimes you may not want to specifically handle all of the exceptions that your program may throw, or you may be unaware that some exceptions may be thrown by your program. You will now explore different ways to deal with unknown exceptions.

One way to handle unknown exceptions is to use a `catch(...)` block to catch any unspecified exceptions in your program. Make a copy of the **testExceptions2.cpp** source file and name it **testExceptions3.cpp**. Modify **testExceptions3.cpp** so that it uses a catch(`...`) block. Write the code of your catch block in the following space.

2b. Add the catch block to **testExceptions3.cpp**. Remember that if the `catch` block with ellipses (in the heading) is used in a program, then it should be the last `catch` block of that sequence. Save, compile, link, and execute **testExceptions3.cpp**. Copy the output of your program in the following space.

3a. Another method to deal with unhandled exceptions in a program is to use the `set_terminate` function. Make a copy of the **testExceptions2.cpp** source file and name it **testExceptions4.cpp**. Modify **testExceptions4.cpp** so that your own handler is executed when an unhandled exception is thrown in your program. You may refer to the text at the beginning of this lab for an explanation on the `set_terminate` function. For an example of how to use this function, visit www.freshsources.com/Except1/LIST6.HTM. List the necessary modifications to the program in the following space.

3b. Save, compile, link, and execute **testExceptions4.cpp**. Copy the output of your program in the following space.

Lab 16.4 Creating Your Own Exception Classes

C++provides many exception classes; however, they do not cover all of the exceptions that may occur in a program. Programmers may create their own exception classes. These classes need not inherit from any other classes.

The exception classes created by the programmer can be very simple and need not contain any members. For example, a class named `ExceptClass` can be defined as follows:

```
class ExceptClass {};
```

The purpose of this simple class is to provide an anonymous object for a throw statement to be caught by a `catch` block. The `catch` block would then provide the action to be taken.

Objectives

In this lab, you will create exception classes and use them in a program.

After completing this lab, you will be able to:

- Create an exception class.
- Use the exception class in a program.
- Use several `catch` blocks with one `try` block.
- Handle an error when the input stream is in a fail state.

Estimated completion time: **50–60 minutes**

Creating Your Own Exception Classes

1a. Design a program that will ask a user to enter a product name not to exceed 15 characters and a weight not to exceed 300. Create and use two `exception` classes and name them **Length** and **InvalidWeight**, respectively. The Length object should be thrown if the product name entered exceeds 15 characters, and the InvalidWeight object should be thrown if the weight entered exceeds 300. If the user attempts to enter a noninteger value for the weight, throw a string containing an appropriate error message. The program should be structured as follows:

- Get all of the input in one `try` block.
- Use three `catch` blocks, one to catch a length error, one to catch a noninteger input error, and one to catch the weight error.
- Output appropriate error messages in each `catch` block.

Write your design in the following space. For your design, write an algorithm (an English language description of the steps required to successfully write the program).

1b. Write a C++ program based on the design you created in Exercise 1a, and name it **ThreeExceptions.cpp.**

1c. Enter, compile, link, and execute **ThreeExceptions.cpp**. Copy the output and save it in a block comment at the end of your program. Run the program at least four times. One run should contain data entered with no errors. The other three runs should each have input that will produce one of the anticipated errors (length limitation, noninteger input, and weight limitation). Save **ThreeExceptions.cpp** in the Chap16 folder of your Student Disk.

The following is a copy of the screen results that might appear after testing the program, depending on the data entered. The input entered by the user is shown in bold.

```
Enter a product's name not to exceed 15 characters: Sofa
The product you entered is: Sofa
Enter the product's weight: 150
The weight you entered is: 150.


Enter a product's name not to exceed 15 characters: TelevisionBlaster
The product name cannot exceed 15 characters.

Enter a product's name not to exceed 15 characters: compressor
The product you entered is: compressor
Enter the product's weight: x215
You did not enter a number for the weight.


Enter a product's name not to exceed 15 characters: Refgrigerator
The product name you entered is: Refgrigerator
Enter the product's weight: 350
The weight cannot exceed 300.
```

17 RECURSION

In this chapter, you will:

- Learn about recursive definitions
- Explore the base case and the general case of a recursive definition
- Discover what a recursive algorithm is
- Learn about recursive functions
- Explore how to use recursive functions to implement recursive algorithms

CHAPTER 17: ASSIGNMENT COVER SHEET

Name ______________________ Date ______________________

Section ______________________

Lab Assignments	Assigned	Grade
Lab 17.1 Using a Recursive Algorithm (Critical Thinking Exercises)		
Lab 17.2 Designing a Recursive Algorithm for a Power Function (Critical Thinking Exercise)		
Lab 17.3 Recursion and Iteration		
Total Grade		

See your instructor or the introduction to this book for instructions on submitting your assignments.

If you are using Visual Studio .NET to compile your C++ programs, you should disable precompiled headers before performing the exercises in the Chapter 17 labs. To do so, change the project properties so that your C++ projects do not use precompiled headers.

LAB 17.1 USING A RECURSIVE ALGORITHM

One way to solve problems in computer programs is to use looping, or iteration. You can also use recursion, which, like looping, is another method of repeating code. A recursive function is a function that calls itself. A recursive definition is one in which something is defined as a smaller version of itself. Recursion, like a loop, stops when a certain condition is met. The condition that causes the recursive function to stop is called the base case of the recursive function.

In recursion, a set of statements is repeated by having a function call itself. Moreover, a selection control structure is used to control the repeated calls in recursion.

Keep the following guidelines in mind as you work with recursive statements:

- Every recursive definition must have one or more base cases.
- The general case must eventually be reduced to a base case.
- The base case stops the recursion.

A function is called directly recursive if it calls itself. A function that calls another function and eventually results in the original function call is said to be indirectly recursive.

A recursive function in which the last statement executed is the recursive call is called a tail recursive function.

A program design for a recursive function is similar to a program design for a loop. As a beginning student, you might find it easier to test your program design using a loop. Then, after you have determined that your design works, use the same design to implement the C++ code as a recursive function.

Objectives

In this lab, you design a program that calls a recursive function to reverse the elements of a string.

After completing this lab, you will be able to:

- Design an algorithm to use a recursive function.
- Use a recursive function for string processing.

Estimated completion time: **50–60 minutes**

Using a Recursive Algorithm

In the following exercises, you design a program that calls a function to display a string in reverse order. For example, a string with a value "Hello" should be displayed as "olleH". To help design the algorithm, first answer a few questions. Because all program designs need to address input, processing, and output, consider how you want to accomplish these tasks.

1. How will your string be declared—as a string or as a character array? If you select a character array, what is the maximum size of the string?

2. How will the value of the string be input—as an assigned value or input by the user?

3. Do you need to know the exact length of the string or only the maximum length of the string?

4. What information (arguments) should the main program pass to the recursive function?

5. How do you know when the recursive function has reached the base case?

6. Will you display the reversed string element by element or as another string? (*Hint*: If you send the string and the length of the string to the recursive function, you always know the last element of the string. What would you do to process the string by a different last character each time?)

7a. *Critical Thinking Exercise*: Write your program design in the space provided.

7b. Write a C++ program based on the design you created in Exercise 7a, and name it **Reverse.cpp**. Step through the code by hand.

In the following space, show what is displayed on the screen after executing the output message.

7c. Enter, compile, link, and execute **Reverse.cpp**. Then copy the output and save it in a block comment at the end of your program. Save **Reverse.cpp** in the Chap17 folder of your Student Disk.

The following is a copy of the screen results that might appear after running your program, depending on the data entered. The input entered by the user is shown in bold.

```
Enter your message to be reversed: Hello, how are you?
?uoy era woh ,olleH
```

8a. *Critical Thinking Exercise*: Design a program that calls a function to input an integer and displays it in reverse order. For example, if you have an integer with a value 5982, you want the integer displayed to be 2895. Do not enter the integer as a string. You must enter it as an integer.

Write your design in the following space. Your design should be a list of C++ comments without any code.

8b. Write a C++ program based on the design you created in Exercise 8a, and name it **ReverseNum.cpp**. Step through the code by hand.

In the following space, show what is displayed on the screen after executing the output message.

8c. Enter, compile, link, and execute **ReverseNum.cpp**. Then copy the output and save it in a block comment at the end of your program. Save **ReverseNum.cpp** in the Chap17 folder of your Student Disk.

The following is a copy of the screen results that might appear after running your program, depending on the data entered. The input entered by the user is shown in bold.

```
Enter a number greater than zero: 5982
You entered 5982. Reversed, that number is 2895.
```

Lab 17.2 Designing a Recursive Algorithm for a Power Function

When designing a recursive function, you must consider that a recursive function executes more slowly than its iterative counterpart. On slow computers, especially those with limited memory space, the execution of a recursive function is visible. On new computers with a large amount of memory space, the execution of a recursive function is not noticeable.

When a statement calls a recursive function as part of an expression, it is a recursive call. Processing a value that returns a recursive function is called unwinding the recursion.

Objectives

In this lab, you design a program that uses a recursive function call to create a power function that raises a base value to a positive exponent.

After completing this lab, you will be able to:

- Design an algorithm that uses a recursive call as part of a value-returning expression to a recursive call.

Estimated completion time: **50–60 minutes**

Designing a Recursive Algorithm for a Power Function

In the following exercises, you answer questions to help design a recursive algorithm. Then you design and write a program that is a power function, which is used to raise a base value to a positive exponent. This power function should be a recursive function. You have already used the power function from the math header file. Design your own recursive function called power that takes integer arguments for base and exponent and returns an integer value. The exponent value must be greater than or equal to zero. The algorithm finds n raised to the power of x, or (n^x). To help design the algorithm, first answer the following questions to determine how your program will handle input, processing, and output.

1. How will the values for your base and exponent be input—by assignment or by interactive input?

2. The main program might restrict valid input. However, your function should accommodate all integer values. How will you accommodate negative exponents?

3. How will you accommodate zero exponents?

4. How will you accumulate the values returned from the recursive function?

5. How will you display the result from the function calls?

6a. *Critical Thinking Exercise*: Design a program from the problem description. Write your design in the following space. Your design should be a list of C++ comments without any code.

6b. Write a C++ program based on the design you created in Exercise 6a, and name it **Power.cpp**. Step through the code by hand.

In the following space, show what is displayed on the screen after executing the output message.

6c. Enter, compile, link, and execute **Power.cpp**. Then copy the output and save it in a block comment at the end of your program. Save **Power.cpp** in the Chap17 folder of your Student Disk.

The following is a copy of the screen results that might appear after running your program, depending on the data entered. The input entered by the user is shown in bold.

```
Enter your base number and your exponent: 3 4
The number 3 raised to the power of 4 is 81.
```

Lab 17.3 Recursion and Iteration

Recursion and iteration (loops) both repeatedly perform the same set of statements. Most, but not all, problems using a recursive solution can also be written with an iterative solution, and vice versa. Iteration is more efficient than recursion in that it uses less memory and CPU operations. Consequently, it is used more often than recursion. There are, however, some problems that are more easily solved with a recursive solution.

Objectives

In this lab, you will design both an iterative and a recursive solution for the same problem.

After completing this lab, you will be able to:

- Design and code an iterative solution to a problem.
- Design and code a recursive solution to the same problem.

Estimated completion time: **60–70 minutes**

Designing a Program Using an Iterative Solution

1a. Design a program that will print out a decreasing pattern of stars in each row for the number of rows input by a user. Use a loop in the design. For example, if a user input 4 for the number of rows, the output would look as follows:

```
****
***
**
*
```

Write your design in the following space. For your design, write an algorithm (an English language description of the steps required to successfully write the program).

1b. In the following space, write a C++ program based on the design you created in Exercise 1a and name it **StarsLoop.cpp**.

1c. Enter, compile, link, and execute **StarsLoop.cpp**. Copy the output and save it in a block comment at the end of the source code file. Save **StarsLoop.cpp** in the Chapter 17 folder of your Student Disk.

1d. Design a program using a recursive function to solve the problem set out in Exercise 1a.

Write your design in the following space. For your design, write an algorithm (an English language description of the steps required to successfully write the program).

1e. In the following space, write a C++ program based on the design you created in Exercise 1a and name it **StarsRecursion.cpp**.

1f. Enter, compile, link, and execute **StarsRecursion.cpp**. Copy the output and save it in a block comment at the end of the source code file. Save **StarsRecursion.cpp** in the Chapter 17 folder of your Student Disk.

2a. An exercise in the text required the design of a program to determine whether a string entered by a user is a palindrome (a string that reads the same if its characters are reversed, e.g., "toot," is a palindrome). If you have completed that exercise, design a program that will accomplish the same task using an iterative solution. You can use either a c-string or an object of the string class.

Write your design in the following space. For your design, write an algorithm (an English language description of the steps required to successfully write the program).

2b. In the following space, write a C++ program based on the design you created in Exercise 2a and name it **PalindromeLoop.cpp**.

2c. Enter, compile, link, and execute **PalindromeLoop.cpp**. Copy the output and save it in a block comment at the end of the source code file. Save **PalindromeLoop.cpp** in the Chapter 17 folder of your Student Disk.

The following is a copy of the screen results that might appear after running your program, depending on the data entered. The input entered by the user is shown in bold.

```
Enter a word to see if it is a palindrome: carat
The word you entered is carat.
It is not a palindrome.

Enter a word to see if it is a palindrome: radar
The word you entered is radar.
It is a palindrome.
```

Notes

NOTES

Notes

NOTES

NOTES

Notes

Notes

Notes

Notes

NOTES

Notes